DATE DUE

20 JUL 61 CK

21 Feb 62 MS

RESERVE ROOM

LC

CATALOG DEPT.
6 JU 62 W

19 Feb 63 SB

8 APR '65 M I

20 MAY 67

JUN 3 1971

21 AUG 1972 MR
DZ

P9-AOP-892

ON ALIEN RULE AND SELF-GOVERNMENT

By the same author

German Marxism and Russian Communism
The Revolutionary Movement in France, 1815–71

ON ALIEN RULE AND
SELF-GOVERNMENT

Petrov

John Plamenatz
Fellow of Nuffield College

LONGMANS

LONGMANS, GREEN AND CO LTD
6 & 7 CLIFFORD STREET, LONDON W 1

THIBAULT HOUSE, THIBAULT SQUARE, CAPE TOWN
602–611 LONSDALE STREET, MELBOURNE C 1
443 LOCKHART ROAD, HONG KONG
ACCRA, AUCKLAND, IBADAN
KINGSTON (JAMAICA), KUALA LUMPUR
LAHORE, NAIROBI, SALISBURY (RHODESIA)

LONGMANS, GREEN AND CO INC
119 WEST 40TH STREET, NEW YORK 18

LONGMANS, GREEN AND CO
20 CRANFIELD ROAD, TORONTO 16

ORIENT LONGMANS PRIVATE LTD
CALCUTTA, BOMBAY, MADRAS
DELHI, HYDERABAD, DACCA

© John Plamenatz 1960
First published 1960

*Printed in Great Britain by Richard Clay and Company, Ltd
Bungay, Suffolk*

325.3
P6980

M;12Ie61 recd. M;239862

Contents

Introduction

THIS book is not an essay in political philosophy, though it comes rather nearer to being that than to being anything else. To deserve the name of political philosophy, it would need to be more rigorous, more precise, more systematic than it is. It goes only a little way in analysing the ideas and assumptions of apologists for and opponents of alien rule, which today means, above all, European rule over non-Europeans; but it goes, I hope, far enough to uncover the confusions of thought and of purpose which make so much of the controversy about self-government blind, irritating, and unprofitable. The book is philosophical only in the sense that it does not aim at describing what is happening but at clarifying the issues raised in a certain field of controversy; it is concerned primarily not with facts but with types of argument.

The book will mean little or nothing to people who do not share the political faith of the West. It is not an argument for freedom and democracy as they are understood in the West; it is only an attempt to make certain issues clearer to people who already believe in freedom and democracy, and who would not, unless they believed in them, find these issues important. This does not mean that the book is addressed more to western peoples than to others; for there are millions outside the West who share, more or less, the political faith of the West. Though freedom and democracy, as ideals, first emerged in the West, there is no reason whatever for believing that they are suited only to western peoples or peoples of European stock. Have not the Indians already come closer to making them real than, say, the Spaniards or the Yugoslavs? There are, of course, conditions, complicated and difficult to describe, which serve to make these ideals more attractive and more easy to realize. These conditions first arose in the West, but are now arising elsewhere, as western influence spreads. Not, however, quite as they arose in the West, for they are effects of alien domination. There are obstacles in the way of liberal democracy outside the West over and above the obstacles found everywhere. But to say this is not to admit that liberal democracy is suited only to western peoples.

What exactly is meant by saying that freedom and democracy are *suited* only to some peoples? That only some peoples can come to value them? But this is clearly not true. For they are today valued, to some extent, in all countries, except where some other political faith which excludes them is imposed by force. And these ideals were not always valued even in the West. There was a time when the English and the French were more ignorant of, or more indifferent to, them than many of the peoples of Asia and Africa now are. Or is it meant that only some peoples can learn to work the institutions needed to realize these ideals? But there is no better evidence for this assertion than for the other. We might as well say that bicycles are suited only to children who can already ride them.

The writer of this book belongs by birth and affection to a 'backward' nation evidently still incapable of liberal democracy. He has therefore felt himself dispensed from the circumlocutions and euphemisms used by persons anxious to disclaim a racial or national superiority which they think might be offensive.

My friends and colleagues, Miss Margery Perham, Mr. Hugh Clegg, and Mr. Philip Williams have read this book in typescript, and I am grateful to them, and to the Rector of Exeter College, Mr. K. C. Wheare, for their criticisms and encouragement.

I

The Claim to Domination and the Claim to Independence

ONLY a generation or two ago, Asia and Africa were full of peoples who did not seem much interested in governing themselves, putting up with their European rulers much as they had done with other conquerors before them. Now we find these same peoples loudly claiming the right to govern themselves, and sometimes even attacking European rule as if it were the most evil they had ever known.

This claim to 'self-government' is not put forward alone. The peoples that make it do not ask for independence entirely for its own sake; they also usually aspire to democracy and to individual freedom. The claim to independence is closely connected with these aspirations, and in ways in which it used not to be until quite recent times. Independent peoples have, of course, always been eager to preserve their independence; alien rule has always been resented, at least to begin with. Independence has been valued and alien rule resented by many more peoples than have aspired to democracy and individual freedom. But before these aspirations were common in the world, conquered peoples did not expect much sympathy in their predicament. The general rule was, in Asia and Africa as in Europe: Independence is for the strong, and those too weak to keep it must lose it. The weak were not condemned for fighting to preserve their independence, nor the strong for depriving them of it. The conquered were thought unfortunate, and their conquerors fortunate. Not until democracy and individual freedom became common ideals was it thought wrong for the powerful nations to use their strength to force weaker nations into subjection. If it is right that governments should be responsible to the governed, then it is wrong for one people to impose their rule on another. Alien rule and democracy are clearly incompatible. And if democracy is, in the modern world, a condition of individual freedom, then alien rule is also incompatible with that freedom. The more democracy and freedom are valued, the more alien rule is apt to be thought humiliating.

Democracy and freedom are European ideals. I do not mean by this that there has never been a popular element in government except among peoples of European stock or peoples influenced by the Europeans. No doubt there has been. In most small and primitive communities, the influence of the people on their rulers is considerable. It is in large and complicated societies that rulers are lifted high above the common people and take little notice of them. And in nearly all societies, simple or complicated, European or non-European, there is a sphere of life private to the family, a shutting of the door against outsiders. When I say that democracy and freedom are European ideals, I mean that it is among peoples of European stock, in Western Europe and North America, that the institutions and processes making freedom secure and democracy possible in vast societies of many millions have been invented. I mean also that it is among these peoples that democratic and liberal ideals have been elaborated and refined. Institutions and ideals develop together, and are indeed so closely related that we can almost say that a people do not fully possess the ideals until they know how to work the institutions. To the extent that the peoples of Asia and Africa subject to European rule demand independence for the sake of democracy and freedom, they can be said to be claiming against the West the right to imitate the West.

This is both the strength and the weakness of their claim. It is the strength because it rests the claim on principles which are more and more widely accepted. Even the Communists accept them, albeit in their own peculiar way. If the claim to independence is made regardless (or even in contempt) of democracy and freedom, it is apt to be much less persuasive. Asians conquered Asians, and Africans Africans, long before the Europeans came among them. Why then should they condemn in others what they have so often done themselves? They can scarcely hope to be listened to unless they pay at least lip service to ideals whose wide acceptance now makes alien rule look wrong, whereas, not so very long ago, it was merely thought to be the misfortune of some and the good fortune of others.

The weakness of the claim consists in this, that it exposes those who make it to the retort that they are not yet fit for democracy and freedom because they have not learnt to work the institutions which make them possible. This retort is often bitterly resented. Yet it may be well founded. I shall not, in this essay, consider whether, in regard to this or that people, the retort is well founded; I shall consider only the kinds of argument that are used to support and resist it.

In no part of this essay shall I assume that western institutions or ideals are better than others. They have, of course, for some considerable time, been gaining ground at the expense of the others, except where they have been successfully challenged by the Communists. That they are spreading is no proof of their superiority. The Europeans have intruded upon other peoples and have so changed them that European methods and ideals are now much more attractive to them than they were. This is an effect, not of the moral superiority of the Europeans, but of their greater wealth and power. No doubt they owe this wealth and power to the growth of science among them; they can control the forces of nature more effectively because they understand them better. They are superior in some forms of knowledge; but it has yet to be proved that they are either the better or the happier for being so.

When methods and values evolved by one people are accepted by another, the first people are likely, at least for a time, to be superior to the second by standards common to them both. This does not mean that the second people admit the superiority of the first. They may do so or they may not, and in any case will want to make the difference between them seem as little as possible. It does, however, mean that there are standards which both peoples share, and which can be used to prove the first people superior to the second. Given the common standards, the argument, provided it takes proper account of the facts, is sound, no matter how reluctant the second people may be to accept its conclusion. Thus, it may well be possible now, as it was not two hundred years ago, to prove that at least some of the European peoples are superior to the peoples of Asia and Africa; that is to say, superior not by standards peculiar to themselves but by standards now accepted even by the peoples they claim to be superior to. But this kind of superiority, if it exists, is an effect and not a cause of European domination. If the Europeans are superior to many other peoples by standards more or less universally accepted, it is only because they have, in one way or another, imposed these standards on other peoples.

Even before the Europeans began to intrude on other peoples, there were doubtless standards common to all the world. Human standards are related to human needs, and there are needs, material and social, common to all mankind. But there is no reason to believe that, judged by these standards, the Europeans ever were, or now are, much better or much worse than other peoples. These standards, just because they are common, are probably pretty well observed in all parts of the world, except in troubled times; and if they are better observed by some peoples than by others, it is by no means obvious that the advanced peoples observe them best. They are not the standards used when some peoples are called more 'advanced' or 'civilized' than others. Only fifty years ago, the Ghegs in the north of Albania were almost untouched by western influences. Even then, no doubt, many of their opinions about good behaviour were shared by Englishmen. Yet a man would have been hard put to it to decide fifty years ago, by the standards common to England and North Albania, whether the English were superior to the Ghegs or the Ghegs to the English. If the Ghegs became inferior to the English (and I do not say that they did), it was presumably after North Albania began to be 'westernized'.

Using only standards which are generally accepted for other reasons than alien conquest or cultural domination, we could no doubt say that some peoples are superior to others in this or that respect. Even if no people had ever conquered another, or impressed them by greater wealth or power, there would still be many kinds of behaviour praised and blamed everywhere, though not everywhere to the same extent. By the standards common to all mankind, not all peoples are equally virtuous in all respects. Perhaps it could be shown, not only that there are values which all peoples share, but that they all put some at least of these values in the same order of preference. If this could be done, we should then have more than just common values; we should also have a common scale of values, which we could use to establish an order of merit among the peoples.

But this exercise of ingenuity would interest only a few persons who like playing intellectual games; it would be of no practical and little academic interest. A scale of values common to a number of persons does not ensure that, provided they all know the relevant facts and do not delude themselves, they will agree about one another's relative merits; unless, of course, this common scale includes all the values they hold. If each person, besides the values in the common scale, has others peculiar to himself or shared with only a few people, and also has his own order of preferences among the values outside the scale, he may still differ widely from the others in his judgements of value.

There is clearly no argument from there being some values in a common scale to the likelihood of general agreement about merit, even where there is no dispute about the facts.

Besides, nations are not interested in assessing each other's merits by reference to some common scale of values; they are not even interested in deciding whether there is such a scale. When they pass judgements on one another, they use standards peculiar to themselves as readily as the ones they share with others, and ordinarily do not bother to distinguish between them. Unless they are brought into frequent contact, they are apt to be indifferent to one another. Until the Europeans moved into Asia and Africa, they were not much given to comparing themselves with other than European peoples. Comparisons inspired by fear or pride, feelings of superiority or inferiority, were long confined to close neighbours. These comparisons were made everywhere, and these sentiments felt; for nations, like individuals, take stock of themselves partly by watching others and passing judgements on them. There was a time when each nation had but few neighbours, and took little notice of peoples whose borders did not run with its own; but in our age every nation has many more neighbours than it once had, and some few, the Great Powers, are neighbours to virtually the whole world.

This coming together of the peoples has not been an effect of forces working equally everywhere. If the world has at last become something like a single community of nations (though a community divided against itself), it is because, in the recent past, a few peoples have forced themselves, in one way or another, on the rest of the world. In the nineteenth century, for the first time in history, one civilization was fast conquering the whole world; and in the twentieth century this civilization split into two parts. Though the two parts differ greatly, they are in some ways very alike, especially in the ideas they proclaim. They are both in favour of democracy and freedom and the equality of nations; they both put themselves forward as liberators of mankind; they both owe their fast-increasing wealth and power to science and technology; and they are both centred in nations of European stock. It is judging by their standards that some peoples are 'advanced' and others 'backward'; and it is largely because they now have two standards, 'Western' and 'Communist', that the non-European peoples are greatly bewildered. Therefore it is equally false to say that the European nations, if they are superior to the others, are so only in power and wealth, and to say that they are superior to them by standards which all the world accepted before European domination began. They are superior, if at all, by standards which first came to be accepted because of that domination.

European conquest and intrusion have had different effects in different parts of the world. In America the natives were either destroyed by contact with the Europeans or else were reduced to something like serfdom. They were also converted to Christianity, and came in the end to appear to their masters, not as alien subjects, but as the base-born and illiterate supports of what were essentially European societies. Though society could not do without their labour, they were too ignorant to be real partakers in civilization. Their masters thought of them much as the privileged orders in mediaeval Europe thought of the peasants; it was not so much that they thought of them as compatriots as that they did not think of them as foreigners. They were included in the church, and therefore in the mercy of Christ, but were otherwise excluded from all the benefits of what was nevertheless called a Christian civilization. They were not outcasts from civilization, for it rested on their backs; they belonged to society and yet profited little from it. Like the mediaeval serfs they had their own dark culture of which their masters had scarcely an inkling; they acknowledged the same God as their masters and worshipped in the same churches; outwardly they shared the same religion, but in their thoughts and feelings differed greatly from them. They accepted their masters, and their masters accepted them, as people do who are permanently settled together; they were intimately connected in some ways and strangers in others. They were neither aliens nor friends nor compatriots; they were members of one and the same social order. It is roughly true to say that in the Americas the European invaders either destroyed the natives or else established such relations with them that the societies so formed, though racially mixed, no longer think of themselves as consisting of native peoples held in subjection by alien conquerors. This is so in most of the states south of the Rio Grande, if not in all. When the lower orders began to aspire to better things, their struggle with their masters took the form of class rather than racial or national conflicts; and where the conflicts were not merely between classes they were racial rather than national. No doubt, in racially mixed societies, even class conflicts have characteristics they would not otherwise have; but that does not prevent their appearing, to the people actually engaged in them, as class and not as racial conflicts. In Latin America there have been, between conquerors and conquered, both social integration and cultural assimilation; there has been a settling down to live together as members of one society, and a taking over of many of each other's practices and beliefs. There has also been a mixing of the races often going as far as intermarriage.

In Asia and Africa relations between the European conquerors and the conquered peoples have been quite different, and for reasons not far to seek. The Europeans dominated Asia and Africa later than America, at a time when it was already much easier for people going abroad for long periods to keep in touch with their home countries and for those countries to control them. True, the Portuguese and Spaniards, the English and the French, who went to the Americas went there as subjects of their kings; they did not form independent colonies there as the ancient Greeks had done all over the Mediterranean. Yet, inevitably, they were largely cut off from the countries of their birth, whether (like the English) they already had a long tradition of liberty or whether they had not. They went in relatively large numbers into sparsely populated lands. But in Asia they went into thickly populated countries, often highly civilized and complicated in their social life; they went in small numbers, not to form new communities, but in search of trade and high and quick profits. Later, when to defend their profits they intervened in the native government, they went as tax-collectors, administrators, judges, and soldiers. They came from what were already strongly organized and powerful states. Militarily they were immensely stronger than the peoples they subjected; and they had evolved political methods enabling them to control vast populations and enormous territories more effectively, and often also more cheaply, than the native rulers could do. The Europeans in Asia had more to lose than to gain by social integration with the native peoples; there was no need for them to merge with the local aristocracy or to form a new ruling class which might be accepted, in course of time, by the other classes as belonging to the same social order as themselves. The Europeans in Asia held aloof from the subject peoples partly because it was their interest to do so and partly because they could do it easily. They governed Asia on behalf of European states in a way in which the Europeans settled in the Americas never did. They were not adventurers or pilgrims who made themselves masters of the countries they conquered or occupied; they were the closely controlled agents of foreign Powers. This close dependence on the governments of their home countries in some ways greatly improved the quality of their rule; but it also had other effects which I shall discuss later.

The empires created by the West Europeans in Asia and Africa have not lasted long. What was the reason? Clearly not the weakness of the nations that created them. If Britain and France now appear much weaker than they did a hundred years ago, that is not because their power and wealth have declined absolutely. A country as powerful as Britain was in 1858 could not wage a war against the Britain of today for more than a few weeks. Nor are they much weaker if we compare their strength with the strength of the peoples still, or until lately, subject to them. If Britain and France and their colonies were the only countries in the world, and if the British and French and the peoples subject to them still thought and felt as they did a hundred years ago, then Britain and France, though considerably weaker than they now are, might find it easy to hold on to their colonies. Or if the European peoples generally still felt about the peoples of Asia and Africa as the British and French felt only fifty years ago, the Asians and Africans would lack the strength to shake off the European yoke. For today the preponderance of wealth and military power rests with peoples of European stock more than ever it did.

European rule in Asia and Africa is coming to an end more quickly than anyone could have foretold a generation ago, mainly for three reasons: because there has been, among the European [1] peoples, a rapid and large shifting of the balance of power to the detriment of the peoples owning colonies; because European rule, unlike the rule of earlier conquerors, has aroused among the subject peoples demands which, for moral reasons, their rulers are hard put to it to resist; and because the European peoples who have colonies have not succeeded in creating a sense of community, a loyalty to the imperial connection, strong enough to make their subjects want to remain closely tied to them politically.

The Europeans remained aliens in Asia and Africa because they deliberately held aloof from the natives, thinking of themselves as servants of European states and missionaries of a superior civilization.

---

1. By 'European' I mean 'of European stock' and not 'living in Europe'. Thus, according to this usage, the United States is a European Power.

It has often been said that this aloofness, even in Asia, was due to the very great differences between the cultures of conquerors and conquered, making cultural assimilation unusually difficult. I do not say that this factor has mattered only a little, but I do say that its importance has been greatly exaggerated.

There have been social integration and cultural assimilation between peoples who differed more than the Europeans and the Asians. Were not the Spaniards even more unlike the Mexicans than the British were unlike the Indians? And if the Spaniards who went to Mexico made themselves at home there, in a way in which the British never did in India, it was certainly not by using gentler methods. Can we even say that the British were much more unlike the Indians than the Muslims who conquered India only a few centuries before they did? No doubt it now seems so. But that is largely because the Muslims adopted many of the customs of the country they conquered, coming as they did to rule and plunder it for their own profit and not as subjects of a foreign state. As a result of European rule in Asia, the predicament of all Asian peoples is now in many ways similar; so that the differences between these peoples seem less important now than the differences between them and the Europeans. Of course, the difference in power between European and Asian peoples, while the Europeans were establishing their ascendancy in Asia, was much greater than differences in power between Asian peoples. But cultural differences do not vary directly with differences in power; though for obvious reasons we attend most to the cultural differences closely connected with differences in power.

Long before the coming of the British, there were very great differences, racial and cultural, between the peoples 'native' to India. How shall we set about measuring those differences to discover whether or not they were smaller than the differences between the Indian peoples generally and the British? Who has established this measure or knows how to use it? And even if the differences from the British were greater, how can we say that that was why the British always remained foreigners in India? Just how much must some people differ from others more than these others differ among themselves to make them 'unassimilable' and therefore permanently foreign? It is only in recent times, and largely as a result of British rule, that the peoples of India have come to regard themselves as one people. If the British differ from the Indians in race, religion, language, and culture,

B

so do the Indians among themselves; and so too have earlier conquerors of India from the peoples they conquered. Why, then, did the British remain foreigners in India as earlier conquerors did not? Why did all the peoples of India come to look on the British as they did not look on one another, in spite of the great differences between them? Not because the British in India treated them worse than they were accustomed to treat each other, and so united them in hatred of the oppressor; but because they ruled them as agents of a Power external to India. They never merged with the privileged classes already there, nor became a new ruling class or community accepted by the others as being as much 'native' to India as they were, nor formed part of a cosmopolitan privileged order recruited in Britain and in the countries subject to her.

The Gauls, the ancient Britons, and many other peoples were ruled from Rome longer than the Indians were from London. No doubt, to begin with, they felt this rule to be alien. Yet they were, on the whole, quickly reconciled to it. Why was this so? Had the Britons or the Gauls less the sense of being one people than the Indians had when the British conquered them? Indian nationalism is an effect of British rule; it has helped bring that rule to a quicker end but could scarcely prevent its establishment. Was it because the Romans, 'racially' and culturally, were closer to the Britons and Gauls than the British were to the Indians? Racially, no doubt, they were closer; but culturally, if at all closer, only a little, for the Romans were a highly civilized people with institutions, political and social, very different from those of the Celtic tribes they conquered. Was it because the Britons and Gauls were barbarians, as the Indians were not, that it was easier to reconcile them to alien government? But the Romans conquered civilized peoples as well as barbarians; not only the Greeks, with whom they had much in common, but the Egyptians and other peoples with civilizations very unlike their own and much older. If the Romans took care to respect local customs and religions, and allowed considerable local autonomies, so too did the British.

How then can we explain the more willing acceptance by subject peoples of Roman than of British rule? The Romans, once they had created their empire, had no rivals to challenge their supremacy. Their empire fell because it decayed inwardly until it was no longer strong enough to withstand the not very heavy blows of the barbarians against it. But Britain was never more than one among the great Powers of European stock. Unlike the French, the Germans, the Russians, and now the Americans, the British have never been strong enough to dominate Europe. They have seemed the most powerful of European nations only outside Europe, among the poor or weak or disorganized peoples of Asia and Africa. And the French, who created the second largest of modern empires, set about it seriously after they ceased to be strong enough to dominate Europe. Again, the Romans, unlike the British and the French, were not the champions of principles, moral and political, dangerous to their ascendancy over other peoples. I shall have more to say later about these two differences between the Romans and the British, French, and other modern imperialists.

The Romans, in the process of establishing their empire, created a cosmopolitan privileged class recruited from all the peoples in the empire. The members of this class had a double loyalty, to Rome and to the places of their birth. Not only did Rome eventually make Roman citizens of all the freemen in her empire; she also allowed men of all nationalities to rise high in her service. The Roman Empire was cosmopolitan in a sense that the British and French empires have never been. If the Roman invaders, in each country as they conquered it, had merged with the native privileged classes, as the Normans did in England, or had formed a new privileged class over and above the others, they might not have kept their empire so solidly together. If they had merged with the natives at the cost of cutting themselves off from the country they came from, they would no doubt have transformed every country they conquered, but without helping to make it an integral part of a large empire; and if they had everywhere kept themselves apart from the conquered, they would then have been felt everywhere to be alien rulers. They did neither of these things, but mixed with the powerful and wealthy among the natives to form a cosmopolitan class sharing a single Graeco-Roman culture. They did it without detaching the members of this class from the countries of their birth; it was not only possible, it was easy and natural, to have a double loyalty. The Romans could not assimilate or romanize all the inhabitants of their empire, who were mostly too poor and illiterate to be more than lightly touched by the sophisticated culture of their masters. But they did not cut off those they romanized from the communities they belonged to before they learnt to be Romans; at least no more than the British and other Europeans have done the Asians and Africans whom they have 'westernized'.

There is nothing unique about this Roman achievement. The Venetians did much the same in the towns subject to them along the Dalmatian coast. They never settled in them in large numbers, either to merge with the native aristocracies or to form a new ruling class superimposed on the other classes; they settled in small numbers, so that most of the 'Italians' in Dalmatia were not Italian by ancestry but only by education. Yet their being Italian did not prevent their being also devoted citizens of their own cities; and they were not accounted foreigners by the poorer classes whose native tongue was Slav. Indeed, the Italianate upper classes were often as much at home in the Slav tongue as the Italian. Not until the nineteenth century, under the pressure of a recently born South Slav nationalist movement, did 'Italians' and 'Slavs' in Dalmatia come to look upon one another as foreigners.

If Joseph II had had his way, the Habsburg dominions would have been ruled by a cosmopolitan German-speaking official class equally at home in all parts of his empire. Perhaps it was already too late by his time to make this acceptable to all his peoples, or perhaps he used the wrong methods. Yet the policy was not in principle unrealizable. People going up in the world in the Habsburg lands in the eighteenth century did ordinarily become German-speaking; to rise socially involved 'Germanization'. Many of those who learnt German were lost to their own peoples, but many were not. Some, indeed, by getting a German education, were better equipped than before to appreciate the culture of their own people. Local patriotism can gain in depth and sweetness for being in harmony with wider loyalties. This happened in the Habsburg lands, but not quickly enough to save the empire. In the end, the various nationalisms so weakened it that it could not survive military defeat. Nationalism in the Habsburg lands, until the latter part of the last century, was predominantly a middle-class affair; the rising middle classes used it as a weapon against the more cosmopolitan classes above them and also against the Austrian and Hungarian governments. For a variety of reasons, it was their interest to do so. If it had not been their interest, if they could have asserted their increasing social importance more effectively by becoming 'cosmopolitan' rather than 'nationalist', the empire might have been saved. If they could have acquired more quickly a larger say in the government of the empire, they might have cared less than they did for national autonomy, or might not have pressed for it in ways threatening the unity of the empire. Patriotism and nationalism are not the same thing; patriotism is a love of one's people which does not carry with it hostility to strangers, whereas nationalism is emotionally in arms against the foreigner, the intruder, the outsider. There was plenty of local patriotism in the Habsburg lands before the rise of nationalism, just as there was in India.

The Indians, comparing the British with earlier conquerors of their country, often say that the British alone were not 'assimilated'. They put this forward as something more than a mere statement of fact, though quite what more they mean to convey by it is not clear. Do they mean that they would have resented British rule less if the British had been assimilated? If they mean this, the statement is ambiguous. British rule may mean the rule of the British in India or the rule of Britain over India. If the British in India had become a native ruling class, either by merging with the older ruling classes or by forming a new 'Indian' ruling class above them, India might have come to resent Britain's rule over her just as fiercely as she in fact did; for that kind of assimilation would probably have cut the British in India off from the mother country more quickly and more sharply than crossing the Atlantic cut off the English colonists in North America. That, under the circumstances, was the most likely kind of assimilation, if assimilation there had been. There has never been much sign in the British empire of a different process of assimilation, of the emergence of a cosmopolitan ruling class, recruited from all races and peoples, held together by devotion to the imperial service and by community of culture, and yet also deeply rooted in every part of the empire. Perhaps the empire grew too quickly for that to happen, and its parts were too widely separate; perhaps the nation that made it was too small in comparison with the subject peoples; perhaps the forces, cultural and external, that disrupted it bore down upon it too soon.

There is assimilation and assimilation, and one kind sometimes limits or excludes another. There is the kind which is social integration, and there is the kind which is a matter chiefly of acquiring alien customs, methods, and values. This second kind, for convenience sake, may be called 'cultural assimilation'. The first kind always involves the second, to some extent, but is not therefore the greater the more there is of the second. In a country like India, having sharply divided castes rather than a more amorphous system of classes, the British, if they had come to belong to Indian society, would probably have done so as a separate caste or community. No doubt they would have adopted more Indian customs than they actually did; the process of cultural assimilation of the British by the Indians would have gone further. But the opposite process might have gone much less far; the Indians might not have adopted European and English ways and ideas to anything like the extent they have done. There has never been more than a sprinkling of Europeans among them; and if these Europeans had been 'assimilated', in the sense of socially integrated, by becoming a caste or community accepted as part of native Indian society, the westernization of India might have been much slower and much less extensive. What is true of India is true also of other parts of Asia and Africa with no caste system; even of the parts which have never been directly ruled by Europeans. The westernization of Asia and Africa would never have gone so far so quickly if the relatively few Europeans who went there, either as conquerors or traders, had not held themselves aloof from the natives, refusing to be absorbed into local society; if they had not kept in close touch with Europe, living as foreigners and masters among non-European peoples. Cultural assimilation, when it is rapid and wide, and of the many by the few, is perhaps incompatible with social integration.

Not for one moment do I suggest that the peoples of Asia and Africa are the better for being westernized; for this process, broad and deep though it has been, has also been disruptive and incomplete. It has greatly changed the lives of hundreds of millions of people without making Europeans of them culturally and politically; it has too often cut them off from what used to satisfy them without giving them anything as satisfying in its place. When I say that the process is not complete, I do not mean to imply that it ought to be completed, or even that it must be if it is to cease being disruptive. It may be that social harmony could be restored in Asia and Africa in countries only partly westernized. I do not wish to deny this, but only to say that, at the moment, there is little social harmony.

The process of westernization will probably never be completed. Nor can I see why it should be desirable that it should be. What is desirable is not complete westernization but the achievement of social harmony. Social harmony is never completely achieved; it is never true of any society that it enables all its members to attain their ideals, or provides for reconciling conflicting interests methods acceptable to everyone. But we can, by taking thought, come much closer than we are to achieving it.

The peoples of Asia and Africa cannot now return to what they used to be before the Europeans forced themselves upon them. For better or for worse, they have adopted many western methods and values, and are likely to adopt more. Though they resent European interference, they now no longer have, either for themselves as individuals or for their countries, the ambitions of their ancestors. They have new ambitions which clearly owe a great deal to European ideas and institutions planted in their midst. They must therefore come to terms with Europe in two senses: they must settle their differences with the European peoples, and they must seek to restore social harmony in countries already transformed by European influences. Even if they need not absorb European people, they must absorb European ideas and practices. They cannot have social harmony unless their ideals are compatible with one another and with their institutions.

History teaches us that different peoples put a value on different things. But it also teaches us that personal happiness and social peace are everywhere thought desirable. To say to another person, 'My ways are better than your ways, and you must live as I think fit', is the grossest impertinence; but to say to him, 'Since these are your ideals, you will not be happy or at peace with your neighbours, unless you do this', may be a friendly act. True, the giver of the advice may be more foolish or inexperienced than the person he gives it to; but he may not be. If the ideals originally came from him, it is not presumptuous in him to believe that he can give good advice. It is not the Europeans who are adopting Asian and African methods and ideas; it is the other way about. This may not be the work of Providence; perhaps God in His wisdom regrets it. Who knows? We can only know the mundane facts. But, given these facts, it is not presumptuous to say that the Europeans have more to teach other peoples than to learn from them.

I have already conceded that European ways and ideas have gained ground at the expense of others, not because they are better by any standard commonly accepted before they began to gain ground, nor because they lead more surely or quickly to personal happiness and social peace (which are everywhere thought desirable), but because the peoples who first acquired them were the richest and the most powerful, and therefore able to impose themselves on others. Men have got happiness (by which I mean, not pleasure, but the sense of well-being that comes of living what is felt to be a worthwhile life) and social peace in the service of ideals different from those of the West; and for all I know, perhaps more successfully. The cultural assimilation of the world by Europe is neither to be praised nor condemned. It is happening and can hardly be stopped, still less reversed. The world must accept it and make the best of it. By breaking in upon them, the Europeans started among the peoples of Asia and Africa a process of change which those peoples now no longer wish to stop or reverse but which they aspire to control; and they cannot control it unless they are self-governing. This aspiration and the desire for self-government are themselves effects of the process started by the Europeans. It is here that westernization differs most conspicuously from other processes started in the past by foreign conquests.

Western science and philosophy, as they have developed in the last three or four centuries, are the most sustained, comprehensive, and rigorous attempt ever made by man to understand himself and his environment, physical and social; just as western industrialism is incomparably the largest effort ever made to subdue nature to human purposes. This attempt and this effort, if they have not brought happiness and peace, have brought power and wealth to the peoples that made them; and power and wealth are everywhere impressive. The methods, the qualities, the values that western man has acquired in this unique and astonishing pursuit of knowledge and mastery over nature are now acceptable all over the world. Not understood everywhere or liked by everyone, not even in the West; but understood at least in part and desired by the bold, the enterprising, the ambitious, by the men most apt to take the lead, especially in times of trouble and quick change.[1]

---

1. Until quite recently the changes set going by European intrusion in Asia and Africa were probably resented by many more people than welcomed them, even in the upper classes. Perhaps they are still resented by most of the people who have definite opinions about them. Change may be widely unpopular among all classes, even in an independent country, and yet be impossible to stop. People are often blind to the connections between things. They accept one thing which brings on others without their knowing that it does so. If they knew, they would not accept it; but having accepted it, these other things come upon them. At first, and perhaps for a long time, they resent them. But in the end they are often reconciled to them, and even come to think themselves fortunate in having them. They have submitted to change and in the process have been changed themselves. Though, if they had foreseen what was to happen to them, they would have deplored it, now that they look back on it, they account it progress.

Alongside this pursuit of knowledge and power over nature has grown European respect for freedom, intellectual, moral, and political. In the West, more than anywhere else in the world, men have asserted the right to criticize all accepted beliefs about nature and about good behaviour, the right to live as they think fit provided they allow others to do likewise, and the right to be consulted by those who take decisions in the name of the communities they belong to. The European, even when he believes in a God whose creature and instrument he is, often insists on his right to define for himself that God's nature and the right to worship Him as he pleases.

No western peoples have cared more for freedom than the British and the French, or have done as much to elucidate it and to elaborate the rules and institutions needed to establish it. They have also created the largest empires in Asia and Africa. True, they did not create them to bring freedom to others so much as to increase their own wealth and power. Indeed, when they started to create their empires, they were still far from having established freedom in their own countries. In England the rights that the West now understands by freedom were confined to the upper classes; and in France were rather claimed than enjoyed, or if enjoyed, then not securely. Yet the enlargement of freedom in Britain and France was not stopped or retarded by the creation of the British and French empires. The two processes went on together, as they had not done in Rome. Roman freedom was destroyed largely as a result of Roman conquests. The Romans did not retain their republican institutions for long after they had extended their rule beyond the frontiers of Italy. Intellectual and moral freedom they never cared for as we do now, but they did set great store by their political rights. They lost them and they got an empire. They did not choose to lose them in order to get an empire; they did not see two alternatives before them and prefer one to the other, as Esau did when he sold his birthright for a mess of pottage. They merely lost their freedom because they won an empire.

So, too, perhaps the British, the French, and other peoples having colonies, could have enlarged their own freedom and given freedom to the peoples subject to them, and still have drawn them as willing partners into a close political union with themselves. Though we may not see how they could have done it, we cannot deny that perhaps they could have. Yet they do not seem to have done it. European conquest has made attractive to the conquered peoples the methods and ideas of their conquerors. At first this attraction was confined to the upper classes and to circles directly affected by the conquest; and was also mixed up with resentment and even contempt. The feelings of the conquered towards their conquerors are always mixed, and remain so until either social integration has gone so far that the conquerors are no longer looked upon as aliens or the conquerors move out. The deeper and broader the process of westernization, the more people share these feelings and the more intensely they have them. This must be so unless increasing westernization means greater social integration of the conquerors with the conquered; but this is precisely what it has not meant. The Europeans have neither come to belong to the peoples they have subjected nor have implanted in them strong loyalties to cosmopolitan empires with which they wish to be closely associated. Yet they have powerfully influenced their subjects. Hence the need their subjects have felt and still feel to imitate and to get rid of them.[1] The Europeans transformed the peoples subject to them in such a way that they created demands which could be met only if they withdrew or else remained on condition that they put themselves on a level with their subjects, ceasing to be superiors and becoming equals. When pushed to it, they have nearly always found it easier to do the first than the second, especially where they were mostly officials or business-men spending only their years of service in the colonies. Where there have been permanent European settlers in large numbers, they have been unwilling to withdraw or to accept equality with the subject peoples.

It has been morally impossible for the West Europeans to reject outright the demands of the peoples subject to them. Freedom, as they understand it, is more than the secure enjoyment of customary rights and autonomies; it is man's right to call all things in question, no matter how hallowed by tradition, his right to choose how he shall live, his right to be consulted when decisions are taken that affect him. These rights are, of course, limited; but they are supposed to be limited to

---

1. This is not always the attitude of the conquered to their conquerors. In the nine-teenth century, the Balkan Christians wanted to get rid of the Turks but did not want to imitate them. During the first two centuries of Turkish rule in the Balkans, many of the natives voluntarily went over to Islam. By the nineteenth century, they had lost all respect for their rulers; they took pride in being 'Europeans', in belonging to a race which was already dominating the world. The Balkan peoples had ceased to feel inferior to the Turks long before they got rid of them, and their hatred vanished as soon as they were free.

ensure that they are the more effectively exercised. They must not be
exercised by some to the detriment of others. These rights are limited,
in theory and in practice, in all kinds of ways. Yet in theory they are
not confined to some peoples and refused to others. It used to be the
fashion to say that they follow from the very nature of man as a
rational and purposeful being; they were called the 'rights of man'.
It is no longer so much the fashion to speak in this way, because the
philosophers have persuaded many people that this derivation is
logically unsound. Yet the rights are still claimed for all men, and the
assumption is still made that the burden of proof rests with whoever
would deny them to any man or body of men.

The Europeans have also produced doctrines, several of them extraordinarily popular, about the 'natural' superiority of some races over
others. Though most of these doctrines emerged after European
domination in Asia and Africa became really extensive, oddly enough
(or perhaps it is not odd) they have flourished most vigorously
among European peoples not conspicuously successful either as imperialists or as architects of freedom. The greatest among the empire-
building peoples have also been the most devoted to freedom. They
have had perforce to reconcile their pursuit of empire with their devotion to freedom; they have had to do more for the peoples subject to
them than ever the Romans had to do. They have had to say that they
were bringing them freedom as well as peace, justice, and prosperity,
and have had to make an effort to make good their words. Sometimes,
no doubt, reluctantly. The Europeans living in Asia and Africa have
been perhaps the most sceptical about the success of this effort, but
they have been under pressure from their home governments, especially since those governments became democratic.

The reluctance is as natural as the effort. It is rare for men to have
power over others, and irresponsible power, without coming to despise
them and to feel superior to them. There have been two forces at
work moulding the behaviour of the Europeans to the peoples subject
to them: the feeling of superiority over them, and the feeling that it is
their duty to give them freedom. This second feeling was long much
weaker than the first, and only gathered real strength in the twentieth
century, after the great imperialist Powers achieved full democracy
and their governments were exposed to strong pressure from domestic
radicals and socialists.

Reluctance to grant independence to subject peoples has had other causes besides the feelings of superiority over the conquered natural to conquerors. The Europeans acquired all kinds of interests in their colonies and were eager to hold on to them as long as they could. They made a profit out of them, or needed them for strategic purposes, or got valuable raw materials or even recruits for their armies. They were also proud of their empires and were admired for having them. But all these advantages are now much smaller than they were. Britain and France are now no longer, militarily, among the greatest Powers, and must rely much more for their security on the United States than on their colonies and what they can get out of them. Colony-owning Powers are now expected to do much more for their colonies than they used to; so that colonies are now often liabilities rather than assets. Subject peoples resent alien rule more fiercely than ever, and are therefore more difficult to govern. Even the prestige attached to having colonies has almost disappeared. Indeed, to have them is to be exposed more to blame than to envy; they are a reproach to their possessors. This, perhaps, is the unkindest cut of all. Many of the peoples who now cry out loud against colonialism would once have been only too pleased to get colonies if they had been powerful enough to do so; others have extended their frontiers and have dealt pitilessly with the nations absorbed by them; and some are still ruled more brutally than the British or French ever ruled their colonies.

It is perhaps a wonder that countries having colonies are not in a greater hurry to get rid of them, for they have now at last become what Disraeli once called them, millstones round the necks of their possessors. There are, I think, several reasons that explain why European governments hold on to their colonies even when they appear to have more to lose than to gain by doing so. It is difficult for them to sacrifice special interests to the common interest, because special interests are better organized and more clamorous. Their democratic principles and the desire to placate world opinion may incline them to make concessions, but they also have to please their own peoples. The special interests know what they want, whereas the people generally may not be aware that the maintenance of colonial rule is costing them much more than the special interests would lose by its ceasing to exist. Besides, even when they are aware of it, they may be willing to pay the price; and not unreasonably, for the special interests are the interests of compatriots. Millions are sometimes willing to lose a great deal so that thousands may not lose everything. This motive is apt to be strongest when the thousands are not just people who have put their money into the colonies but have gone there to make their homes.

Another reason for reluctance to let go of colonies is injured pride. The possessors of colonies feel that the outcry against them is cheap, ignorant, or hypocritical. They feel that they have not been given credit for the good they have done and tried to do, or that their accusers are worse than they are. When denunciation of 'colonialism' is confined to the subject peoples, even the owners of colonies can sympathize with it. Though many of these peoples, when they had the chance, behaved as badly or worse than their 'oppressors', it is natural that they should resent foreign rule and being treated as inferiors in their own countries. Or if this denunciation were left to the Swiss and to one or two other more or less blameless peoples, it would still be bearable. But why should the Americans, who tricked and bullied the Indian tribes, who took half Mexico by force, and who still ill-treat their own Negroes, preach virtue to others? If there is no question now of California or Arizona or New Mexico or Texas being lost to the United States, as Algeria may soon be lost to France, is it because the Americans have treated the Mexicans better than the French have treated the Algerians? Or is it not rather that these once Mexican provinces have been swamped by the Americans as Algeria was never swamped by the French? And why should the Russians denounce colonialism? This question, too, is often put, though with less indignation and more contempt. Who can suppose that the Russians, white or red, ever had the right to condemn anyone for oppression? A woman who has sinned in the past and who now preaches virtue as if she had never sinned is apt to make people angry, but a woman of the streets still on the streets who does so only makes them laugh.

There is yet another motive for reluctance to grant independence to colonies. It is the most honourable and reasonable of all the motives, and also the most resented. It is the desire not to leave people whom you have taught to care for freedom to their own devices before they are ready for it. This desire has not, I dare say, been the strongest of motives for holding on to colonies clamouring for independence, and has no doubt often been put forward as an excuse by people who did not really feel it. But it can be genuine and is not the less resented for being so. Freedom is difficult to establish, and is not to be had for the asking. It depends on institutions and habits that do not emerge of themselves as soon as a colony gets independence. Any people can have independence provided other peoples are willing to let them have it; but it is not enough that others should wash their hands of them for them to get freedom. If then a subject people want more than independence, if they want freedom as well, they may fail to get freedom for getting independence too soon. When they hear this said to them by their rulers, they find it hard to bear; and yet it may be true. Also, of course, it may be false; for their rulers are not dispassionate judges. Independence or self-government may come too soon or be too long deferred. If we agree that freedom is desirable, then it does matter to us that we should know when self-government is likely to hasten and when to hinder its coming. This essay is written, not to recommend freedom to people who have no use for it, but to consider in a general way the connections between independence and freedom. It is much easier now than it was for colonies to get independence, and they are tempted to use any means to get it. There is also less to be gained by holding on to colonies, and their possessors are therefore much readier to give them up. But because independence is easier to get it does not follow that freedom is so too.

True, independence cannot always come at the moment most opportune for freedom; it must often come either too early or too late. A colony may not be ready for freedom, and yet it may no longer be possible to hold on to it, except by methods which make it even less likely that its people will get freedom. Or independence may have been deferred too long, and the people driven to forms of resistance destructive of freedom. Certain methods of government make the governed less capable of freedom, and so too do certain methods of fighting government. It is important to discuss these methods; important, that is, on the assumption that freedom is worth having. Under what conditions is independence most likely to promote freedom? It may often be out of our power to create these conditions. If, however, we believe in freedom, we must think the question worth putting and answering. What is the use of holding on to a colony on the ground that it is not ready for freedom if it is out of our power to make it ready? Or what is the use of fighting for freedom in ways that are destructive of it? Whether we attack 'colonialism' or defend it, let us at least understand what we are doing.

Capacity for freedom is not, of course, the only test of fitness for self-government. There are many countries now independent which are not free, and no one would suggest that they ought to be deprived of their independence in order to be made capable of freedom. It is one thing to intervene in other people's domestic affairs, and quite another to wash your hands of them when you have long been responsible for running their affairs. Even if there was no excuse for your first thrusting yourself upon them, there may now be good reasons for not turning your back on them in spite of their eagerness to see the last of you. I shall discuss tests of fitness for self-government other than capacity for freedom, but my prime interest will be in self-government in its relations to freedom.

Rousseau once spoke of people being 'forced to be free'. As he used the words, it is difficult to fix their meaning. It is, however, possible to induce people to put a value on something which otherwise would mean nothing to them, and the inducing may be more than persuasion. There is a sense (which is not exactly Rousseau's, though connected with it) in which most persons who now cherish freedom have been 'forced to be free'. They have been educated to it, and all education involves some compulsion, though not always the kind that is physical force. This 'forcing to freedom' is easily justified in the education of children in countries where freedom is thought desirable. Nobody believes that children ought to be allowed to do what they please, or ought only to be prevented from doing themselves an injury; everybody admits that they must be brought up, even though the process is sometimes painful to them, to be tolerable and useful neighbours. Whatever the standards accepted by society, children are brought up to conform to them whether they like it or not; and they are said to be well brought up when this conformity comes easily to them. Education for freedom is as much a form of discipline as any other education; though of course certain kinds of discipline are excluded by the nature of the end aimed at.

The lover of freedom, however strong his love, will seldom allow that free countries can rightfully intervene in the affairs of countries that are not free in order to compel them to freedom. He will not have one country treat another as a parent or a teacher treats a child. A child must be provided for by others, and will in any case look to them for guidance. It needs education as it needs food, shelter, and affection. It is not a question of someone else deciding what is good for the child and setting about providing it, when all the time the child has its own ideas about what is good for it. It is not a question of someone's imposing his will on the child when it already has a will of its own. The child has no conception of its own of how it should live, which its parents and teachers can pronounce to be inferior, and so feel justified in imposing their own superior conception on it. The child literally does not know how to live, and must be taught to do so. If it is not taught in one way, it will be taught in another; it feels the need to be influenced, to be guided, to be put on its feet morally and spiritually. If then we live in a free society, we have the right and the duty to educate the child for freedom; or in other words, to 'compel it to be free'. But men in societies different from our own, however repulsive their ways to us, are not children. They are as much at home in their world as we in ours. We have no right to impose our preferences on them; they already have their own, and are no more at a loss what to be and what to do than we are. They have received their education as we have received ours. They may by our standards be greatly inferior to us; but at least they have their own standards. We impose our standards on our children, not because our standards are better than theirs, but because they have none of their own and look to us for guidance, and also because they too will live in the society which is both ours and theirs. We must not interfere with others, individuals or peoples, merely to impose on them what we think is good for them.

I speak, of course, of independent peoples. If we have already long been interfering with an alien people, if our government over them is already well established, and our interference has created problems that otherwise would not exist, and has raised demands unknown before, the matter is not so simple. If they need our help to solve these problems and to meet these demands, it is our duty to give it, provided we are really able to do so. We are not absolved from this duty merely because the more ambitious among them are eager to have us go. The people generally may hate us so much that it is out of our power to help them. But if we can help them to get what they want (and not just what we decide they should have) we ought to do it; our duty is to the whole people and not only to those of them (often the loudest) who have most to gain by our going quickly.

Even with independent peoples, whose difficulties and demands are not of our making, we are not always bound to refrain from interference except when they are openly aggressive. One country can be dangerous to others without being guilty of actual aggression. Its rulers may be preparing aggression. If their preparations are obvious, we can expect other countries to sympathize with us in our danger.

We can then call upon the future aggressors to cease their preparations, and if they refuse, we can attack them. But the preparations for aggression may not be obvious, and if we take a strong line with the would-be aggressors, we may find other countries sympathizing with them rather than with us. In that case, the less dangerous course may be secret interference in their domestic affairs to put obstacles in their way or to help put other rulers in their place. Both these courses are dangerous, and ought not to be lightly undertaken. Yet they may be legitimate.

Again, if a country supposed to be independent is not so in fact, we are not bound to treat it as if it were. We ought not to question the right of its rulers to rule it merely because they got power by methods we dislike; but if they do not really have the power they claim to have, if they are the instruments of a foreign government, we need not respect an independence which is not genuine. We have not a positive duty of interference, unless we are bound by treaty to protect that country's independence, but equally we have no duty not to interfere. Our right of interference is not here, as it is with a truly independent country, essentially a right to defend ourselves or our neighbours. It is not a right of interference merely in order to avert danger. We may interfere even when there is no pressing danger to avert provided we do not do more harm than good by interference. For example, if it was true that we ought not to have interfered in Hungary when the Russians gave power to Kadar, it was so, not because the then condition of Hungary added nothing to our own danger or the world's, but because our interference would have been useless and might have been dangerous. We are no more bound to accept the covert than the open subjection of one country by another. But if we do accept it, we thereby limit our right of interference to a right to take action to avert danger. If we treat a nominally independent country as if it were truly independent; if, say, we establish normal diplomatic relations with it, we have no more right to interfere with it than if it were in fact what it purports to be.[1]

Some people may not like this conclusion, that when we have established normal relations with a satellite country, we have no more right to interfere with it than if it were genuinely independent. Surely

---

1. This does not mean that recognition implies approval of the regime which is recognized; recognition implies only an undertaking to respect the conventions which govern relations between independent countries.

C

(they may say), though we have had, for one reason or another, to accept a great injustice for the time being, we are not thereby precluded from trying to set it right when occasion offers? At the moment we may do more harm than good by refusing to have normal relations with the satellite, by refusing to treat it as if it were independent; but later on it may be within our power to restore its independence. Why then should we not do so? Surely, it is one thing to respect the authority of an established government, no matter what its kind, in a truly independent country, and quite another to respect the authority of men who are the tools of a foreign Power?

This line of argument can lead to dangerous conclusions. If we are to undermine the authority of a satellite government on the ground that it is not independent, why should not other people undermine the authority of a colonial administration? True, the dependence of a colony is not masked; it is public and open. There is not (or there need not be) any hypocrisy about it. But what relevant difference does that make? If we claim a right to interfere with a satellite government's authority, it is presumably not because it purports to be other than it really is, but because it is a form of alien rule. It is not the hypocrisy we object to but the foreign domination. If that is our principle, we should apply it impartially, as much to ourselves as to other people. The government of an independent country may be hypocritical; it may pretend to be democratic when it is not. Does that give us the right to seek to undermine its authority? We need not condone aggression, but if we do, we cannot afterwards use it as an excuse for making trouble for the persons guilty of it. Or if we can, we must expect the same treatment from them, remembering that nearly all colonies are, in one way or another, fruits of aggression. This is not to say that, once we have established normal relations with a satellite country, we may do nothing to try to restore its independence; it means only that we ought not to do so by subverting the authority of the government established in it.[1]

Since the second World War the position of the colonial Powers in

---

1. To Englishmen or Frenchmen this will not appear a hard saying, but to refugees from countries under the heel of the foreigner it may well do so. I am sorry for it, for there is no class of people for whom I have greater sympathy. I should say that I am here speaking only of what *governments* are entitled to do or to allow to be done. It is not private persons but governments that recognize or do not recognize the independence of foreign countries. Private persons may have the moral right to do what governments ought not to do and even what governments forbid.

relation to their subject peoples has been greatly weakened. This is an effect of a change in the balance of power, not so much between European and non-European peoples, as between some European peoples and others. The British and French are relatively much weaker than they were, the Russians and Americans much stronger. Though the Americans and Russians have attacked many peoples weaker than themselves, taking vast territories from them, they have also been severe critics of 'colonialism'. Fortunately for them, the territories they seized touched their own and were sparsely populated; they could therefore absorb them as integral parts of their own countries. Russia and the United States extended their frontiers, while Britain and France remained the same size as before and reduced other countries overseas to subjection. This difference has seemed to the Russians and Americans to put them morally on a higher plane than the peoples guilty of 'colonialism'.

Now that the two greatest Powers are against colonialism, the pressure to grant self-government to colonies is much greater than it was. Whether or not this is to be regretted depends, from the point of view of the believer in freedom, on whether it increases or decreases the chances that freedom will spread. If it increases them, then what-ever the motives of these Powers, their influence will, from that point of view, have been good. For instance, it is not illogical to condemn Communism for what it is, and still to hold that the threat of it has had a salutary effect in parts of the world not overrun by it. I do not say that it has had this effect, at least not everywhere; but it probably has had it to some extent, and it is worth enquiring to what extent. Communism is clearly a challenge to the peoples who both own colonies and believe in freedom; it moves them to treat their colonies differently, sometimes more wisely and sometimes more foolishly than they otherwise would.

The threat of Communism has also affected America's attitude to colonialism. The countries owning the most colonies are America's chief allies, and the Americans have sometimes been embarrassed by this fact. When America was isolationist, Americans could denounce colonialism as much as they pleased without anyone being the better or the worse for it. But now that they think of their country as the champion of what they call 'the free world', they are anxious to put an end to what looks like a reproach to that world, the subjection of some peoples to others. They want all the peoples not yet captured by

Communism to be united against Communism; or if not united, not to be so bitterly divided as to enable Moscow to play some of them off against the others. They want 'colonialism' to end. At the same time, they want to avoid offending their more important allies. Their attitude to colonialism is therefore vacillating; they do not like it but they hesitate to condemn it. They condemn it less wholeheartedly than they did, and yet find themselves obliged by their self-chosen role as the supreme enemy of Communism to intervene as they used not to do between the old colonial Powers and their colonies. They are less censorious and more assiduous.

They are less censorious also for another reason. To them, as to others who care for freedom, it now seems less obvious than it once did that to give a country independence is to put its people in the quickest way of getting freedom. The colonies now claiming independence are not societies of the same kind as the thirteen colonies which signed the Declaration of Independence in 1776. The freedom of the individual was about as well respected in those colonies as in the mother-country, and they were already much closer to democracy. If capacity for freedom is our test, the thirteen revolted colonies, in spite of negro slavery, were fit for self-government; or at least not less fit than the country they rebelled against. It is by no means clear that the colonies now clamouring for independence are all fit for self-government in the same sense.

The Russian Communists are not, like the Americans, hesitant critics of colonialism; they can afford to condemn it utterly. Not because their record is cleaner, for it is incomparably worse by any standard, Marxist or otherwise, accepted by Europeans before 1917. They can afford to condemn colonialism relentlessly because the Asians and Africans know almost nothing about how the Russians have treated the peoples subject to them. The colonial Powers are not allies of the Russian Communists, who have nothing to lose and perhaps much to gain by making difficulties for them. Besides, the Communists have the cynicism always begotten by the ruthless exercise of power; they are not in the least put out by the accusations made against them. They have committed stupendous crimes, but they have never behaved like guilty men—except, perhaps, when on trial for their lives in their own countries.[1]

---

1. And really not even then. There is still a certain dignity about the man who feels guilty and behaves as if he were so, and therefore does not behave like a terrified animal.

I have said that the peoples until recently or still subject to European rule, impressed by the power and wealth of the Europeans, have adopted many of their methods and ideas. At least the more enterprising and influential among them have done so. Among these ideas is freedom. To some, perhaps to many, Asians and Africans freedom has come to mean a great deal. That the idea is European in origin does not mean that it is suited only to Europeans. It is a European idea only in the sense that it first arose in Europe; it is not European in the sense that there is something innate in Europeans which makes the idea more attractive to them or them more capable than others of making it real. It first arose among them for reasons which have nothing in particular to do with their natural aptitudes. Still, since the idea is European, and the Europeans conquered or otherwise made themselves masters of large parts of Asia and Africa, Asians and Africans often value the idea less for its own sake than in the hope of using it to raise themselves on a level with the conquerors and intruders from overseas. 'We want what you have got' is one way of saying 'we are as good as you'.

It is not, however, the only way of saying it. While the power and the wealth that shone brightest in Asian and African eyes came from the West, it was western ideas that seemed the most attractive apart from their own, to the extent that they remained loyal to them. But now it is no longer so necessarily. With the growth of Russian Communist power and wealth, and with the Russians more active all over the world, this pull of the West (a West as much hated as admired) is no longer as strong as it was. Or if as strong is no longer the only pull. There are other ideas, moral and political, as much associated with overwhelming power as western freedom and democracy. These other ideas are presented to the world as superior to western ideas. How tempting it is to say to alien, and often arrogant, intruders, 'Here is something as good as anything you have to offer, and better; if you try to prevent our having it, we must push you out of our way'. Conquerors, especially conquerors who stand aloof as aliens from their subjects, inevitably humiliate them; and it is pleasant to feel that the people who have humiliated us have been surpassed by others who not long ago were also thought of as inferiors. There are no doubt millions in Asia and Africa for whom Communism offers little or no attraction because they are still attached to their own traditions. It may even be that they are still the most numerous. But the times are against them. In a fast-changing world, they are the passive millions fated to be the victims of the ambitions of others. They are the dead weight of opposition to what the active and the strong thrust upon them in the name of progress. The conflicts that decide the fate of the Asian and African peoples will be fought out by minorities: by those who want freedom as the West understands it, by those who are Communists or sympathize with Communism, and by those, caring nothing for either freedom or Communism, who want to get independence for their countries and power for themselves by playing the Europeans off against one another.

Only the first of these groups is in any way attached to the West; though, of course, all three are keen to get material aid from the West and to use methods, industrial and military, first discovered in the West. Even the group who dislike both freedom and Communism are great innovators; they want to make their countries powerful and rich, and must use European methods to do so. Though they usually dislike Communism more than western democracy and freedom (to which they are often no more than indifferent), they resent the West more than they resent Communist Russia. They have known the western peoples more intimately and have been more humiliated by them. Fearful of Communism though they are, it is the western countries that they feel the need to be rude to and to defy. Indeed, even the group who really care about democracy and freedom have very mixed feelings for the West; they too are often suspicious and resentful. Both these groups feel that Communism stands in their way: either in the way of their getting what the West has taught them to value or in the way of their getting power. Yet they dislike the West more than they dislike Communist Russia, for they have scores to pay off only against the West. It gives them pleasure that there should be a rival to the West strong enough to vex and frighten peoples who have long treated them as inferiors.

The great attraction of Communism for the weaker and poorer nations is that it has, in one generation, raised the most 'backward' of the European peoples to a level with the most 'advanced'. What it has done once it may do again. Of course, it cannot do as much for other countries as it has done for Russia, since no other 'backward' country has natural resources so great. Yet it will do what it can do more quickly than other political movements, being harder and more reckless than they are. It appeals to the bold and the desperate, to fanatics in a hurry to make up for lost time; it appeals also to the ambitious who have no hope of making good in the accustomed ways. In countries where everyone is literate, where all interests are organized and articulate, where scarcely anyone has more to gain than to lose by violence, it makes sense to speak of government by persuasion and agreement. But where most people can neither read nor write, where they do not know what is happening around them or whom to trust, where 'progress' means nothing to them, though they are caught up in it, what is the use of persuasion? The dull, the silent, the long-suffering millions cling desperately to what is familiar, not because they understand and cherish it, but because they know nothing better. They must be torn free of the stupidity they are stuck in; they must be shaken into life and hope and intelligence. Before they are fit to be led, they must be driven. That is how many Communists and sympathizers with Communism think and feel in backward countries. That is certainly how they thought and felt in Yugoslavia; they were moved by anger and shame more than by pity. And they were angry, not only with the rich, but with the poor also. They were ashamed of the 'backwardness' of their country; they felt their ambitions and ideals as much kept back by the inertia and stupidity of the 'exploited' classes, whose cause they said was their own, as by their 'exploiters'.[1]

Communism has yet another attraction apart from the promise it seems to give to add quickly to the power and wealth of backward peoples. If it rejects freedom, moral and political, it does so in practice and not in theory. The Communists have never, as the Fascists have done, condemned democracy. Nor have they ever repudiated the belief which Marx shared with all the nineteenth-century socialists: that society must control production so as to make every man more free, more his own master, than ever before. The Communists condemn only the 'false democracy' of the West, claiming that their own kind is superior to it. And if they predict that eventually there will be no democracy anywhere, it is only because they also predict the end of the state, the end of all force used to oblige men to obedience. What is to come when there is no democracy is the perfect freedom of the full communist society, without exploitation or violence or the manipulation of man by man. The Communists say that their system

---

1. I speak of the Yugoslav Communists as they were in the years before they got power and immediately after they got it. Since then they have become milder, to their country's benefit and their own.

is already more democratic than what the West calls democracy; or else they say that the methods they use lead more quickly to genuine freedom. While some classes exploit others, they say, there can be neither true democracy nor true freedom; what matters, therefore, is to put an end to exploitation as quickly as possible. Sometimes the Communists are moved to denounce the hypocrisy of western political methods and to boast that their own are better; while at other times they are less concerned to make comparisons between methods in current use than to claim that the future belongs to them. They like to use many arguments and to get the best of them all, even though to the intellectually fastidious some seem to go rather badly with others. 'You boast of democracy,' the Communists say, 'while we admit that our government is a class rule, the dictatorship of the proletariat, but still we are at bottom more democratic than you are.' And they also say, 'We know what is happening in the world, and we call things by their true names; we are waging a ruthless war against our class enemies, and we stop at nothing to prevent them misleading and corrupting the people.'

These Communist arguments will not impress the logician or the close student of recent history. Nor will they impress the millions in the West who live comfortably, innocent of both logic and history; who, though they cannot refute Communist arguments, care nothing for them. No doubt, in Asia and Africa, too, the millions are indifferent to these arguments. But there are people who are attracted by them, and who have a chance of getting power. When western democracy is called a fraud, is not the accusation likely to seem most plausible in the countries least experienced in working western institutions? The bad workman blames his tools. This is as true of political as of other instruments; and is not the less true because it is not the workman's fault that he lacks skill. Men are not excited by ideas and hopeful of institutions in the measure that they understand them; they expect too much to begin with, and are afterwards too greatly disappointed. They are embarrassed and frustrated by what they cannot use, and are eager to throw it away and to try something different. If they are told that the fault lies, not in themselves, but in their institutions, they are only too willing to believe. What they have taken from the West is shoddy. Let them make ready for a better freedom by using better methods. Communism does not, like Fascism, renounce what the West proclaims; it offers to surpass it. Marxism, like all the other brands of socialism, is rooted in the individualism and rationalism of the eighteenth century; it adds nothing to, and abates nothing from, the idea of freedom defined by English and French radicals. Marx aimed at the same end as they did, though he differed from them in advocating different methods and in predicting different social and political conditions when the end was attained. He came not to deny the radicals but to fulfil them. Since the Communists have not repudiated Marx, they can say that they too are aiming at the freedom praised by the West; but with this difference, that they are sincere and also know how to get what they are aiming at. To people not fully at home with European social and political ideas, and thus disappointed in western institutions, this argument sometimes carries conviction.

Even in the West there are hundreds who detest Communism because they are shocked by its brutalities for every one who sees how far its achievements fall short of its principles. Outside the West, there are even fewer people who can see the strength and the weakness of the arguments used for and against Communism and western democracy, and there are many more who are indifferent to, or sceptical about, the stories (coming mostly from western sources) of Communist atrocities. Perhaps also there are fewer people shocked by these stories even when they believe them to be true. The tale of the Communists as friends of freedom does not sound everywhere as hollow as it does in the West. To Asians and Africans it comes at least as easily to take the West Europeans for hypocrites. Have they not heard them preaching freedom and equality? And have they not often been treated with contempt by them? Not merely refused the rights they asked for on the ground that they were not yet ready to use them properly, but insulted and despised?

Communism has one great advantage over democracy; it offers easy solutions in 'backward' countries. I do not mean that there are no hazards to being a Communist. Indeed there are, and sometimes they are great. It is safer to be a Communist in England than in Russia, and even than in Yugoslavia. But in a backward country, if you are a democrat, it is often extraordinarily difficult to know what to do for the best. You may know that, socially and economically, there is a need to take drastic action. But how can you take it if you renounce all methods likely to destroy what little of democracy and freedom you already have? You cannot rely, as you can in England, on deep-rooted prejudices and habits that support the elaborate structure of democracy and freedom in the modern state. In England, to be a good democrat and liberal, you have only to behave as most people expect you to behave; but to be so in a 'backward' country, without being ineffectual, you need rare intelligence, self-control, and moral courage. To be a good Communist in a 'backward' country, you need to be aggressive, sly, bold, and quick to seize your opportunities. Admittedly, the last two of these qualities are far from common, but they are not all that rare.

Whether in a 'backward' country it is easier to be a Communist or an authoritarian of some other kind depends on circumstances. I shall say more of these circumstances later.[1]

---

1. It is, however, important to distinguish the non-Communist authoritarian regimes of Asia and Africa from European Fascism. Except in Europe, most non-Communist authoritarian regimes have been established by the educated classes or by nationalist movements which have arisen in the armed forces or have gained control over them before capturing the state. The peculiarity of Fascism is that it is a revolt of the gutter against both the educated classes and the egalitarian movement which gave birth to democracy and to socialism.

2

Capacity for Self-Government

I⊤ follows from what was said in the first chapter that the very conception of capacity for self-government is due to the spread of ideas which were originally European. The peoples subject to the Europeans governed themselves for centuries before the Europeans came among them. There was then no sense in saying they were not fit to do so. They may have been governed badly by European standards, but those standards were not then relevant. What has made them relevant is the domination of the world by the Europeans and the acceptance by other peoples of European methods and ideals. Asians conquered Asians, and Africans Africans, without anybody seeking to justify these conquests on the ground that the conquered were unfit to govern themselves. Nobody then cared for the responsibility of conquerors for the good government of the conquered. And when the Europeans first acquired dominions outside Europe, their doing so was not wrong either by their own or by other standards. The need to justify their conquests and the possibility of condemning them both came afterwards, as the European conquerors evolved liberal and democratic ideals and institutions at home and preached their virtues abroad.

We have seen, too, that the Europeans have not, by their brutality or weakness, proved themselves unfit to govern other peoples. They have not been less humane to their subjects than Asians and Africans to theirs. Their wealth and their power are now greater than ever. If they were united in the resolve to keep other peoples subject to them, there would be no hope of independence for those peoples.

The general acceptance of European ideas about democracy and freedom does not, of course, condemn their conquests retrospectively. If what the European conquerors did was not thought wrong at the time they did it, it is absurd to say to them now: 'Because what you took was not rightfully taken by principles that have come to be

widely accepted since you took it, you now have no right to keep it.'
We should never use this argument about private property. No
matter how our ancestors came by what is now ours, we have a right
to keep what we have inherited. The right, of course, is not absolute.
We may sometimes be rightly deprived of our property for the benefit
of others; but then the ground of the deprivation is that benefit and not
the wickedness, by present standards, of the methods used by our
ancestors to get the property. Indeed, even if those methods were
thought evil at the time they were used, our title to the property is not
shaken. Those who decide whether or not we shall keep it must ask
themselves, not how our ancestors got it, but what good can be done
now by taking it away from us. This is as true of government as of
property. However little interested conquerors were in the good of
their subjects at the time they conquered them, it may now be for their
subjects' good that they should continue to rule them. Or, however
justified the conquest was when it took place, it may now be right that
the conquerors should withdraw. Right, not for some high philosophical reason intelligible only to the learned, but because withdrawal
is necessary to give the people concerned what they most want.

I have said that European wealth and power have imposed European
standards on the rest of the world. This imposition has not been
merely by force. The Europeans first went to Asia and Africa to get
rich by trade, without wishing to conquer and rule. True, they sometimes forced their trade on reluctant peoples; but more often, at least
to begin with, they were welcomed. The first concessions and privileges granted to them were not usually extorted by force; they were
freely granted because it was thought to the advantage of both parties
that they should be. Later, they were often found irksome and
arbitrarily revoked or restricted; and the Europeans, if they felt strong
enough to do so, used force to get them restored and to enlarge them.
Or else, having got some concessions willingly made, they afterwards
extorted others as they came to know their 'hosts' better and learned to
exploit their weaknesses. Thus, gradually, they ceased to be privileged
foreign communities and became conquerors and rulers.

The attitude of their hosts [1] to the Europeans was mixed even after
force was used against them. They resented European domination

---

1. I use the word 'host' deliberately for two of its meanings: sometimes it is the correla-
tive of 'guest' and sometimes of 'parasite'.

and the social changes following upon it, but they also valued many of the things brought to them by the Europeans. Their feelings were mixed in two ways. They admired their guests and also hated them; and again, they wanted what the Europeans had to offer and yet disliked some of the effects of their coming. Their feelings were mixed both towards the Europeans themselves and towards what the Europeans were doing to their countries. Unfortunately, it was usually beyond their power to sort out their feelings, and to adopt a well-considered policy towards these guests who stayed too long. They behaved capriciously and incoherently, partly because they often did not understand what was happening to them as a result of European intrusion, and partly because they were weak. It takes both knowledge and strength to decide what to absorb of foreign influences and how to control them. Only the Japanese have come near to deciding for themselves how they would come to terms with the dominant civilization of Europe. Other peoples have been much more at the mercy of a process incomprehensible to them. Some among them, the upper classes, gained more than the others materially from European trade, while the others perhaps gained more in the end from the peace and security brought by European rule. But they all lost many of the old ways dear to them.

It would be idle to pretend that the Europeans knew what their intrusion meant to the peoples affected by it. They had, however, the advantage of being masters of the situation; they could impose their own solutions even when they did not understand the problems that faced them. Moreover, the further their influence penetrated, the more the societies they dominated came to need the services which they were the best able to render. Without perhaps seeing very deeply into the processes started by their coming, they came nearer to having the knowledge required to deal effectively with the problems of societies rapidly becoming westernized. The more they transformed the lives of the peoples dominated by them, the more necessary they became to those peoples. Not until they had passed their knowledge on to their subjects could they cease to be necessary to them.

The Europeans have also another advantage. They have been pioneers not only of the natural sciences but of the social sciences as well. It is often said that the social sciences are not properly sciences at all. I shall not dispute this verdict, although it is profoundly misleading. It would need many pages to sift out the error and the truth in it. But no one, I think, will contest that the Europeans have devoted more time than other peoples to the systematic study of social institutions, past and present. They have long been accustomed to the idea that societies differ greatly from one another and are all in process of continual change. They have also, more than other peoples, been deliberate reformers; they have often tried to change institutions in order to improve them. This reforming zeal has itself been largely an effect of a closer study of society and social change. The myth of progress was born at about the same time as the serious study of history began. Since then, of course, history has been the powerful ally of philosophy in exploding that myth; but the fact remains that the Europeans, whether they believe in progress or not, have been the longest and closest students of society. They have come nearer than other peoples to creating a vocabulary adequate for the description of social institutions and social change. Both the academic and the practical language of modern politics is theirs. That is to say, where political and other social institutions are systematically discussed, they are discussed in terms of concepts invented in Europe, and the actual business of government is everywhere carried on largely in idioms of European origin. To understand the modern world, to explain what is happening to it, and to know how to act effectively in it, a man must be able to think and speak about it in European ways, even when he speaks of Asia and Africa. It may be a pity it should be so, but the fact remains.

To say that Europeans and people who have learnt to think in European ways understand the modern world best is not, of course, to say that they understand other people's feelings and wants better than those people do themselves. To understand social institutions and social change is not to understand how people feel. The English, who are the most successful politically of all European peoples, and who have contributed as much as any people to the social sciences, are perhaps rather slow at understanding feelings they do not share. Few things are more striking about them than the contrast between this dullness and their acuteness when they discuss impersonal matters.

(1) *Capacity for self-government short of capacity for democracy*

The gradual extension of European trade over the world brought with it the first notion of fitness for self-government: *the ability to afford to modern trade and industry the security they need.* Not only the Europeans, but the natives who traded with them, stood to gain by this security. At first the security depended mostly on special privileges granted to the Europeans, and on extra-territorial rights. But as trade with Europe grew and affected more and more widely the economies of non-European countries, it came to depend on more than that. It came to depend on courts of law and governmental practices enforcing European types of contract and European notions of right. The need for these courts and practices was felt by everyone engaged in the lines of trade and industry introduced by the Europeans. Thus, by good government was understood efficient and not too corrupt government. If the native rulers could provide it, with more or less of European 'advice', they were left to do it; but if they could not, the Europeans often took their place. They excused their action by saying that the native rulers had proved 'unfit to govern'. They usually did not even attempt to justify themselves by an appeal to local or universal standards; 'fitness for government' meant for them merely willingness and capacity to give scope for and protection to economic activities of the European type. By the time they took over the government of a country, whether openly or otherwise, there were often considerable sections of the native population who stood to gain by their doing so. These people might dislike the foreigner and resent his arrogance, but they needed the same kind of security as he did.

The Europeans soon came to take an interest in more than trade. They did not become conquerors and rulers only to provide better security for their trade; but rather, having become conquerors and rulers, they acquired in time other than economic interests in the countries they ruled. They acquired a sense of mission. They thought it their duty to bring good government and personal security, as these things were understood in Europe, to the peoples whom they ruled. Except towards the end of the nineteenth century, during the 'scramble for Africa', they seldom took possession of a country in order to 'civilize' it; but, having once got involved in it in one way or another, they quickly persuaded themselves that they were there to do more than protect their own interests. And so, in a sense, they were; for as soon as they were actually responsible for the government of any country, they usually did more than was needed merely to protect European trade and industry. That is not to say that they did not continue to prefer European to native interests, or that when they acted in what they honestly believed to be the interests of the natives, the natives agreed with them or were wrong if they disagreed.

This sense of mission carried with it another conception of fitness for self-government: *the ability to afford security of person and good government by the standards of western Europe.* This second conception is not unrelated to the first. On the contrary, it is in some ways closely related to it. Yet the two conceptions do not coincide, and the second is more demanding than the first. A country could be well enough governed to afford security to European trade and industry and yet not be well governed by this second standard. For example, most of the Balkan countries, even before 1914, were fit for self-government by the first standard, and yet some of them were not so by the second; whereas Austria and Hungary were so by both standards. Good government, by this second standard, means a great deal more than respect for rights of property and the enforcement of contracts; it means constitutional government in the sense of government which scrupulously respects definite rules and conventions in the exercise of power. True, there cannot be security of person where there is no security of property, but it does not follow that where property is secure the person is so too. The person is not fully secure unless those in authority scrupulously respect the rules that define their authority, and unless those rules are precise. Moreover, there can be greater security for some kinds of property and contract than for others; namely, for the kinds involved in trade and industry of the European type. Where this is so, a country may be fit to govern itself by the first criterion and unfit by the second.

There is a third criterion of capacity for self-government different from, though in line with, the first. We may say that *a country is capable of self-government when it can produce native rulers strong enough and responsible enough to respect international law.* This criterion is in line with the first because it takes into account primarily a government's attitude to people other than its own subjects. If a government respects international law, then the country it governs is a tolerable neighbour. Yet this third criterion is clearly different from the first. A country may be so far from giving adequate protection to foreign traders and industrialists as not even to allow them in, and yet may respect international law in its dealings with other countries. Even more obviously, this third criterion differs from the second. A country may not provide security of person and may not have constitutional government, and yet may be a good neighbour in the community of nations. Some people say that the Communist countries are, or might easily become, good neighbours; they say that the difficulties we have with them are due much more to mutual distrust (for which we are to blame as much as they are) than to Communist contempt for international law. This may well be true. Certainly, if a government does respect international law, it does as much as other governments are usually held to have the right to expect from it. If it allows foreign traders and industrialists to establish businesses within its territory, it will be expected to protect their interests, and if it allows foreigners to settle there, it will be expected to give them security of person; but its right to keep them out will not ordinarily be contested. If it lets them in, it can create special conditions for them, or it can treat them as it treats its own subjects. In the first case, it carries out its obligations to them so long as it scrupulously respects the conditions it has itself laid down, and does not arbitrarily change them, but gives due notice of its intention of doing so; so long as it either sees to it that foreigners can take action to avoid being seriously damaged by its change of policy, or else compensates them for the damage done to them. In the second case, it carries out its obligation by treating foreigners (and therefore also its own subjects) consistently; by making it clear what rules it means to enforce, and enforcing them impartially.

The emergence in the West of several powerful and independent states in close and continuous contact with one another, the creation overseas of other West European States (as much West European as the Greek cities outside Greece were Greek), and West European cultural influence and political domination over the Slavs, the Asians, and the Africans, have created, for the first time in history, a world-wide community of states. Another way of saying the same thing is that these developments have brought into existence very widely accepted notions about how governments should treat one another and how they should treat persons subject to their authority. These notions cover more than is covered by international law, public and private; for international law includes only rules for the breach of which a government can be held responsible before some international body or which other governments have by tradition a moral right to require it to obey and to take reprisals against it for not obeying. Still, these notions and international law, public and private, are very

D

closely connected. A government is expected not only to conform to certain rules in its dealings with other governments; it is also expected to conform to rules in its dealings with foreigners within its own territory; and these last rules are derived from notions about how any government ought to treat all individuals within its territories. The great difference between its own subjects and foreigners is that foreigners have other protectors besides itself. The criteria of capacity for self-government so far discussed derive therefore, ultimately, from notions wider than international law.

These notions, and also the rules of international law deriving from them, are of European origin because it was in western Europe that there first arose several strongly organized states in close contact with one another. Though today these rules and notions are widely accepted outside the area of their birth, they are not all accepted everywhere. Communist countries have their own ideas about how governments should treat their subjects. Their respect for international law clearly does not rest on their accepting western ideas about this matter, though they sometimes speak as if they accepted them. They do, however, respect international law in their own way and for their own purposes. If they allow foreigners into their territory, they give them security, not because they care for individual rights, but because they need the services of foreigners and wish to avoid trouble with foreign governments. Communist countries are not markedly less scrupulous than others in keeping the agreements they make. Because they are suspicious, they keep to the letter of them rather than the spirit; they are punctilious rather than loyal. But perhaps the same can be said of the western Powers in their dealings with the Communists. They are apt to be more loyal in their dealings with one another than with the Communists. This is only to be expected. The less people trust one another, the more they accuse each other of bad faith and the more narrowly they interpret their mutual obligations. Like misers they push meanness as far as the need to preserve the appearance of honesty allows. The Communist states have, in practice, a considerable respect for international law; but they have it without accepting the principles on which this respect often rests in other countries. They do not even pretend to care for the security of private traders and industrialists in foreign countries; and they do not really care for individual rights or national independence for their own sake. They are, however, strongly organized states in a world where all countries are brought into closer relations with other countries than they used to be; they are ruled by political parties which keep firm hold on power and take the long view. In their behaviour towards other states, they are at least as consistent and far-seeing as the western Powers. They respect international law because it pays them to do so; and with this respect there necessarily goes an outward concern for the independence of other nations.

That capacity for self-government, in our first two senses, means nothing to the Communists is obvious, since they care nothing either for the security of private traders and industrialists or for individual rights and constitutional government. The reader may object that it is unfair to say that it also means nothing to them in our third sense. If they respect international law, do they not thereby admit the right to self-government of other countries which respect that law? And does not this involve accepting our third criterion of capacity for self-government? I do not think so. The Communists do not really believe that they ought to respect a country's independence if that country respects international law; they do not believe that its being a good neighbour to other countries is a sufficient reason for not interfering in its domestic affairs. Since they believe that it is their duty as Communists to help people who share their faith to come to power in any country, provided they can give this help without doing more harm than good to their own countries or to the Communist movement generally, they do not believe in respecting the independence of non-Communist countries. They may often respect it in practice because they find it expedient to do so, but they do not believe that they ought to respect it. The rule they accept is, 'Let us do nothing that harms our country or our movement', and not, 'Let us respect the independence of every country that is a good neighbour to us and to others'.

The Communist states are a good deal more nationalist than they were, and perhaps set less store by the duty to help foreign Communists get power; and no doubt, too, western governments, in pursuing national interests, sometimes forget the duty to respect the independence of countries that are good neighbours. Still, the difference between the Communist and the western states remains; the social philosophy of the Communists makes capacity for self-government a meaningless, or at least an irrelevant, criterion to them, whereas the social philosophy of the western Powers does not. This is so, even though it is often the plain interest of Communist states in their dealings with other states to respect their independence by respecting international law.

A country's incapacity for self-government by one or more of these criteria has never, even by the Powers that accept the criteria, been held enough in itself to justify intervention in its domestic affairs. The Powers are interested in maintaining peace, and any intervention by one country in another's domestic affairs which threatens war is likely to be condemned by them. Hence, in practice, incapacity for self-government has seldom been held to justify intervention except of the strong in the affairs of the weak. This has always made this excuse for intervention seem hypocritical. The victims of it have said, 'You only do this to us because we are weak; if we were strong you would not dare'. The reproach is natural but perhaps also rather beside the point. If it is right to use force to protect your interests, you cannot be condemned for using it against someone weaker than you are merely because you would not have used it against someone stronger. There is no point in your using it unless you can do so effectively. The proper reason for condemning interference by a strong country in the domestic affairs of a weak one is the same as for condemning the interference of any country in the affairs of another country which has offended it: the plaintiff ought not also to be judge and executioner. If, however, there is no impartial judge strong enough to enforce his judgements, the plaintiff, if he thinks he stands to gain by it, will try to be judge and executioner; and other people liable to be offended as he has been will not condemn his action.

Thus it was that, before 1914, the stronger European Powers with interests to defend in weaker countries often sympathized with one another when they interfered in the domestic affairs of those countries. All they asked of each other was that they should respect the interests of other strong Powers. Sometimes they divided parts of the world where there were only weak governments into 'spheres of influence', each being given by the others a free hand to intervene in the domestic affairs of the countries within the sphere allotted to it, provided it took care not to harm the interests of the other Powers. At other times, where the Powers could not agree upon spheres of influence, they undertook to consult one another and to deal jointly with any country that offended them. Whether they acted separately or together, they acted on the assumption that what they required of weaker countries was required justly. If those countries did not behave as they were required to do, they were pronounced unfit for self-government. Even if they were not reduced to formal dependence on one or other of the European Powers, their independence was often in practice severely limited. Not all the Powers of European stock were agreed about how to treat weaker nations. The Americans, on the whole, disliked the establishment of permanent European rule over non-European peoples, though they did nothing much to stop it except in China. They were also generally suspicious of punitive expeditions undertaken by the other Powers, believing that they would lead to some kind of permanent rule, open or disguised, over the peoples receiving 'punishment'. They were, however, quite willing at times to take punitive action against weaker nations in the western hemisphere. Perhaps they thought that the right to punish belongs only to the virtuous.

The attitude before 1914 of the stronger European Powers to the weaker peoples in the Balkans and in Asia and Africa is clear enough; it is revealed in their actions. In the weaker nations, the attitude of westernized persons to western intervention is less clear. They accepted western criteria of capacity for self-government, but they probably condemned western intervention, looking upon it as nearly always a cloak for aggression. They may well have thought that intervention is wrong in practice, because the real motive behind it is likely to be the desire to dominate; or else that, even when that motive is not the strongest from the beginning, it is apt soon to become so. But where western rule was long established, they did not always want to put an end to it immediately, realizing that it had created problems which could not be easily solved without the help of the rulers. They probably wanted the western Powers to keep out of weak countries that were still independent, and to prepare to leave in the fullness of time the countries already subject to them.

After the first World War the old ideas about intervention were either abandoned or modified. The Powers at war had accused each other of atrocious crimes and had spoken of their enemies as uncivilized peoples. Thus, confidence in the moral superiority of civilized Europe was greatly diminished even among the Europeans. The Powers established a League of Nations, and by setting up the system of mandates admitted that they could be responsible to an international body for how they ruled peoples not yet capable of ruling themselves. True, the victors refused to admit this responsibility in the case of peoples already subject to them before the war; only colonies and provinces taken from the vanquished were mandated territories. True also that the rulers of these territories often resented the League's interest in them. Yet the principle was established that European Powers could be responsible for how they ruled 'backward' peoples to an international body which included many more than European states. Though from time to time one of the great Powers, entirely on its own initiative, took action against some weak nation accused of behaving in a manner unworthy of an independent state, the need for such action was often deplored even by the Power that took it, which usually hastened to assure the world that it had no intention of establishing its permanent rule over the offending nation. It was coming to be more and more widely admitted that intervention, to be justified, must be undertaken by or on behalf of a world community of nations, and even then must not be a cloak for establishing *permanent* foreign rule. When Japan and Italy, in Manchuria and in Abyssinia, did what had often been done by the old colonial Powers before 1914, they were solemnly condemned as aggressors. If they were not punished for what they did, it was because it was thought too dangerous to punish them. They had not intervened merely to protect their interests; they had established their own rule, disguised or open, over a foreign people. They had offended against new canons of decent international behaviour.

The old colonial Powers dominating the League of Nations were accused of hypocrisy for condemning in others what they had themselves often done. Their actual motives do not concern us; for this essay deals with theoretical rather than historical questions. From the point of view of the political theorist the accusation of hypocrisy is irrelevant. The League of Nations was created to enforce new standards of international behaviour, and both Japan and Italy had joined the League without being compelled to do so. These new standards were not arbitrarily set up by the Powers that condemned Japan and Italy; they were entirely in keeping with conceptions of justice widely accepted long before the League was created. It had long been held that independent states, in their dealings with one another, ought to conform to definite rules. Not, of course, to the same rules as individuals, but to rules resting on similar moral assumptions: that independent communities ought not to interfere in one another's domestic concerns, and that disputes between them, when they arise, ought to be settled by an impartial judge. It was because this sentiment had been gaining strength for a long time, not least among the great colony-owning Powers, that it had at last been possible to set up an International Court at the Hague and a League of Nations at Geneva. The setting up of these bodies had inevitably altered the rules of international behaviour, and had not done so for the special benefit of the old colonial Powers. These bodies, in so far as they were effective, made it easier for the weaker nations to resist the stronger. That, however, was not necessarily against the interest of the stronger nations even in their dealings with the weaker ones. It all depended on what they wanted of the weaker nations. If they wanted to use the failure of weaker nations to protect foreign interests as an excuse for gaining control over them, these new bodies were certainly a nuisance to them; and the greater their authority, the greater the nuisance. But if all that the strong nations wanted was to protect their own interests abroad, they could do it best by strengthening the authority of the International Court and the League. These new bodies did not reject the old conceptions of capacity for self-government; they merely gave a new status to them; the reasons which the European Powers had given, sometimes sincerely and sometimes not, for intervening in the domestic affairs of weaker nations and for taking over their government were now put forward by international bodies as rules of conduct for all nations to conform to. Nations accused of breaking the rules were in future neither to be reduced to subjection by their accusers nor to be allowed to break the rules with impunity. That at least was the hope of those who created these bodies. What had too often in the past looked like European excuses for extending European rule were to be raised to the level of principles acceptable to all peoples.

(2) *Capacity for liberal democracy*

The fourth criterion of capacity for self-government, which is *the ability to work the institutions that make democracy and freedom effective*, differs from the other three so much as to deserve to be put in a separate class. Unlike the others, it has not been used to justify either the intervention of a stronger country in the government of a weaker one or the taking of disciplinary action by an international body. It has been used only to justify the continuance of alien rule where it is already established or (as with the mandated territories) the transference of an already subject people from one master to another. It is not, of course, the only criterion that can be used for this purpose. The continuance of alien rule can also be justified on the ground that it is needed to make a 'backward' country capable of taking its part in the community of nations. Unless it can produce a government able to maintain effective authority, it cannot give adequate protection to person and property or have normal relations with other countries, and will therefore not be thought fit to govern itself. The peculiarity of the fourth criterion is therefore not that it alone is used to justify continued alien rule but that it alone is used for no other purpose than this. The other criteria have been used to justify foreign intervention or the setting up of foreign rule or punitive action by an international body; this criterion has not.

It might be objected that this criterion differs so much from the others that it ought not to be treated as a criterion of capacity for self-government. Self-government, after all, is not the same as democracy; at least not in the sense in which different countries are interested in each other's capacity for self-government. Countries, like persons, are interested in the behaviour of others primarily as it affects themselves. It matters less to them how other countries manage their own affairs than that they should not be a nuisance to their neighbours and to foreigners living in their midst. What more can we decently ask of other people than that they should be good neighbours? If a country is capable of self-government in the three senses already discussed, it is by definition a good neighbour to other countries. If it allows foreigners in as traders or in other capacities, it gives them security of person and property, either treating them as it does its own subjects, whom it treats fairly by standards generally accepted, or else giving them a special status which it respects; and it maintains normal relations with other countries. While it does this, what right have other countries to expect more of it?

Nothing more, no doubt, provided that the country in question is independent. Independent countries have no rights against one another except that they should respect international law and whatever agreements they have freely made; and their duties to each other flow from these rights and agreements. But the duties of a country to its colonies and dependencies are different from, and greater than, these. It has a duty to do justice to all its subjects while it rules them, and therefore a duty to see to it (in so far as this is possible) that justice will be done to them when it ceases to rule them. In other words, quite apart from the duty to make what provision it can to ensure that a colony or dependency, when it becomes independent, will be a good neighbour to other countries, it has also to ensure that it will deal justly with its own citizens. It may be out of its power to ensure this, but it ought to strive to do so as far as it can. In theory this need not mean that it must ensure that the colony, when it gets independence, is as fit for democracy as alien rule can make it; though under modern conditions, for reasons that I shall discuss later, it is in practice likely to mean this. In any case, if the subject people aspire to democracy and freedom, the alien ruler ought, if possible, to see to it that they do not get independence under conditions likely to prevent their getting the freedom and democracy they want. Therefore, where it is a question of granting independence to a subject people, capacity for self-government, in the sense of the ability to work the institutions that make democracy and freedom effective, is a very relevant criterion. That, no doubt, is why the phrase 'capacity for self-government' is as often used in this sense as in the other three.

Capacity for self-government, in the first and third senses, requires above all strong government. If a political system provides strong government, the rulers can pursue consistent and rational policies. They may not always do so, but at least the system does not prevent their doing so; and the longer it has lasted, the more likely they are to pursue such policies. Where a system provides only weak governments, they cannot maintain stable relations with other governments or give adequate protection to foreigners in their territories. A strong government can refuse to admit foreigners and cannot be bullied by foreign Powers into admitting them; or it can admit them on its own terms. If they come in on those terms, it is strong enough to keep to those terms itself and to oblige them to do so. If it is weak, it cannot keep foreigners out or give them adequate security when they have come in or prevent their taking advantage of its weakness. It cannot control foreigners unless it can control its own subjects; and if its subjects can be used against it by foreigners, it cannot avoid losing its independence.

To be strong enough for this purpose a government must be able to know what is going on in its own territories and must be able to enforce its decisions. True, in the early Middle Ages all governments in Europe were too weak to do this; but in those days that did not much matter, for there were also no governments strong enough to take permanent advantage of this weakness. The modern state in full control of all its subjects did not yet exist. Where all countries have weak governments (or rather all countries in contact with one another), then none is incapable of self-government merely because it is weak. Notions of strength and weakness vary from age to age. As soon as some countries become much stronger than others, there arise new conceptions of what governments owe to their subjects and their subjects to them, and also new conceptions of how governments should treat one another. These conceptions arise, of course, first in the strong countries. The strong countries, just because they are strong, are more enterprising than the others, and so too are their citizens, who move into foreign parts, demanding everywhere the same protection from government that they are in the habit of receiving at home. If they cannot get it, they either take matters into their own hands (as so many traders and adventurers have done) or they call upon their home governments to protect their interests. Iron pots are not more beautiful or even more useful than earthenware, but they give and take harder knocks. Put them among the others and the others are no longer safe.

Clearly a small country can have strong government in this sense. It can even be militarily weak and have it. Switzerland is a small country and its armed forces are not very formidable; any one of its large neighbours could overrun the country in a day or two. That none is tempted to do so is doubtless largely due to Switzerland's being neutral and to their all having an interest in respecting that neutrality. But Switzerland has a strong government; it can afford to all men, citizens and foreigners, the protection which they feel is their due, and it can also maintain normal relations with other countries. Strength, in this sense, depends, not on the size of the armed forces, but on efficient administration; on the government's knowing what is happening and being able to take quick and effective action. Nearly all European governments are strong by this measure if we compare them with many governments outside Europe. This sort of capacity for self-government does not require humane and decent administration. Any country, however brutally governed, however much its citizens are liable to be victims of secret and arbitrary power, is capable of self-government in this sense if it has a powerful police force and a well-disciplined, watchful, and energetic hierarchy of public officials large enough to control all communities and organizations inside it. Russia and China are both, by this standard, more capable of self-government than they used to be before the Communists took control of them; but they are not therefore more civilized or more decently governed by Marxian or liberal or any other standards except those evolved by the Communists since the Bolshevik revolution. They are, however, strong enough to give ample protection to foreigners whom they choose to admit within their frontiers, and to maintain equal and stable relations with other states.

Capacity for self-government in the second sense requires a good deal more than in the first and third senses. It requires, not only efficient administration, but an independent judiciary with high professional standards and, in all branches of government, a scrupulous respect for rules, written and unwritten, governing the exercise of power. What these rules are must be known to more people than those who actually have the power supposed to be limited by the rules, and it must be possible to lodge effective complaints against those people when they are suspected of breaking the rules. This means that there must be, in the broad sense, constitutional government. Not democracy, and not even parliamentary government, but the kind of government that Montesquieu had in mind when he distinguished the French monarchy from what he called oriental despotism. Under the old monarchy in France the courts of law were, he thought, in fact (though not in name) independent of the king; judicial offices were hereditary and there were also exacting standards of competence and impartiality, at least in the highest courts. There was already an elaborate machinery of government, clumsy perhaps and dilatory, but bound by rules and traditions widely known and openly discussed, which it was difficult even for the supposedly absolute monarch to change. Government depended considerably on an informed and critical public opinion. Its authority was limited, in much more than the minimal sense in which all authority is limited because the people, if they are pushed too far, will refuse obedience or openly revolt. It was limited also by a strong belief among the educated part of the nation (including the public officials) that it ought to be exercised in definite and established ways, and that new processes ought not to replace old ones unless it could be shown that change was in the public interest. Though the king's authority was legally absolute, its exercise in his name by his subordinates was elaborate, clearly defined, and already subject to independent, diverse, and informed criticism. Less subject, no doubt, to this kind of criticism than the exercise of authority in England, but yet subject to it considerably and continuously. Though this was less true of other absolute monarchies in western and central Europe, it was true also of them to some extent. Government in most of them was carried on at the top by a hierarchy of well-educated officials, executive and judicial, with fairly high professional standards, and who belonged socially to classes with a considerable tradition of rational criticism and independent thought. For reasons I need not go into, these old monarchies found it much more difficult to adapt themselves to changing social conditions than the parliamentary monarchy of England. Yet they were not, in the eighteenth century, before the French revolution shook them, very noticeably less attentive to the needs of the poor or less respectful of established rights or less open-minded than the English House of Commons. They did not give foreigners a special and more secure status than that of their own subjects; they afforded much the same protection to everyone living in their territories, or if they discriminated between them did so less on grounds of nationality than of class. They were capable of self-government in the second of the senses I have discussed, and therefore in a sense different from the sense in which Russia is now capable of it. It may not matter much to foreigners that a country should be capable of self-government in this sense rather than in the sense in which Russia is so. But still the two senses are different, and both are and have been widely used; and it is therefore worth while distinguishing between them.

To be capable of self-government in the fourth sense, that is, to be able to work the institutions that make democracy and freedom possible, a people must have other qualities besides the ones we have discussed already. They need not all, or even many of them, understand how the system that gives them democracy and freedom works, but they must know how to act in order that it should work; they must know what to do. What I have just said may sound like paradox, and I must make my meaning plainer.

It is only in highly sophisticated societies that there are many people—and even then they are a small minority of the whole population—who know how the political system, taken as a whole, works. Their knowledge is imperfect, as all knowledge of anything vastly intricate must be; there are many parts of the machinery of government of whose internal workings they know scarcely anything. They understand the system as a whole, not because they understand every part in detail, but because they understand how the parts fit together to form a whole. These people are mostly not active politicians; they are mostly critical observers inspired by curiosity. They lack the experience that an active politician needs, and are often by temperament unfit to take any larger direct share in the government of their country than the ordinary citizen who does no more than cast a vote at elections. Yet they have a special and great importance: they help to refine the language of politics and to create the climate of political opinion. A free society is always a politically conscious and critical society, and the persons who by their work form that critical consciousness are essential to that type of society. A free society, unless it is small and simple, tends to be, politically, a highly sophisticated society. It not only tends to be sophisticated, but needs to be so, if it is to remain free. Sophistication is not skill. In all large societies, free and unfree, many kinds of political skill are needed; wherever the machinery of government is elaborate, this must be so. But a society which is both large and free (and most modern states are large by the standards of Aristotle or Rousseau) will tend to become and will need to be politically sophisticated. This sophistication is not confined to the persons who, in the sense explained above, understand the political system as a whole; it is shared by many others. The function of these observers and critics is to promote this sophistication by providing the ideas, explanations, and arguments on which it thrives.

There are, of course, many people in a democracy who have ideas about how the system works. Their ideas are often crude and even mistaken, and they cannot be said to understand the system in the sense of being able to give an adequate description of how it works. It is astonishing how often even politicians, who have spent a lifetime in the business of government, lack this understanding. That need not make bad politicians of them. To do their work properly they have to know what to do; they must have practical knowledge, but they need not know how what they do fits into the whole machinery of government. They may know it, and may even be better politicians for knowing it; but they need not know it. Critical understanding is different from practical understanding, and few men can have much of both. That is not to say that a man who has mostly one kind of understanding is not the better for having some of the other. Life, however, is short and man's abilities are limited, and few can go far in the one direction except at the cost of going only a little way in the other.

Yet the whole atmosphere of politics is different where there is political sophistication, where the influence of theorists and critical observers is widely felt. The run-of-the-mill practical politician, though he does not see clearly (even in general outline) the whole system in which he is involved, is aware that there is a system, that it has changed, that it will change, that there are many opinions about it. Though his understanding of that system is limited he is not a mere routine politician, who does what always has been done (or what he thinks always has been done) without even imagining that it could be done differently. He is not without ideas about the political system, and though they may be inadequate, he is (if he is aware of the inadequacy) the better for having them. He is open-minded, and therefore persuadable. There are, among his colleagues, some at least who combine practical skill with critical understanding; he is impressed by their skill, and he sees that they take history and philosophy and social theory seriously. Because he respects them he is not without respect for what seems important to them; he has a lively sense of the value of activities different from the ones in which he excels. He is more than merely without contempt for them, more than merely impressed by them. He is not like the peasant who looks up to the priest or the doctor because they have powers which he believes are salutary though he knows nothing at all about them. He has also, in his own way, dabbled in these activities; living in a sophisticated society given to critical and many-sided discussion, he too is necessarily (though without any special aptitude for it) a man of ideas. In his case, a little learning is not a dangerous thing. He has been brought up in a society where ideas and systematic study are taken seriously and yet are always open to criticism; where theories are respected but are not worshipped.

At the same time, his not having a special aptitude for theory and systematic study does not make him feel inferior or inadequate. He too has his special knowledge, his skill, which the mere theorist and student lacks. He sees that this knowledge is valued by people who do not share it but who understand its importance. In a free society, where everything is open to criticism, even the most learned and the most acute have their deficiencies continually brought home to them,

No one is infallible, no one has the last word, no one has magical powers. Intelligence (practical and theoretical) is respected, but opinions are not sacred.

In complicated and fast-changing societies, this attitude to politics is essential, both among those who practise and those who study it, if there is to be stable democracy. If there were no political sophistication, if there were only practical skills, it would be difficult to make the frequent reforms that have to be made if political institutions are to be nicely adjusted to changing social conditions. If a single theory is sacred and beyond question, then, since all theories are in fact inadequate, the appearance of adequacy must be preserved at the cost of freedom of thought. The theory must be interpreted, now in one way and now in another, to suit the circumstances, and without regard for consistency, and yet the claim to perfect consistency must never be abandoned. The theory is then perhaps less a guide to action than a means of discipline; those who have made good their claim to interpret the theory use it to confute and destroy their opponents. Not that their actions are never, or even only slightly, affected by their theory; for they either are or pretend to be sincere believers. They are inspired or inhibited by their faith as well as by other things; so that it can truly be said of them that, but for their faith, they would not behave as they do. That, however, does not make them scrupulously true to their faith or unwilling, when the need arises, greatly to distort it. Even the conscious hypocrite is a victim as well as an exploiter of his professed beliefs; and no body of men wielding great power in the world ever consisted only of hypocrites. But the inhibiting and inspiring effects of a faith beyond question are different from the influence of theories and ideals on political behaviour in a free society. Unquestioned faith does, of course, allow of deliberate change on a scale impossible where there is only respect for tradition and practical knowledge. Wherever men take it upon themselves to master their environment, they have a high regard, in some form or other, for social and political theory, descriptive and utopian. In a free society, social and political theory, the systematic study of institutions, and also systematic argument about what is desirable, are as much respected as anywhere; but there are few who suppose that any one theory can serve as a complete guide to action. This is not only because it is recognized that every theory, in so far as it claims to explain the facts, contains error as well as truth and fails to take account of a great deal that is relevant, and in so far as it lays down what should be done, makes judgements of value that many people cannot accept. It is also because in a free society, precisely because it is free, the relation of theory to practice is understood differently from the way it is understood in, say, a society dominated by the Communist party.

The function of social and political theory in a free society is to increase people's understanding of their environment and themselves, and also of their moral assumptions and ideals, so that they can see what follows from them, and thus more easily decide what they want, what they must do to get it, and how they can best accommodate their wishes to the wishes of other people. Nobody has the right to say to anyone else: 'I understand your circumstances and I understand you better than you do yourself, and therefore I shall rule you in your own interest.' No one can use the claim that he possesses that truth as an excuse for controlling the lives and beliefs of others. The rules that are generally accepted in a free society are not derived from any theory about how society functions or how it is likely to develop or what are its permanent interests; they are merely the rules that must be accepted if there is to be both freedom and social peace. What people's permanent interests are, and how society functions or is likely to develop, are always, in a free society, open questions; anyone can say what he likes about them and challenge the opinions of the 'experts'. Even the rules which have to be generally accepted if society is to remain free are not beyond question; they are as open to discussion as anything else. Their stability does not depend on their not being criticized; it depends on people's learning by experience that unless they conform to them they cannot long remain free to criticize either them or other things. In a free society nothing is sacred, not even freedom itself, because nothing is left untouched by criticism.

It does not follow that because nothing is sacred nothing is cherished. Beliefs and loyalties are not necessarily the weaker for being subject to careful scrutiny and criticism. No doubt, people who have been accustomed to accept everything on trust are apt to be bewildered and dismayed when their beliefs and loyalties are first exposed to criticism. Freedom can be disheartening and therefore dangerous, and that is often a good reason for not giving too large a dose of it all at once to people who have not yet acquired a stomach for it. But there is no reason for believing that freedom, however men come by it, makes it impossible for them (or for all but a few of them) to have a faith to live by; to have beliefs and loyalties strongly enough held to give substance and purpose to their lives. There is perhaps only one man in a thousand who can be a thorough-going sceptic and yet quite happy, in the fashion of Montaigne, living on curiosity and on doubt as the bees do on flowers and honey, buzzing with contentment. There are more Pascals than Montaignes among us; more people who feel a need for beliefs beyond their own questioning than who dare question everything. They too can have what they need in a free society; and indeed are not the less likely to have it because society is free. If a man needs faith, and the need is strong, his faith is not disturbed by the scepticism of others. It is only when his faith is weak or is not the fruit of his own thought and experience that he is disturbed by other people's doubting what he believes. A society which allows all beliefs to be questioned does not thereby prevent a man from acquiring some beliefs which he treats differently from all others in the sense that he 'lives by them'.

To get faith is to solve a problem. Not, of course, to solve it in the manner of the scientist, by putting forward an hypothesis tested by methods generally accepted; for the problem solved by the getting of faith is always a personal problem. It is a problem different in kind from the problems that interest the mere scientist. The man who needs a faith needs more than beliefs that can be verified or rules of conduct which he can accept because they enable him to live comfortably with other people; he needs to believe that there is a larger purpose in the world than the purposes of creatures like himself, or else that there are, among human purposes, some so much nobler than others that life is ill-spent except in their service. Where in a man this need is strong but unsatisfied, he is profoundly unhappy. Is this need so strong and so general that a society which leaves it unsatisfied is thereby condemned? Is it less likely to be satisfied in a free society than in another?

Primitive man accepts many beliefs on trust, and so too does civilized man, but this kind of acceptance is not faith as I have defined it. All men, most of the time, when they act deliberately, do so on the strength of beliefs accepted on trust and rules of conduct not questioned; and no society could subsist unless they did so. They also often act without thinking at all, merely because they have been conditioned to do so. Every society (and not least an advanced and sophisticated one) is so complicated and so imperfectly understood by its members that it simply would not hold together unless people mostly

E

acted from habit without thought or were moved by unquestioned beliefs and principles. A sophisticated does not differ from an unsophisticated society in having inside it less action from habit or fewer beliefs accepted on trust. Indeed, there will probably be more, precisely because in a sophisticated society men are apt to be more active and more diverse in their actions. The simpler a society and the lazier its members, the fewer the habits and the beliefs accepted on trust needed to hold it together. But as habits and beliefs accepted on trust multiply in a varied and sophisticated society, so too does the questioning of them. Sophisticated man needs both a greater store of habits and beliefs usually accepted on trust, and a greater capacity to examine that store critically. The capacity to criticize and improve does not take the place of the need to accept on trust, but is added to it. With a heavier load to carry through life, sophisticated man does not make less use of the old horses that pulled his carriage but puts others in harness with them.

As men get used to criticizing old beliefs about how things happen and looking for new ones which explain the facts better, they also come more frequently to doubt conventional opinions about right behaviour. They do so partly because the quest for knowledge changes society and thus makes these opinions less well adjusted to social needs than they used to be, and partly because doubt in one sphere easily gives birth to doubt in another. Scepticism, scientific and moral, flourish together, and in the beginning both are disturbing. Yet neither is destructive of belief in the sense that it leaves man with nothing that he can hold on to. Man is not left a wanderer in a pathless universe. All the explanations of the scientists are provisional; they are accepted for the time being until better ones are put in their place. But scientific method cannot be provisional in the same way; for unless it is accepted, it makes no sense to prefer some explanations to others or to call any inadequate. True, there is not the same limit to scepticism in the moral sphere; there is nothing we have to accept before it can make sense for us to reject anything. There is, however, one moral rule that it always makes sense for us to accept, no matter how varied and how changing people's opinions about what makes life worth living: and that is the rule of freedom, which requires us to respect everyone's right to live as he thinks fit provided he allows other people to do likewise. To accept this rule is clearly not equivalent to having a purpose in life; it does not fill the void created by the rejection of other values or provide us with a method for acquiring them or for deciding that some are intrinsically better than others. It is a purely formal rule, and does not of itself suffice even to tell us how we should treat other people. Before we can apply the rule, we must know what other people want, what they think makes life worth living. Though the rule does not enable us to decide what purposes we or other people should have in life, it does require us to destroy or frustrate in ourselves and in them the ambitions that cause men to seek to enslave one another.

But, because the rule of freedom is essentially negative, men in a free society are not therefore left without positive and satisfying ideals to live by, and are not less likely to come by them than in a society which is not free. There is no good reason for believing that the cynicism which takes the flavour out of life flourishes more where there is freedom than where governments take it upon themselves to indoctrinate their subjects. There is, no doubt, in a free society, a greater variety of opinions about what is worth doing and striving for; there are more kinds of ambition deemed respectable and more ideals thought worthy of discussion. There should therefore be a greater chance that a man will find, among the pursuits and ideals brought to his notice, the kinds that suit him best. There is also the chance that he may be more bewildered than inspired by the variety open to him. But this bewilderment, I suspect, is due less to the wide range of possible choices than to faulty upbringing or defect of temperament. Even in the freest society the choices open to a man are not many; what he can do, what will attract him, and what will satisfy him are determined, within fairly narrow limits, by his talents, education, and circumstances. If he does not know what he wants, it is not because there is too much for him to choose from; it is because he has not been taught to think and choose for himself or because he is by nature undecided. He might be happier in an authoritarian society. But to the extent that this indecision is an effect of faulty upbringing, it can be prevented in a free society. In a free society men can be made capable of freedom if they are not congenitally incapable of it; though admittedly in a society which is not free, they can be saved more easily from some of the painful effects of this incapacity.

For all that anyone knows to the contrary, there may be as much (or more) cynicism and distaste for life in societies where everyone is disciplined by government in the name of some doctrine that no one is allowed to question. Who can tell? Who has measured these things, or made the necessary comparisons? Where fanatics rule, it is dangerous to be openly cynical or to show disgust. It may even be that men cease to question what is repeatedly dinned into them, and what it is safer to believe than to disbelieve. Even in the privacy of their own minds, they may not consciously question it. What could they gain by doing so, except the painful sense of their own impotence? If a man has a need for self-respect, it is intolerable to him to feel that he is at the mercy of other men; and he will sometimes, to keep that self-respect, persuade himself that he wants what they require of him even when he does not. He cannot bear to look upon himself as their tool and yet dare not revolt against them. He therefore makes their ideals his own, and yet, at a deeper and less conscious level, cannot help but reject them. To reassure himself, he may even work harder and shout louder than others in the service of these ideals; he may cheat himself to avoid humiliation. Or he may cease to think clearly or feel strongly about anything, which will still not prevent his being enthusiastic, almost by habit, when the occasion calls for it. Because he dare not question ideals repulsive to him, he will be angry with others who question them, and will even mistake this anger for evidence of the sincerity and depth of his own belief.

Primitive society is neither free nor authoritarian; there is in it neither freedom of criticism nor conscious indoctrination. There is not much room for either doubt or faith. The primitive man, even when he breaks the rules of his community, does not do so because he has examined and rejected them; he is moved to break them by mere passion or interest. He normally accepts them, as he does ceremonies and superstitions, because he has been conditioned to do so, and indeed must do so if he is to live comfortably with his neighbours. If he is perfectly at home in his society it is because he is thoroughly conventional; it is not because he has acquired for himself an adequate faith to live by. Doubt and faith are both intellectual needs, and I suspect that in any society where the one exists the other does so too. Where faith is imposed from above, doubt is not suppressed; it is only hidden or put aside, sometimes consciously and sometimes not. The same capacity for sustained thought about matters that are not merely practical, which makes faith possible, also stimulates doubt. Where faith is imposed from above, those who are not capable of this kind of sustained thought do not really acquire faith; they merely acquire images and phrases which stir their emotions; whereas those who are capable of it may or may not be attracted by the only faith offered to them. If they are, so much the better for them. But if they are not, they are still left with a need unsatisfied. Not only that; for as I have said already, they are often moved to pretend, even to themselves, that the need is satisfied when it is not. Now this condition is as painful and blighting as the bewilderment of the man who, in a free society, though he needs a faith, has not been able to find one among the many ideals, religious or social or personal, which are thought respectable and are openly discussed.

However, my purpose is less to weigh the advantages of free and authoritarian societies against each other than to explain the function of social and political theory, and of all systematic thought about man and his condition, in free societies. These theories and this thought do not provide all men with the same beliefs and preferences nor governments with a single comprehensive guide to policy; they do not, and indeed must not, create a faith which the powerful can use to decide how society shall change and even to justify sacrificing the happiness of the present generation to posterity. The fundamental rule which everyone at all times is expected to obey (even though he is allowed to criticize it) is the rule that all men are to be allowed to pursue their own good as they choose to see it provided that their good does not require them to make other men subservient to themselves. This formal rule looks utilitarian but is not so in the strict sense; for by a man's good we must understand whatever he willingly strives for no matter how indifferent he may be to happiness. The function of theory and doctrine, social, political, and moral, is to explain to man his own nature and environment, and the implications, logical and practical, of his own principles, so that he can decide for himself what he shall make of his life. There are thus produced, not one faith, but many, putting every man who needs faith in the way of acquiring the moral and social beliefs comforting and encouraging to himself. He can learn how to live at peace and friendship with men whose beliefs differ from his own; he can learn also what needs to be done to give him and them what they severally want.

Strong beliefs go as well with tolerance as with intolerance, and indeed much better. The man who cares deeply for freedom has confidence in his own beliefs and tastes, and is not put out by other people's not sharing them. He is not tolerant from diffidence or cynicism or indifference; he is tolerant because he sets great store by what he has made his own, by the faith and the loyalties and the affections which make him what he is; and therefore he understands that what his spiritual possessions are to him other people's are to them. If he is modest, it is not from humility, but from self-respect and respect for others. Only the free man is truly just, because he alone can afford to give all men their due. He alone can add nothing to his own dignity in his own eyes by taking away from theirs.

Perhaps no man is completely free in this sense. But a society, if it is to be fit for self-government by the last of our four measures, must at least respect this freedom. Most of all among the politically active minority, among those who govern and who between them make the demands and create the currents of opinion which help determine how the authority of government is used, there must be a firm hold on this idea of freedom and a high value put upon it. I say 'a firm hold' rather than 'a deep understanding' because I want to avoid suggesting that the politically active and the politically intelligent need to be moral and political philosophers. Yet I mean by this firm hold what often goes by the name of understanding, and not without good reason. For though it is not the power of lucid and vigorous exposition and criticism, it is also more than merely knowing what to do as a man with practical skill knows it. The merely practical man knows what to do in familiar circumstances, he knows how to behave as he has been trained to behave; but when circumstances change, if he has no more than practical skill, he is lost. In the modern world circumstances are apt to change quickly. To have a firm hold of a moral or social idea, to understand the spirit of it, it is not necessary to be able to write or speak about it as the philosopher or social theorist does; it is enough to know what to refuse and what to demand for its sake as circumstances change. This is a kind of critical, as distinguished from narrowly practical, understanding; and yet it is clearly not the understanding of the theorist, of the professional man of ideas, who knows what assumptions he is making and what arguments he is building upon them.

A man does not get this kind of understanding, which is neither practical skill nor theoretical knowledge, merely by doing his job competently and conscientiously; he gets it by listening to and taking part in discussions of much broader than immediate interest, by having some idea of how things have come to be as they are and how they differ in his own country from what they are among foreigners. To the discussion of these broader topics, institutional, historical, moral, and psychological, he may have no significant contribution to make; he may say nothing that impresses other people; he may even be confused and illogical. He may come to the feast bringing no food with him; and yet he comes to it and partakes of it, and is different for doing so. He is nourished by the discussion that goes on around him continually; he is affected by it in ways beyond his power to describe. He is educated politically; he grows in sophistication, in maturity of judgement. He does so, not merely in the process of transacting political business, in the process of negotiation, but also because he lives in a society where forms of government and moral and social problems are discussed repeatedly and vigorously and without restriction. He acquires a sense of what is and what is not compatible with freedom; a sense which need not be the less sure because it is more than he can do to define freedom satisfactorily or to discuss broad issues except in worn-out phrases. This critical understanding, which is neither practical skill nor the ability to analyse and expound, is the heart of what I call political sophistication. It is in this sense that the active minority must be sophisticated if the institutions making for freedom and democracy are to be preserved and successfully adapted to changing conditions. This sophistication, though not to be confused with either practical skill or analytical ability, is the product of the one and the other. It exists where political leaders at all levels of activity are 'exposed' (as the sociologists say) to intellectual discussion of a fairly high quality. If it is a mistake to underestimate the critical intelligence of people who are not lucid, exact, and systematic thinkers, it is no less a mistake to suppose that they can develop that intelligence merely by reflecting on their own experience. Every man's experience is narrow; it is often only a small part of the experience to be gained even in his own profession. In the modern world everyone who has acquired much knowledge has acquired most of it by reading other people's accounts of what has happened and is happening in the world. The practical man's debt to the theorist and the student is immense, even when what they discuss is his own line of business.

So, too, of course, is the debt of the theorist to practical men; and not only when he explains what they do. The more sophisticated the public interested, say, in the academic discussion of moral or political principles, the more the theorist must take account of all the relevant facts, and the more carefully he must distinguish between verbal and moral and factual problems. If he does not do this, he risks more than talking nonsense; he risks being found out. The sophisticated can often recognize nonsense when they see it, even when they cannot explain why it is nonsense.

So far, I have spoken of the sophisticated, of the people who, at one level or another, are the leaders, the spokesmen, the organizers, the negotiators. They are only a minority of the nation, and the health and vigour of democracy depend more directly on them than on anyone else. There can, of course, be freedom for a considerable part of the nation, even where there is no democracy. Where there is freedom without democracy, the preservation of free institutions depends as much on the temper of this minority of leaders as it does where there is freedom with democracy. The only difference is that democracy requires a larger and more varied politically active and sophisticated minority. But I shall not speak of free societies that are not democratic. Not that freedom in them is limited to the upper classes, for it is not so always; for though the upper classes are apt to have more freedom than the others, all classes may have a good deal. The opportunities given only to the rich and the educated may not be understood or coveted by the poor and the illiterate; and it is surely absurd to say that freedom is diminished because people cannot get what they do not want. It is when the voteless learn to demand what they do not have and what those who have the vote stand in the way of their getting, that it comes to matter greatly to them that they too should have the vote. A society can be free without being democratic. It may even, as a result of the voteless being given the vote, lose what freedom it had; though it cannot be truly democratic unless it is free.

But in the modern world it is almost impossible for a society to be free if it is not also democratic. Democracy and freedom go together now as they never did before; and that for a simple reason. Where the larger and poorer classes are illiterate and passive, where they accept their lot because it seems to them that it cannot be otherwise, where they have (as in these cases they always do have) a primitive culture of their own which makes the ideals of the upper classes meaningless to them, there can be great freedom for the privileged and considerable freedom for the unprivileged, though these freedoms differ not only in degree but in kind. The freedom of the privileged is personal and political, and is also secure; their rights of property are well defended, they can rely on the courts for protection against arbitrary power, and they have the vote and can criticize government freely. They are the ruling classes and therefore are not without responsibilities; but the business of government is not great, for the rich ask little more of government than that it should protect their property and other rights, and it need do scarcely anything for the poor. Privileges are great and responsibilities small, and the upper classes enjoy a wide freedom. The poor, no doubt, are exploited; services, rents, and taxes are required of them. They have little property to defend, and the courts, if the poor resort to them, are often careless of their rights. Yet they may, for all this, have a considerable freedom. When they have paid, in labour or in kind or in money, what is required of them, they may be left very much to their own devices; and sometimes, for one reason or another (for instance, because the value of money has fallen, or dues and services fixed by custom are levied on an out-of-date census where population has greatly increased) the burden of exploitation is lightened. Where government is remote and there are few contacts between the upper and the lower classes, the lower classes can sometimes enjoy a considerable freedom, provided they have not learnt to aspire to what is not already theirs by custom.

When, however, the poorer classes cease to be satisfied with what custom allows them, when they cease to be (what they have long been) a world apart and in the shadows tributary to a world of light, when they become demanding and formidable, concessions must be made to them or else the privileged classes must close their ranks against them, submitting themselves to a harsher discipline than they knew before. One country may resist the claims of another subject to it, and yet itself remain free. But it is much more difficult for one part of the community still to preserve their own freedom when they have to make great efforts to keep the other part down. How long can the Europeans in the Union of South Africa remain free if they persist in refusing to give to the Africans the rights which contact with European civilization has caused them to demand? Already they have lost some of their freedom, and they are bound to lose more if the struggle grows fiercer. The spread of industry and education makes the poor more demanding everywhere, so that conditions are now fast becoming such that no section of the community can have freedom unless all sections have it. Today, as never before, a free society must be democratic. I shall therefore use the expressions 'a free society' and 'a democratic society' as if they were synonymous, except when I make it plain that I am doing otherwise.

That a democratic society must be free can, I hope, be taken for granted; though some have contested it. Unless those who govern can be freely criticized by their subjects, and unless there is competition for popular favour between groups genuinely independent of one another, government can never be truly responsible to the people and therefore democratic. The word 'democracy' is always so used that it follows that if a democracy is of the representative type elections inside it must be free; or at any rate, the word is always so used by people claiming that their own system of government is democratic. They may sometimes, speaking of other systems, use the word ironically or elliptically, to suggest that a system is often called democratic though it is not so, or is democratic in some other sense than the senses current in their own part of the world. Thus, it sometimes happens that people in the West who are not Communists, and who claim to have no illusions about Communism, call Russia a democracy without intending to convey thereby that Russian elections are free and the government responsible to the people. But when Russian Communists call Russia a democracy that is precisely what they intend to convey. They may not always believe what they say but that is what they mean when they say it. They assert that Russian elections are free, though they deny that the conditions of freedom are what western critics say they are. That is to say, they deny that where there is only one party and where the right to criticize that party is severely limited, elections cannot be free. It is easy to prove them wrong, but it is not worth while.

For democracy to be real there must be in the community, not only at least two independent parties, but a great variety of other organizations speaking for all sections of the people. There must be at every level of society experienced negotiators and organizers who can bring effective pressure to bear on government. Unless there are these organizations, the people are not able to make definite and moderate demands on government. Indeed, it is not too much to say that it is through them that the people acquire the kind of interests that government can take notice of. The business of a democratic government is supposed to be to give the people what they want. But how do governments know what the people want? The 'programmes' which the parties proclaim at general elections are altogether too vague to give much information; they lay down general principles that can be interpreted in many different ways. In any case, the electors do not take much notice of these programmes; they vote for one party rather than another because they think it friendly to the interests of people like themselves or because they trust its leaders or from habit or for some other reason that gives the party only vague notice what it should do. If the people had no other means of making their wishes known than by preferring one party to another, they would be hard put to it ever to make those wishes clear. Programmes are pieced together more to look attractive than to create definite obligations, and even the party leaders that make them are not certain what they are committing themselves to by means of them. If they get power, they can, within broad limits, interpret their promises to suit themselves; or at least they could do so if they had to reckon with the people only at general elections. This is so even where parties are few and well organized. Where there are many and they are loosely organized, the promises they make to their electors commit them to almost nothing at all.

Governments know what the people want because, through all kinds of bodies (trade unions, producers' and professional associations, societies to promote this and that), the people make definite, and therefore negotiable, demands on government. These bodies do not so much convey the demands of their members to government as create them; they are not only the tongues that speak for the people but the brains that think for them. Not that the people are dumb and thoughtless without them. Even in a society consisting only of men of great talent, there would soon arise a division between an active minority and a passive majority; the minority would do the proposing, amending, and arguing, and the majority would do the listening, consenting, and dissenting. This would necessarily be so unless the society were very small indeed. Just because a number of men are placed in similar circumstances or have similar tastes or belong to the same trade or profession, they do not have the same notions of what their interests are, of what they would like to have done for them. Their purely personal opinions are vague and various; or, if they are not, it is because they have banded together to further their interests and have acquired, as a result of doing so, common and definite opinions. If they had not felt that they had something to gain by banding together, they would not have done so in the first place; but they in fact did so to discover their interests as much as to promote them. And once an association has been formed and has lasted some time, people join it because it is the thing to do, often without even knowing what they stand to gain thereby. It is only afterwards (and not always then) that experience teaches them what, if anything, they have gained by it. We must always distinguish between a man's desires and his interests, between what he wants and what he can decently ask for himself or have others ask for him. It is as an associate or as a member of a class or as a person having a social status that a man has interests. When we ask what his interests are, we are not asking what he wants; we are asking what demands are made by people like him. True, the range of his interests, taken as a whole, may be unique; he may be the only person who belongs to all the groups and classes of which he is a member. But he acquires his interests by belonging to these groups and classes; so that his interests are not even necessarily the sum of his strongest and most persistent desires. They are the sum of his socially permissible demands, whether he makes them himself or they are made by others on his behalf. They may not be approved by everyone or by most people in the community, and may even be illegal; but they are socially permissible in the sense that, when they are made, they find supporters. A man may, of course, make some demands for himself alone and still get wide support because his position in society is unique, as when he is a king or in some other way set alone above (or beneath) other men.

In a democracy which is genuine and enduring all classes and groups and professions are organized to make definite demands on one another and on government. They are all articulate in the sense that they all have spokesmen trusted by the people they speak for; they all have leaders who cannot lead effectively unless they enjoy the confidence of the men they claim to lead. If they lose that confidence, other leaders can make use of the discontent either to take their places or to form rival organizations to draw their supporters away from them. Of course, there is always the inertia that favours those who already have power against those who would deprive them of it. Everywhere the dice are weighted in favour of established authority. But in a free society they are so weighted as much by the people's natural conservatism as by the skill and ruthlessness of the powerful. Trust is a moral investment, and is not readily withdrawn by the people from the leaders in whom they have placed it. Why, indeed, should it be? Are those who challenge authority any more likely to be acting for the public good than those who have it? Once, however, that trust is seriously weakened, it is easy for the challengers of authority to take advantage of its being so. In a democracy with innumerable organizations speaking for an immense variety of 'interests', leaders are peculiarly sensitive to the feelings of their supporters. They are also watchful critics of one another. They are experienced negotiators; they know what to ask for, when to be firm, when to give way. Between them they create standards of decent behaviour in the making, resisting, and compromising of claims. They are the agents of the public and not of the government; they are independent of one another; they come from every section of society. Experience has taught them moderation. Because of them all interests are articulate and nearly all claims can be negotiated. No important group in society is left unspoken for and without the means of making its needs felt.

The failure of democracy in backward countries is often attributed to the low standard of morality among public men. This explanation is perhaps too simple. The United States, the largest and the oldest of the great democracies, is not the least corrupt. I shall not deny that democracy in the Balkans, while it lasted, was as corrupt as it ever has been in the United States. Perhaps it was more corrupt. Who knows? No one, I think, has taken the trouble to compare these democracies at their worst. Rough and uneducated men have reached high office in the Balkans, but perhaps not more often than in the English-speaking democracies beyond the seas. Certainly in the Balkans, while German and French cultural influences were the strongest (which they were until the Communist regimes were established), men of intellect were highly respected. Nor was it really easy to be a successful politician in the Balkans; it required skill that was peculiar but also rare. I doubt whether democracy failed in the Balkans because Balkan politicians were more corrupt or less well educated or less skilled than the politicians of several countries that have been democratic for a long time and are likely long to remain so. I think it failed largely because there were not enough pressure groups, not enough organized interests, independent of one another and of the political parties. Who could tell what the peasants really wanted? For the peasants were inarticulate as a class, though not as individuals. The peasant is often narrow in his views but also hard-headed. Rather more often than the intellectual, perhaps, he knows what he wants. But as Marx saw, millions of peasants, each of them knowing what he wants for himself, are still not a politically conscious class. Before they can be that, they must decide what interests they have in common; and this they cannot do until they are organized. It is not enough that there should be competing politicians to make a variety of promises to them; for the promises may be vague in themselves or unintelligible to the peasants. If the promises can be interpreted equally plausibly in several different ways, the peasants in preferring some promises to the others really decide nothing. As a class they do not know what they want government to do for them; they have no one to make clear demands on their behalf, demands intelligible to themselves and to the government; no one to take legal but vigorous action to oblige the government to take notice of their needs. They have no real political spokesmen, no trusted leaders to teach them what can and what cannot be done for them. Between them and the politicians, between them and the other sections of the people, there are no effective intermediaries.

While the peasants—and this could be said of any other class— expect nothing from government, it matters little that government does nothing for them. But when they have been taught to believe that government ought to look after their interests, it matters greatly that it should be seen by them to do so. If they expect something without knowing what it is, if they have no one to interpret their common needs and in the same process to form their collective wishes, no one to find words for them, no one close to them for them to trust (and to repudiate when not trusted), there is then a wide gulf between them and their rulers. Even if government tries to do something for them, they will not understand what is being done, and will be suspicious and ungrateful. They may not be driven, but neither are they led. It is then easy to persuade them that they are the victims of government, and that democracy is a trick to enable them to be exploited in the name of liberty and justice. And indeed the chances are that little will be done for them, because under a parliamentary regime the unorganized and inarticulate are apt to be neglected. Not bullied but neglected. Parliamentary politicians are not usually fanatics; they are usually content to get power at as cheap a price as possible. They exert themselves most for those groups and classes who make their exertions most worth while; or in other words, for people who know what they want and how to induce politicians to give it to them.

Democracy does not necessarily work best where there is the greatest social equality. In the Balkan countries, even before the coming of Communism, there was as great social equality as, say, in Australia.

When the Balkan peoples got rid of the Turks, they had no native aristocracy and no middle class. To begin with, their states were peasant states just as Australia was a colony consisting mostly of working-class Englishmen. The men who ruled the Balkan states between the two world wars were socially about as close to the people generally as the men who ruled Australia. In Australia, as in the Balkans, as everywhere in the world, most people most of the time took little enough interest in politics. Indeed, the Balkan peoples, while they could still do so safely, probably (despite their illiteracy) took a greater interest in politics than the Australians did. And who shall say that it was a less intelligent interest? Who, merely by comparing the intellectual quality of political conversation among ordinary people in Athens or Belgrade and Sydney, could have told that the Australians were much better fitted to work a parliamentary democracy than either the Greeks or the Serbs? The Australians owe their much greater competence, not to the superior political intelligence of the masses nor (if I may say so) to the higher general culture of the ruling circles among them. They owe it to the political character of those circles and to how they are related to the people generally. This character is partly a result of Australia having been a British colony for several generations, and of the Australians being men of British descent eager to work British institutions in a new country. The emigrants who went to Australia from the British Isles came mostly from the poorer classes who had scarcely more political experience than the same classes on the European continent; they had not learnt how to govern a country in British ways before they left Britain, and therefore had to learn it after they had settled in Australia. They too were novices. But they had the advantage of knowing what model to take and where to find willing instructors.

Though this advantage has been great indeed, it does not alone explain why the character of ruling circles in Australia has been so much more propitious to democracy than in Greece or Yugoslavia. It is also partly explained by the much greater proliferation in Australia of trade unions and pressure groups of many other kinds whose spokesmen make clear demands on government and are experienced negotiators.[1] The politicians therefore know what is expected of

---

1. Mr. Hugh Clegg has pointed out to me that a fanatical movement, nationalist or Communist, may become the more formidable for getting control of these bodies. Therefore, where these bodies exist, the obstacles in the way of building up a liberal

them; they know what they have to do, or try to do, to satisfy the people. And the people know that their 'interests' are being looked after. However little they may follow the course of day-to-day politics, however ignorant they may be about the political system of their country, they know that they have effective spokesmen. They know what is being asked for on their behalf, and they see that real efforts are made to get it for them. They acquire confidence in the system, not because they understand it or even because they are (as individuals) wiser than Balkan peasants, but because they see what the system does for them. Though they are not politicians seeking to reconcile diverse interests in order to get or to retain power, and though their business is to get as much as they can for the groups they speak for, the spokesmen for the many 'pressure groups' which between them include the whole people, soon learn that they must in practice adjust their claims to the claims of other groups. In other words, they soon learn to do business. They are effective and moderate, and effective because moderate, and yet they do not lose the confidence of their 'clients'. The politicians, the seekers after power,

---

democracy may be greater than where they do not exist. I acknowledge the force of this argument. I should say in reply to it that a fanatical movement will seek to create such bodies where they do not exist in order to consolidate its hold on the people, and also to create the illusion that the people's interests, in all their variety, are being looked after. It is true that these bodies are means to democracy only where they are independent; and that they can easily lose their independence, especially in backward countries. Nevertheless, they are indispensable to a free democracy, and it is better to foster them, even though there is a risk of their falling victims to a fanatical movement, than to forbid them. They will come eventually, in any case, for they are part of the apparatus of modern industrial society. If they arise while nationalism or Communism is still weak, the chance of their acquiring an independence which they are eager not to lose is all the greater. Every organization throws up leaders, and men who have acquired the habit of authority do not like to be made the pawns of others.

Miss Margery Perham tells me that the missionaries, by setting up church communities and associating the natives in their government, taught them European political methods. The missionaries often opposed the European officials, and so made the natives familiar with the idea that opposition to government can be legal and stubborn.

I am sorry that I have said nothing about the missionaries, whose influence has been great and often good. Social anthropologists, who want the peoples they study to be untainted by the West, have scolded the missionaries for their interference with native customs which they thought immoral or indecent. Government officials have resented their obstinacy and have denounced them as trouble makers. Yet the missionaries had two great virtues: though they sometimes treated native customs with scant respect, they came closer than other Europeans to acting on the belief that all men are equal in the sight of God, and they also set an example of resolute but peaceful opposition to authority. They knew how to be firm without being cold or contemptuous.

have to take notice of them; they are faced with concrete demands which they have to meet with limited resources. They can explain their predicament and expect to be understood; the men who make these demands on them are also, to some extent, their interpreters with the people.

In the Balkan countries the politicians were divorced from the mass of the people, and especially from the peasants. The fact of this divorce has often been noticed but not so often satisfactorily explained. True, the politicians were much more 'westernized' than the peasants, and spoke a different political language from them. They worked a political system not understood by the peasants. But everywhere, even in western countries, politicians speak a 'different language' from the common people, and are busy doing things not understood by them. Politics is everywhere mostly talking and writing, and is carried on in an idiom often unintelligible except to the politically active and to those who study their activities. There are, admittedly, degrees of understanding; and I do not doubt that the language and activities of parliamentary politicians were much less understood by Balkan peasants than by working-men in western Europe. The peasants enjoyed talking politics and were often shrewd judges of the motives of politicians, but they understood very little about how political institutions work. We can allow that working-men in the West understand a great deal more without having to admit that they understand much; and this comparative ignorance is by no means confined to them, even in the West. Nor were the politicians in the Balkans divorced from the peasants in the sense that they found it difficult to mix socially with them. On the contrary, social intercourse between the educated and uneducated was much easier in the Balkans than in the West; for in the Balkans, much more often than in the West, a highly educated man might have close relatives who were completely un-lettered. Educated people in the Balkans enjoyed the company of peasants, and found it refreshing; and they certainly came as near to understanding the peasant as educated men in the West have come to understanding the manual worker.[1] But they did not know what to do for the peasants, socially and politically; they either imitated what had

---

1. Even in Tsarist Russia, which was quite undemocratic, educated people understood the uneducated at least as well as they did in England. The peasant occupies as large a place in Russian literature as the working-man in English literature, and is portrayed with greater truth and understanding.

F

been done for them elsewhere, or more often neglected them. The peasants, as a class, did not know what they wanted, and the politicians had uncertain or meagre notions of what to do to satisfy them. The peasants never learnt to have confidence in the political system imported from the West, because it was never borne in upon them that that system was beneficial to them. The politicians were not faced with a wide variety of organizations speaking, clearly and moderately, for every section of the population; they never learnt to be skilful conciliators of definite, openly proclaimed and diverse interests. They were not supported and restrained by a civil service with high professional standards. Compared with western politicians, they were less conciliators of stable and open interests than intriguers for power often working in secret. That, of course, is not the whole story; they were also plagued by hatreds between different nations inside their countries, and they could not count on the familiarity which, though it is not understanding, draws people to what has long been established among them. But it is part of the story, and an important part usually neglected.

Respect for freedom among the politically active and sophisticated and a feeling widespread among all sections of the community that their interests are being adequately cared for are, I think, the two most important psychological conditions of stable democracy. If I have spoken of them at considerable length, it has not been, I hope, to labour the obvious, but to try to make clear just what these conditions involve. The friends of democracy too often speak loosely and carelessly in its favour, seeming to make impossible claims for it. If these claims are taken literally, what democracy is in fact falls so far short of what it is in theory supposed to be, that it looks a fraud. It is better to make more modest claims. Unfortunately, these more modest claims are also less simple, and it takes time to explain them.

3

The Arguments For Continued European Rule Over Subject Peoples

I HAVE already explained that the purpose of this essay is not to consider how colonies are governed, or how their government could be improved, or what should be done to enable colonies to attain independence. This is an essay in political theory; it deals with certain kinds of arguments and with the assumptions on which they rest, and deals with facts only to the extent that they are relevant to the arguments. Of course, there are many facts relevant to these particular arguments and they have to be considered. It is not, however, within the scope of this essay to determine whether or not statements of fact are true. For if that were within its scope I should not be competent to write it. The essay does not deal with arguments which concern a particular colony or situation; it deals only with general arguments and typical situations.

All the arguments considered in this chapter and the next rest on assumptions of European origin which are now more or less accepted by most other peoples. It was on the basis of these assumptions that I tried in the last chapter to define and explain certain criteria of fitness for self-government. There are still, no doubt, many people who do not make these assumptions, or who do not make all of them. Nothing said in this essay condemns them. Indeed, it may even be that they are right; for though some of these assumptions are ultimate moral principles which must either be accepted or rejected, it may be that most people, if they could see clearly what they lead to, would reject them. I do not say that they would do so or that they would not; and I refrain from giving a definite opinion, not because I want to appear impartial, but because I do not know. These assumptions, in so far as they are ultimate moral principles, cannot be derived logically from whatever was common to European and other moralities before European domination began, and there is no reason to believe that they are peculiarly in keeping with needs universal to mankind. It may well be that there are other principles as well or better suited to give men security and happiness.

I say nothing for or against these principles; I make only statements of fact about them, and in particular this statement, that the more active and enterprising people in the world accept them. They do not always accept them all, but they accept some of them. Even the Communists accept some of them together with other principles peculiar to themselves. They are principles which happen now to be attractive to men who have or who seek power. These men are believers in what Europe has taught the world to call 'progress'; they think progress inevitable or desirable or both together. They are eager to bring progress to their countries, partly because they approve of it and partly because that is the best way of serving their own ambitions.

I shall take in this chapter five arguments commonly used to justify the prolongation of European rule over non-European peoples.[1] I shall begin by putting each argument as simply as I can, and then go on to make my own comments on it. The arguments against prolonged European rule I shall consider in the next chapter.

(1) It is often said that the institutions necessary for effective self-government in the modern world are outside the experience of many non-European peoples. They are so, whether by effective self-government is meant democratic and free government or merely efficient government by natives. We can say this without in the least implying that tribal or feudal government, or government as it existed outside Europe before European domination began, was inefficient in any absolute sense. There are different standards of efficiency in government depending on what people expect of it. Tribal or feudal or any other 'backward' form of government may be very well adapted to certain conditions and needs, and therefore in that sense efficient. But, given that non-European peoples (or the most active and forceful among them) have acquired European needs and standards, material, moral, and political, it can be argued that they ought, in their own interest, to consent to learn from those who first set these standards how they are to be realized; and that it is for their

---

1. They could be used to justify other than European rule, and sometimes are. But they are mostly arguments devised by Europeans to justify their rule over Asian and African peoples, though sometimes also over European peoples deemed more 'backward' than themselves.

European rulers, who are apt to be better judges than they are in these matters, to decide when they have learnt what Europe has to teach them. Thus goes the argument.

For subject peoples to admit that Europeans are in these matters better judges than they are themselves is not to admit an inferiority degrading to themselves. Europeans are just as inferior by non-European standards as Asians and Africans are by European standards, and it is nobody's fault that Europeans have not come to accept other peoples' ideas as those peoples have come to accept many of theirs. It just is so, and it is no use pretending otherwise. Since, for a number of reasons already discussed, the whole world has accepted the European myth of progress and has learnt to speak of 'backward' and 'advanced' peoples, it is right that the 'backward' peoples should take lessons from the 'advanced' ones. They cannot be expected to put up with subjection for ever, and it would even be against European principles that they should do so. But they ought, in their own interest, to be willing and patient learners. This is the gist of the argument I want to consider.

The idea of progress, as it has emerged in Europe, can hardly be rejected. I do not mean that it is beyond criticism. I can easily conceive how it might seem shallow or repulsive to people just as intelligent and sensitive as any who accept it. Individuals may reject it and even loathe it with all the strength of their souls; but entire communities are not likely to do so. They cannot isolate themselves from European influences; they cannot build walls to keep these out as they sometimes did against the barbarians. As European ways gain upon them so too must European ideals and ambitions. It is therefore their own interest to make the best of what Europe has to offer them, not because what Europe offers is better than what they had before, but because there is now no resisting the forces that bring European ways to them.

How can they make the best of what Europe has to offer? Not by acting as if they had already made it their own when in fact they have not done so. The idea of progress once accepted, it is mere common sense to agree that progress is made by stages; and it is surely also common sense to acknowledge that those who have made this progress before you, know better than you do how it is made.

If political progress, as Europe understands it, is to be made by a non-European people, they must first acquire a civil service and a system of courts dispensing justice in the European way. Without a civil service and law courts with high professional standards, there is no efficient government as governmental efficiency is understood in the West. If the people are governed by a European Power, and have European officials and judges over them, it is probably not very difficult for them to acquire a civil service and a judiciary of fairly high quality. Natives can be trained to be competent administrators and judges almost as easily as Europeans can; indeed, just as easily except to the extent that their social environment prevents it. Where governmental efficiency depends on the careful training of a relatively small number of persons, it is not all that difficult to get it. It may have taken centuries for western countries to acquire their high professional standards, administrative and judicial, but it need not take much time for them to pass them on to select minorities in other parts of the world. Just as foreigners who come, say, to England or France for their education are at no great disadvantage compared with native Englishmen or Frenchmen, provided they are treated as equals by them, so Asians and Africans who receive a good European training in their native lands are at no great disadvantage compared with Europeans, if their environment does not undermine their training.

The foreigner who comes to England for his education, if he stays in England, does not really find it harder than the Englishman to behave well by English standards. He does, as most men do, what is expected of him, what makes him acceptable and respected. If he feels himself despised or excluded, he resents the treatment meted out to him, and is sometimes moved to behave in ways which surprise his neighbours and even himself. But if he can earn respect and equal treatment by good behaviour according to the standards of his adopted country, he will have a powerful motive for behaving well. Only if he cannot, will he be moved to defy those standards, to trample them underfoot, in order to avenge himself for his humiliation. Or, if he is timid, he may betray them secretly rather than defy them openly. Though his treachery will hurt him more than it hurts others, he may not be able to resist the temptation to it. He may be ashamed of it because he accepts the standards which he feels the need to reject, and yet also moved to give way to it and even to revel in it. The motive for treachery is sometimes fear and sometimes greed, but it is also (and perhaps mostly) the need of the humiliated for vengeance; a vengeance which is often both secret and futile.

So, too, in a dependent country, those who are trained by the ruling Power to be competent officials and judges, and are thus raised up above the mass of their compatriots, may be humiliated at the same time as they are exalted. They may find themselves despised and excluded by their European colleagues. If they do, then, while there is still no prospect of getting rid of European rule, they may vent their anger on the people below them, hitting out where they can do so with least danger to themselves. This brutality and this arrogance, which Europeans too often treat as marks of inferiority in the natives trained by themselves, are sometimes merely effects of their own behaviour. Cold disdain begets hot resentment, and the behaviour caused by that resentment seems to justify the disdain. Later on, when the end of European rule looks nearer, the resentment that used to be shown openly only against inferiors is turned upon the Europeans themselves, who are astonished to find themselves hated even by the small section of the people whom they have raised high above the others. They feel that they have been 'betrayed'; for the 'traitors' are often those among the subject people who have come closest to understanding and living up to European standards.

It is not enough for foreign rulers to give to a select minority of their subjects the kind of education that makes them highly competent in this or that profession; they must also accept them socially as fully equal to themselves as soon as they have proved their competence. Anger and resentment are harmful wherever they are found, but they do the most harm when they flourish among persons specially trained to be leaders in their own communities. It is absurd to put yourself forward as a foreign ruler anxious to raise a subject people to full equality with yourself, and still to treat those of them who have risen highest by your own standards as if they could not, whatever they did, become entirely fit for the company of people like yourself. But this is precisely what many Europeans have done and still do.

Even where the native minority highly trained by European standards are not humiliated and resentful, either because they are treated as social equals or because they have learnt to rise above the resentment caused by unequal treatment, there is still a danger that what their training gives them may be spoilt by their environment. While European ascendancy is secure and they enjoy European esteem, they take pride in their achievements. In nearly all communities, whatever gives power and secures reputation is generally esteemed; or if not generally, then by all who are respectable enough for their opinions to count. The maintenance of high professional standards, whether in the public service or elsewhere, depends on more than the proper training of those who enter the professions; it also depends on public opinion, or in other words, on what is felt and thought about professional conduct by the groups and classes whose opinions count. It is not enough that professional training should be good; there must also be a social environment which encourages the maintenance of high professional standards. In a colony where European rule is still unchallenged, the public opinion that counts is the opinion of the Europeans and of the professions created by them. A native belonging to one of these professions is sustained partly by the corporate spirit of his profession and partly by educated public opinion dominated by the Europeans. Though the standards he accepts are understood by only a small section of his own people, he is secure and respected while he lives up to them. He may even be respected by people who do not understand why he is respectable; they know only that he is respected by their 'betters', and that is enough to make them respect him.

When a subject people gain their independence, and even before they do so, these high professional standards may decline. They may do so, not because there is in general a moving 'backwards' to the conditions that existed before European rule began, but for a quite different—and an almost opposite—reason. As the subject people become more westernized, the number of the politically dissatisfied and vociferous grows. All kinds of demands come to be made on government which were not made before. Political parties are formed and grievances are more skilfully exploited. Both the leaders who create the parties and the supporters recruited into them are much more alive to European ideas and methods than their ancestors were. Yet these parties are often very different from political parties in the West, more fanatical, more ruthless, more cynical, and more corrupt. When independence comes, power passes to them. An efficient and incorruptible civil service and judiciary may be obstacles which they feel the need to undermine though without admitting that they do so. The old civil servants and magistrates trained to high standards feel themselves isolated in a political system where their virtues are perhaps still praised but no longer tolerated if they stand in the way of the ambitious. Thus, though the country, taken as a whole, becomes more 'western', the standards of the classes who, as the West sees it, are the best educated, intellectually and morally, may greatly decline.

This process is not confined to colonies and subject peoples; it can also happen to a primitive people who are already independent. When the Serbs in 1833 gained so wide an autonomy from the Turks as to be virtually self-governing [1] they were still a peasant nation only slightly touched by western influences. The process of westernization went on steadily right up to the outbreak of the first World War in 1914. Its first achievement was the setting up of government departments and courts of law which were soon more efficient and less corrupt than the Turkish administration had been. Their quality improved considerably until the eighteen-eighties, when a country which, until then, had been a bureaucratic oligarchy tempered by monarchy acquired some of the characteristics of a western parliamentary and liberal state. Political parties were formed, and the struggle for power between them became so bitter and ruthless that the monarch was able to corrupt them and play them off against one another to establish an oppressive personal rule. The party in power, whichever it was, tried to fill the government departments with its own supporters, and to tamper with the courts when it was its political advantage to do so. All this was an effect of increasing westernization, for Serbia was much more like a western country in the last (and politically more sordid) decades of the nineteenth century than she had been for a generation or more after 1833. The government of the old oligarchs was cleaner than that of the new parliamentarians.

The increase of popular influence and popular participation in government need not, of course, lead to a decline in public morality and the suppression of liberty. In England and in several other western countries it did not do so. But in primitive countries moving rapidly 'forward', it can easily do so. The select minority who are the first to get a western education often get a very good education of its kind. Perhaps their country is conquered by one of the more civilized European peoples, or else the first students sent abroad go to the best schools. The first to be 'westernized' are usually deeply excited by what they learn. They may be few in number and able to make only small beginnings in bringing 'progress' to their country; and yet,

---

1. The complete independence of Serbia was not recognized by the Powers until the Congress of Berlin in 1878.

isolated though they are among their own people, they are more thwarted than corrupted by the great uncomprehending and unorganized majority. They work in a small way, but hopefully, and they keep their standards high. The process of westernization must go a good deal further before they are up against native movements strong enough to deflect them from their courses or to corrupt them.

The dilemma that faces 'backward' peoples is this: they cannot have constitutional government and impartial justice, let alone democracy, unless they have an efficient and impartial judiciary and hierarchy of officials, but the process which begins (or at least ought to begin) by giving them these two things also, if it goes too fast, threatens to take them away. Therefore, if constitutional government or democracy and freedom (which require constitutional government) are what they want, they will not get them unless it is so contrived that, as they move from stage to stage towards their goal, they do not lose at one stage what they gained at stages before it.

If constitutional government or democracy is to be preserved, there must be much more than a popular clamour for self-government, much more than an organized nationalist movement. There must be a considerable variety of well-organized parties and pressure groups, accustomed to disagree strongly with one another and yet also willing to respect law and convention as they compete for power and for influence with the government. If none of them is allowed to eliminate or dominate the others, experience will eventually teach them all that this respect is in the interest of all. If, however, democracy is introduced all of a sudden or by too rapid stages, there is a danger that one or more of these bodies will destroy the others or will get such a monopoly of power as to prevent other bodies which otherwise might have emerged from doing so. As a backward people become politically active, there is always the danger that the first organized political groups will get too tight a hold on power, or else, in the attempt to get it, will resort to practices fatal to freedom and democracy. If they resort to these practices, their rivals will do so too; for it is not much use their being clean fighters if their rivals are dirty.

Therefore, if what you want is to establish freedom and democracy on a sure foundation, you must extend the popular element in government by stages, doing your best to encourage the formation of a diversity of political parties and pressure groups accustomed to negotiate with the government and with one another. You must be willing to listen to them and to take their aspirations seriously, but you must not allow any of them to get much power until they too have proved themselves willing to listen to and to take one another seriously.

The essence of democracy is competition for power and influence by persons and groups who respect each other's equal right to compete. This respect is not easily learnt. And among a 'backward' people subject to foreign rulers more 'advanced' than they are, who is better placed to teach it than these rulers, especially if they intend to withdraw when their subjects are fit to govern themselves? This argument for prolonged European rule, taken by itself, has considerable force to it; though, as we shall see later, there are also strong arguments on the other side.

(2) Another argument sometimes used in favour of prolonged European rule is that most of the subject peoples now claiming the right to govern themselves were never properly one nation before the Europeans conquered them. They are only now in process of becoming one nation, and if they are given self-government too soon, some tribes or communities may come to dominate the others. If that were to happen, there would still be alien rule, though it might not be apparent to the outside world. No doubt, even before the coming of the Europeans, there were tribes and communities dominating other tribes and communities, but there were not then the instruments that there now are in the hands of those who rule; their domination was looser and more easily shaken off. Also, there were not then widely accepted principles of European origin condemning foreign domination and serving to make it more humiliating where it exists. But now it is surely, on these principles, the duty of a ruling Power not to give a subject people full self-government until they have become one nation or until they have proved themselves willing to accept loyally a federal system which prevents the domination of some tribes or communities by others. This second condition is perhaps only a corollary of the first, for a people willing to accept a federal system are already well on the way to becoming one nation.

In order that there should be self-government, there need not be democracy, but those who govern must be held to belong to the same nation as the people they govern or else must belong indifferently to any of the nations under their rule. Thus, if there were a West European federation, it would be self-governing, even if it were not democratic, if its government were recruited indifferently from the nations of western Europe. It might happen that some nation was not represented in the federal government or was less fully represented than its size might seem to warrant, but that would not prevent the federation's being self-governing provided that nation did not mind. If, however, it did mind, if it was or felt itself to be excluded on purpose, it would look upon the federal government as an alien government. Its not minding would be strong evidence that a broader patriotism had already come into existence alongside the narrower. The federation could, however, appear to be entirely self-governing to outsiders and yet not seem so to several of the nations included in it.

In the same way a unitary state can be independent, and in that sense self-governing, and yet be denounced by some nation inside it as a form of alien rule. This was so in the United Kingdom before the Southern Irish broke away from it, and it has been so in several European countries. Yugoslavia between the two World Wars seemed to the outside world to be a self-governing state, but to several of the peoples inside it the self-government was a cover for Serbian domination over non-Serbian peoples. The Croats resented being ruled from Belgrade even more than they had resented being ruled from Budapest. At least they often said so, though there are reasons to doubt their sincerity, for they were certainly a more noisy and important people in Yugoslavia than ever they had been in the Habsburg Empire. So, too, the Sudeten Germans, the Slovaks, and the Ruthenes looked upon government from Prague as alien rule, even though they had, as individuals, exactly the same political rights as the Czechs in the only Slav country that was a genuine parliamentary democracy.

If the withdrawal of alien rulers from a country whose people have not yet become one nation were to lead to a relapse into tribalism or feudalism or some other more primitive social order, it might perhaps be justified. For that might suit the people just as well or better than the 'progress' brought to them by the Europeans. Many 'backward' peoples now subject to alien rule were quite well governed by their own standards before they were conquered by peoples more 'advanced' than themselves. Who will venture, nowadays, to assert the right of 'advanced' peoples to put an end to tribalism or feudalism or anything else which satisfies those who have it, on the mere ground that it is not in keeping with 'advanced' principles?

But a relapse into tribalism or some other social order which existed before the intrusion of the West is most improbable. Contact with the West has destroyed the old life beyond recall. It has, as I have said before, changed the peoples exposed to it in ways which are often unintelligible to them. Some will want to force the pace of 'progress' so as to prove themselves as good as other people, while others, though conservative or reactionary in some respects, will want to retain or procure some of the benefits of western civilization. Even if there is a partial relapse into the old order, the people will still be socially and morally at sea; they will not be at home in their environment, and will not, even if they know what they want, know what to do in order to get it. The old unquestioned customs will no longer be there in their pristine strength and purity, a buttress to the spirit and a guide to conduct. There may be no full turning back; and yet there may be, if alien rule is withdrawn prematurely, no sense of going forward, no sense of direction at all. Yet the old tribalism or whatever else it was, though now half dead, may still survive and be dangerous.

I have not assumed that it is better to be westernized than not to be, or even that it is better to be fully than only partly westernized. Complete westernization is scarcely possible and not even desirable. It is, however, in a people's interest, once a process imposed on them by the intrusion of foreigners in their midst has begun, that it should go far enough, before they are left to their own devices, to enable them to get their bearings. When a simple society begins to change rapidly as a result of contact with a more complicated and sophisticated society, the people involved in this change often lack the ideas they need to make sense of their own experience. They are caught up in something they cannot understand, and therefore cannot control; they can neither put an end to it nor control it. It is therefore not arrogant to hold that they ought not to be left to themselves until they do understand it well enough to have some hope of controlling it.

If they still half feel and think as tribesmen or as members of separate communities, racial or religious, they will not know how to use the institutions of the modern state impartially, and may use them to try to establish the supremacy of their own tribe or community. People who are partly tribal or feudal or communal in their habits and ideas and partly western (with some of them much more western than others and yet without the habit of authority) must find it difficult to pass without external guidance from the bewildered and mixed-up condition brought upon them by foreign intrusion to some better and more harmonious condition acceptable to them all. They must find themselves torn between incompatible conceptions of how men ought to live; they must be confused and uneasy, and therefore easily brought to violence. This will be the more so the more passive they have been hitherto in the hands of their alien rulers and the less experience they have had of organized co-operation, social and political, of the western kind. It is therefore the duty of those rulers to see to it, as far as they can, that the institutions of the modern state arising among them are not used to make some tribes or communities or castes supreme over others.

We must distinguish here between really primitive tribal societies and societies which, though the Europeans call them 'backward', are complex and sophisticated. In several regions of Asia conquered or dominated by European Powers, the educated classes were able, to some extent at least, to take stock of what was happening to their countries. They too were greatly confused by rapid change but much less so than the rulers of tribal societies. They could adapt themselves more easily to it and could devise more realistic policies to resist or control it to defend their own or the public interest. But greater ability does not always carry with it greater willingness. In Asia, too, narrower loyalties to clan or community or religion or 'race' have got in the way of broader loyalties to the nation newly emerging largely as a result of European intrusion. In Asia, as in Africa, the apparatus of the modern state has been created either by Europeans or in imitation of Europe, and the nation, as a self-conscious unit, is mostly the product of this apparatus and of common reactions to foreign rule. Nationalism is strong, no doubt, but so too are tribalism, provincialism, caste, and other tighter loyalties, which are less vocal politically but not therefore a smaller influence on political behaviour. There is the danger that these narrow loyalties may get the better of nationalism or even may use it as a cloak. It is the duty of the ruling Power to see that this does not happen; it is its duty to hand over authority to men who are accepted as having the right to speak for the entire people in the country gaining independence, to men who are looked upon as national representatives, even if they are not democratically elected. Otherwise, in the eyes of all the people except the tribes or communities that get power, one form of alien rule is put in the place of another, and the condition of the people generally is perhaps no better than it was before, or even worse.

True, the new rulers, even if they are felt to be alien, will probably be less alien than the old ones. Neighbouring tribes and communities, especially when they have been subject together for several generations to the same conquerors from overseas, are likely to have a good deal in common. They will all have been made to feel inferior by the same remote master race; they will all have been treated as 'natives' who differ from one another much less than from the people who have come from afar to teach them how to live. Surely, the departure of rulers who by temperament and in their habits and appearance are so different from themselves will be felt by them all as a blessed liberation raising their common dignity?

This is true but not the whole truth. Unless they can identify themselves with them as full compatriots, men often resent the power over them of rulers close to themselves more than of rulers remote from them. Conquerors from afar who have proved themselves incomparably stronger than the conquered, and who have imposed on them many of their own methods and ideals, are apt to be as much admired as hated. Their superiority, in a sense, is incontestable; their strength and skill cannot be denied, and if the conquered accept their ideals, they must judge themselves by standards which for a time diminish them in their own eyes and add to the dignity of their conquerors. They may hate their conquerors and yet also respect them. But the 'native' rulers who take over from the conquerors, unless they are accepted as full compatriots entitled to speak for a whole nation, will not be respected in the same way, and may soon come to be as much hated. They follow in the footsteps of rulers felt to be more admirable than themselves; and they follow, not as creators and innovators, not as men bringing new and wonderful things with them, but as imitators of those who ruled before them. Only if the nation newly emerged is as close (or closer) to the hearts of the people as the old tribes and communities, only if the paramount loyalty of the first 'native' rulers is to the entire nation and is felt to be so by the people generally, will the people feel that the withdrawal of the conqueror has made them self-governing.

In these days when self-government is widely accepted as desirable, the remote and obvious foreigner actually in power may be felt to be less dangerous than the probable future ruler, even though he is closer to the people, if he is not accepted by them all as one of themselves. As I have tried to explain, the spread of European political ideas cuts at the roots of European rule over non-Europeans, and also more generally at the roots of all foreign rule which looks obviously foreign. Therefore, the days of the foreign ruler, powerful though he may be, seem to be numbered, at least in those parts of the world where western rather than Communist ideas prevail. It was not so some thirty or forty years ago, but it is so now. Most people now take it for granted even when they belong to the ruling nations; so much so indeed that anyone who refuses to admit it or acts on the contrary assumption is usually condemned as a 'reactionary'. But when different tribes or castes or communities are close neighbours and have for some considerable time been included in the same colony or dependent state, they are apt to appear to outsiders as one people. Often, of course, they are in the process of becoming one people. But if, before they have become one people, one section of them establish an ascendancy over the others, this ascendancy may well not look like foreign rule to outsiders. Indeed, even the other sections may hesitate to give it that name; for if they are already on the way to becoming one people, it will not come naturally to them to do so. Yet the ascendancy may still seem oppressive to these other sections, and not the less so because they cannot count on the sympathy of the outside world. In their own country they will be denounced by the supporters of the dominant section as traitors to their 'own' people, or as 'reactionaries' trying to hinder progress. The 'forces of history' will be invoked against them. It will be said that a new nation has come into the world and that they are trying to strangle it at birth. There are also often excellent reasons put forward, economic, political, and of other kinds, why *this* nation should exist within just *these* frontiers. To break it up or weaken it is held to be a retrograde step. The dominant section refuse to admit that they are not spokesmen for an entire nation, that they are one group seeking to dominate others, that they are using nationalism as a cloak for oppression. They are there to stay. That is the assumption they act on, and are loath to make concessions to 'traitors' and to 'enemies of progress'.

It can sometimes happen that people who have long been clamouring for the departure of foreign oppressors blame them for leaving too suddenly or too soon. I have heard Hindus blame the British for precisely this reason. If, they said, the British felt sincerely that they ought not to leave the Muslim minority at the mercy of the Hindu majority, they ought to have stayed in India until they had persuaded both Muslims and Hindus to accept a compromise that left India intact. The partition of India was a retrograde step, against the best interests, in the long run, of the Muslims as well as the Hindus, and even of the British themselves, since a united India would probably have been more strongly attached to the Commonwealth than either of the two parts into which India was broken. I make no comment on this argument as I am not concerned with particular problems; I merely use it to illustrate my point. Just as some Hindus have blamed the British after their departure for leaving so suddenly, so many Muslims, before that departure, feared that it might come too soon. They feared that the British might be in such a hurry to go that they would leave the Muslims unprotected in a united India dominated by the Hindus.

(3) Another argument used to justify continued European rule over non-Europeans is in practice often closely connected with the one we have just been considering. It is said that European rule is much less resented than it appears to be because those who shout loudest against it are only a minority eager to take the place of the Europeans. They alone are politically articulate, and since only their voice is heard, it looks as if all the people want what they demand. They are often the most westernized section of the people, and at the same time the most hotly against the West, for it is precisely because in some ways they have ceased to feel as their ancestors felt and have begun to feel as Europeans do that they think themselves humiliated by foreign rule. The rest of the people bear it meekly enough as they have always borne whatever was their lot. This articulate and half-westernized minority, though still unfit to rule, do their best to arouse hatred of the foreigner in the hope of riding to power on a wave of nationalism. The people generally must be protected against their ambitions.

Even when it is allowed that the articulate minority are popular with the people generally, it is still argued that they ought to be resisted. For the people, though they are taught to hate the foreigner and to share some of the passions of the minority, may still be more their victims than their followers. They probably do not know what the minority mean to do with power when they get it, and might repudiate them if they did know. They do what they are told willingly enough, but they do it blindly, without an idea of what is likely to happen to them as a consequence. The skill of the minority is the effective and unscrupulous exploitation of grievances, but this skill is no evidence of the capacity to govern.

G

Also, the popularity of rebels and extremists can often seem greater than it really is, especially if they can create the impression that their victory is certain. The passive, the indifferent, the inarticulate, the people who care most for their own safety, are always prone to submit to the powerful and even to flatter them. While the cause of the rebels seems hopeless they readily support established authority against disturbers of the peace; but when the victory of the rebels begins to look probable, their feelings change, and they think it more prudent to gain the favour of their future rulers than to retain the favour of their present ones. If nothing succeeds like success, it is not owing to mere chance, it is not the luck of the bold; it is because men are timid and are flatterers. They see the semblance of power and run to abase themselves before it, not knowing that by their servility they themselves make real the power they bow to. Now that it is generally agreed that 'colonialism' is coming to an end, the ultimate victory of its enemies is taken for certain. These enemies can therefore afford to intimidate the quiet and the passive; they can use terror much more profitably than they could before. Some of them may be caught and punished for using it; but the future, so they think (and so think also their potential victims), is theirs. Meanwhile, the colony-owning Powers are either milder than they used to be for fear of offending world opinion, or if they are not, are much more loudly condemned. The boot is now on the other foot but the kicking is as cruel and vicious as ever.

This line of argument, often abused and therefore not much to the taste of people on the Left, has a good deal to it. Foreign rule is often less generally resented than it seems to be; and it makes sense to say that foreign rulers ought to see to it that, when they withdraw, the passive and inarticulate do not fall victims to a ruthless minority of exuberant patriots. European withdrawal from a non-European country can lead to misgovernment by half-westernized and self-styled 'progressives'; and the misgovernment may not be merely government carried on in ways not approved of in western Europe and North America. If it were only that, if it were in keeping with the standards and preferences of the people themselves, this European condemnation might be dismissed as irrelevant. But it may be misgovernment by the standards of the people living under it, partly no doubt because it does not accord with ancestral folk-ways still only in the process of dying, but partly also (and perhaps even more) because it belies principles and expectations which the people have acquired from the West. It is true that the loudest enemies of the West are often among the most westernized, though not always westernized in the best sense. They may have been attracted to western civilization for the good living it offers, the comforts and luxuries, or for the power to be got by using western arguments and methods against the West. Even when they are honest, as they often are, they may be narrow and vindictive. In spite of their honesty, they may be less idealists than angry and ambitious men. Collectively formidable, they may not be impressive, morally or intellectually, as individuals. They may not revert to the old ways nor try to establish the ascendancy of old tribes or castes or communities over the rest of the people; they may be hot for progress and for using the most modern methods, and yet may care little for the people's good as the people themselves conceive it. Their rule may be odious both by western standards and by whatever standards (part western and part native) prevail among their subjects.

It is also true that, given the assumptions and prejudices of our day, people can be more defenceless against 'native' rulers than against foreigners. Not, perhaps, in the Communist part of the world, but outside it. However much they may proclaim their right to govern what belongs to them as they think fit without interference from outsiders, the colony-owning Powers feel the need to justify themselves to the world, and in giving vent to this need they tacitly admit that the world has a right to take more than an academic interest in what they do in their colonies. In minding their colonies' business they are not minding their own; they are minding other people's. They can perhaps produce as good arguments in their own favour as the arguments used against them. Yet the burden of proof rests on them; for the indifference of the old days is now past and they cannot resort to the cynicism of the Communists. Their business in their colonies is also, in a way, the world's business; and all the more so today that the world is divided into two 'ideological' camps. The colony-owning Powers have, they claim, a civilizing mission in their colonies, and what they do there therefore matters not only to them but to all who share the values used to justify that mission. The English are not Cypriots and the French are not Algerian Muslims, and there are nowadays many fewer people, even in England and France, who believe that what the English do in Cyprus or the French in Algeria is their business alone in the sense that they admit that what Nehru does in India is the business of the Indians. Now this fact that the

English and the French (no matter how reluctant they are to admit it) are morally responsible to the outside world for what they do in their colonies in a way that native rulers would not be, does act as a powerful restraint upon them; and if a dependent people have learnt to care for humane government and for personal freedom, it may well be that they have less to fear from the English and the French than from the rebels who are fighting to liberate them.

It is odd to see violence so little condemned, in the part of the world which delights in calling itself 'free', when the violence is directed against the foreign ruler. True, foreign rule, in the very nature of the case, is undemocratic; the foreigner imposes or has imposed his rule by force. Therefore, and perfectly rightly and sensibly, it is said that there cannot be democracy until the foreigner goes. If then democracy is desirable the foreign ruler must go. But people who care for democracy often go further than this; they often speak as if the sooner the foreigner went the quicker democracy would be established, which is by no means obvious. I shall not, however, consider this point in detail here, for I discuss it in several other places in this essay; though the point is often taken as if it were obvious, especially by politicians and journalists on the Left. They may even admit that the nationalist rebels, when first they get power, will behave tyrannically in spite of their openly declared democratic principles. But, they say, it takes time for any people, and especially for a people who have to fight for their independence, to settle down to democracy. The illegal and brutal actions of the first native rulers are explained as fruits of inexperience, of the arrogance that follows on victory, and of past oppression. None but the politically innocent can expect full and true democracy from the very moment of independence. There is an unpleasant phase to be lived through, and the sooner it comes the sooner it will be over. Besides, even if democracy does not come quickly after independence, or even at all, the people are no worse off, from the democratic point of view, than they would have been under continued foreign rule; for foreign rule, the longer it is maintained against strong native opposition, the more oppressive it becomes. While foreign rule lasts, there is no hope of democracy; but once it is brought to an end by men who are patriots and profess to be democrats, there is always some hope, even though they do not fully understand the principles they profess. This kind of argument (as often taken for granted as made explicit) does powerfully incline people on the Left to consider the victory of rebels against 'colonialism' or 'imperialism' as being somehow also a victory in the long run for democracy, even when they admit that the rebels are probably very inadequate democrats. Their violence is seen as part of a struggle for democracy and freedom, whereas the violence of their foreign rulers is called oppression. Hence a much greater reluctance to condemn the violence of the rebels and a readiness to blame their oppressors for it. So that even in the country having dominion over a rebellious colony, the rebels can count on strong and wide sympathies, especially if they can make it look as if they are popular with their own people.

But what is popularity? If a man is popular, does it follow that he is liked and trusted? It all depends on the circumstances. I have already drawn attention to one obvious point: that most people are anxious not to offend and even to placate those who, they believe, will soon get power; those whose victory they take for inevitable. It is no less obvious that this anxiety varies, not only with their estimation of the chances of victory, but with the apparent ruthlessness of the parties or groups fighting for power. The more ruthless they are thought to be, the more ordinary people will feel the need to insure themselves against their victory by currying favour with them. Of course, if it is thought that there is little chance of their victory, their addiction to violence and terror will usually count heavily against them. But if their chance is thought to be considerable, the position is often reversed. There may be other groups with apparently a greater chance of victory because they are better liked and trusted, who lose in the end largely because there is less to be feared from their victory. If they are less inclined to use terror, or if it is thought more likely that they can be prevented from using it, it is safer to oppose them or to refrain from supporting them than to oppose or ignore their enemies. In times of trouble the chances of victory are peculiarly difficult to calculate, except that there is a general feeling that the ruthless are more likely to win than the mild. Therefore, at such times, even a small group, known to be cruel and vindictive, are apt to be greatly feared. We may therefore hazard this generalization: the greater the disorder and uncertainty, the greater the apparent popularity to be gained by violence and terror. To the group that gains this 'popularity', it does not much matter that it should be more apparent than real if it moves men to behave in ways that bring power to the group. It would be a waste of time for the group to try to win the affection and trust of the people; the quickest and surest way to power is for the group to create the impression that their victory is almost certain and will bear hardly on all who oppose them. They make fear their ally just when that ally is likely to be strongest.

Fear affects more than men's outward actions; it affects their beliefs also, sometimes even to the point of making them think they like what they dislike. They want to assure themselves that it is not fear but some nobler passion which moves them to behave as they do; they make excuses for the bullies so as not to have to admit, even to themselves, that they submit only because they are afraid. They feel the need to think not too badly of the men who bustle and scare them so as not to have to think badly of themselves. If the group they fear have a cause that can be made to look respectable, if they demand discipline and sacrifice for the sake of some high-sounding ideal, this process of self-deception is made the easier.

I do not deny that there are perhaps many sincerely and passionately attracted to the cause, or who need it to give a sense of purpose to their lives, nor yet that there are many who submit without being truly won over and yet also are without self-deception. There are several motives that can move us to submit quietly to the strong and the unscrupulous. But I suspect, none the less, that the self-deceivers are often numerous, as is borne out by recent German experience. When Hitler fell millions of Germans who had until then appeared to be his devoted followers renounced him and even denied that they had ever really supported him; they had, they said, merely put up with him and acquiesced in what he did because there was nothing else they could safely do. They were accused of hypocrisy; and yet most of them were probably not hypocrites, at least not in the crude sense. They were probably not deliberately pretending to be different from what they knew they were. Many of them probably did feel a kind of devotion to Hitler while he was strong and dangerous, and yet afterwards, when it had become openly shameful to have felt this devotion, denied having felt it without being aware that they were not telling the truth. Indeed, in many cases, they probably were telling part of the truth: their devotion to Hitler had never been entirely sincere. While Hitler was strong, it had made life easier for them, ministering to their self-respect, not to admit this even *in foro interno*; after he had fallen it eased their minds to say and to believe that they had never been devoted to him. No doubt, this was not true of all the Germans who denied Hitler after his fall, but I suspect it was true of many. Others, of course, first praised and then blamed him, not to lighten the burden on their consciences, but only because they were by temperament persons who worship success and despise failure. These states of mind are not peculiar to Germans; they are much too common to be written into the specifically national character of any people.

The leaders of nationalist rebellions are closer to their own people than alien rulers can be. They may be the more liked and trusted for this closeness or they may not be; but even when they are not, they are better able than foreigners to work on the feelings of the people, shaming and bullying them into support of their cause. Hatred and resentment are catching; the bitter and the ruthless carry the others along with them or stampede them like cattle, especially when they are disorganized and do not know their own minds. First they disturb them, making them angry and restless, and then find an outlet for this anger by directing it against the foreigner ruling over them. A man, however mild he may be by temperament, who has once allowed himself to be shamed or coaxed or frightened into a violent movement will soon be affected by its spirit, even though in his inmost heart he still dislikes it and finds it oppressive. Anyone who watched the Communists struggling for power in the Balkans during the last war could see a process just like this at work. Persons frightened into support of the movement worked for it as loyally as those who were genuinely converted; to feel secure inside it they had by their outward behaviour to prove their loyalty to it, until at last they acquired a half faith in it. They paid more than lip service to it and less than heart service.

In saying all this, I do not deny that there is often much genuine patriotism behind a nationalist movement, just as there is often true revolutionary fervour among Communists and others like them. A nationalist movement can be truly and widely popular; but it can also have a kind of false popularity for the reasons I have tried to describe. It is the popularity of the violent, the ambitious, and the pitiless which thrives on the need felt by the weak, the confused, and sometimes even the scrupulous to excuse their docility; the need felt by men driven like sheep by a cruel and restless shepherd to assure themselves that they are men who can insist on being treated like men.

Some people may be tempted to say, What of it? Have not the weak always been the victims of the strong? Are not great historical changes often made by hard and pitiless minorities? Why should the colony-owning Powers care what the nationalists do to the majority of their fellow-countrymen? Why should they not hold on to their colonies while they can do so profitably to themselves, and then abandon them when they prove too costly to keep?

These are almost rhetorical questions, and are perhaps not worth answering, except that the people who put them seem to expect answers. These people often pride themselves on their lack of senti-mentality, and will not be put off by soft or moral answers. It is not much use saying to them that the colony-owning Powers, because they have (even though not always with perfect sincerity) preached freedom and democracy and have taught the peoples subject to them to want these things, are in honour bound to do what they can to put them in the way of getting them. They are perhaps more likely to be moved by the argument that the more the colonies, after they have gained their independence, share the ideals and adopt the practices of their former rulers, the safer and stronger these rulers are likely to be among the nations. It is certainly not less their purely selfish interest that democracy should spread than it is Russia's that Communism should do so.

The questions, at bottom, are much sillier than they appear to be on the surface. Who, after all, are the strong? What evidence have we of their strength? I am speaking now, not of individuals, but of political groups and their leaders. Their strength is their ability to get their way; or, in other words, it is their success. We might as well ask, Why should we resist the successful or try to help the unsuccessful against them? But this is an absurd question; for the less we resist people, the more successful they are apt to be. Admiration of the strong, when strength is more or less equivalent to success, is a childish emotion because it rests on a simple mistake; it takes appearance for reality, it takes men for larger than they are, ascribing to qualities in them effects which are due rather to the inaction or foolishness or miscalculation of others, or merely to chance. There are, of course, strong men in the world, men who know what they want and are patient and bold and resilient in the pursuit of it. If they are successful, they no doubt owe their success largely to their strength; but such men are often un-successful because what they happen to want is hard to get. Or else, if they succeed in getting it, their success interests few but themselves because what they want is not wanted by most people and perhaps not understood by them. It takes, perhaps, greater strength of mind, more courage, and a larger and more controlled expenditure of spiritual energy, to make an artist than a political leader; to make a Beethoven than a Bismarck, let alone a Hitler. Was there ever a time when power belonged less to the inwardly strong than it does now; when a man's influence on his fellow-men depended so much on the public image of him created by propaganda?

(4) Where there are Europeans settled in large numbers in a colony, the European Power ruling that colony regards it as its special duty to protect these settlers. Two arguments are used to justify this position. The first appeals to simple patriotism: everywhere men care first for their own people and only afterwards for strangers. If the natives want to get rid of their foreign rulers on the ground that they are foreign, if they make a point of treating them as foreigners, then they must expect these rulers in their turn to show particular solicitude for their own compatriots. The settlers came there under their protection and must now rely chiefly on that protection. When the present rulers leave, the settlers will be more exposed to attack, or to have their interests neglected, than any other section of the community. Therefore, the ruling Power must not grant self-government until the position of the European settlers has been made secure.

This first argument is often buttressed by another: that the special interests of the European settlers, though they conflict with the actual demands made by the nationalists, are in harmony with the permanent interests of the colony as a whole, because the settlers are more progressive than the people taken as a whole. They have often brought such prosperity as there is to the colony, and they are best able, for the time being, to exploit its natural resources efficiently. They are a kind of aristocracy in the colony, not so much because they are richer and have more influence with the government (though this also is true), as because they are the best exponents of ideals and methods which the natives have learned and are learning to accept. Their predominance ought to pass away only gradually as the natives acquire the same abilities. If the European settlers were landowners and capitalists doing no more than draw rent and interest from the country and contributing only money to its development, they could easily be displaced without loss to the community; but they are much more than that. They are a supremely useful aristocracy, the bearers of a dominant culture; and aristocracies of that kind ought to disappear by absorption or assimilation rather than by abrupt elimination.

These arguments are less cogent than the others we have discussed. Not that the others are the whole truth in their particular spheres, for, as we shall see in the next chapter, there are also counter arguments; they are only part of the truth but they are an important part. These two arguments, even if we consider them on their own, are less persuasive; and this is specially true of the second.

No doubt, the ruling Power ought to see to it that justice is done to the European settlers. This, however, is too often interpreted as seeing to it that the settlers retain the advantages they have already acquired, and above all their property. If a ruling Power has decided not to withdraw until it has made sure that, after it has gone, the settlers will retain their property, the chances are that it will not withdraw until it is driven out by force. The settlers in all probability have taken the best lands, and there may not be enough good land left for the natives to raise their standards to the level that contact with Europeans has caused them to aspire to. Their standard of living may have risen in the past as a result of the settlers having come among them. It may be easy to show that all classes are better off for what the settlers have done, and yet just as easy to prove that they cannot be nearly as well off as they might be until the settlers have been deprived of much of their property and have ceased to be a privileged community. The most that the settlers are entitled to ask for is that, if they are expropriated, they shall be fairly compensated; and there is no reason why the compensation should come from the colony rather than from the mother-country. The colony may have profited from the efforts of the settlers, but so too has the mother-country, which is ordinarily much the richer of the two and the better able to bear the burden.

The people of the colony may, of course, want to keep the settlers among them, and may therefore be willing to leave them most of their property or to undertake to compensate them for whatever part of it is taken from them. That the ruling Power should want to make as good a bargain for them as it can is only natural. But it ought not to insist on making a better bargain for them than is likely to survive the grant of self-government. If the natives believe that concessions which are excessive have been extorted from them as the price of self-government, they will soon, after they have taken over control of their own country, find an excuse for repudiating them. On the other hand, if the ruling Power refuses to leave until it has obtained all the concessions it asks for the settlers, it may soon cause the natives to despair of getting self-government unless they resort to violence. And the natives, once they have resorted to violence, will quickly become much more obstinate than they were before. It does not then much matter whose the fault was that blood was first shed; for when blood is shed, the quarrel is soon raised above (or below) the level of rational argument. It is then that men feel themselves committed, as they think, irrevocably, to what has come to seem to them a sacred cause. It is then that they feel it dishonourable to give way; and men are apt to prefer their 'honour' to their interests, when the two conflict in times of trouble.

The ruling Power cannot have a greater duty to the settlers than to the natives, even though the natives strive to get rid of it on the ground of its being alien to them. The natives, if they are to get what they want (which is largely what their alien rulers have taught them to want), must get rid of alien rule, and it is right, by the very principles proclaimed by their rulers, that they should do so. By these same principles, their rulers owe it to them to help them get what they want, and to resist their demands only because giving in to them will prevent or retard their getting it. Having established their rule over the colony, they are bound to deal impartially with all the peoples in it, no matter what their race or culture; they ought not to prefer the settlers on the ground that they are their own people or are racially and culturally closer to them or are eager to retain the connection with the mother country when the natives want to break it. Their duty to the settlers is merely to help them reach a settlement with the natives which will enable them to live in harmony together after independence has come, or else, if that cannot be done, to help them withdraw from the colony with as little loss as possible. The natives are usually the great majority, and their interests must be preferred to all others, even (should the need arise) to the extent of removing from among them the alien settlers who came uninvited and often took the best of whatever was to be had. This is not required by principles generally accepted two or three hundred years ago, but it is required by principles which the West Europeans have come to adopt in recent times and which they have propagated all over the world.

It cannot be denied that the settlers are usually more 'progressive' than the natives. They are Europeans and usually come much nearer than all but a few of the natives to understanding European ideas and practices, which are in fact dominant. They live much more as believers in 'progress' would have men live. So much must be admitted, but not, I think, much more. After all, as much could be said for the nobles in central and eastern Europe in the eighteenth and early nineteenth centuries; they too were much larger participators in western culture than the classes beneath them. They dealt with one another more considerately, more politely, perhaps even more gently, than did the other classes; their womenfolk were more emancipated; and in general they were more inclined to be tolerant of personal idiosyncrasy and to let a man live as he pleased. They were, within the limits of their own class, more liberal, more truly respectful of personal freedom, than the other classes. All this, however, did not prevent their also being, in their attitude to the claims made by those other classes, quite illiberal. By the standards of the modern believer in progress they were the class that had progressed furthest, they were the most civilized; but they also often stood in the way of the progress of others. They were not 'reactionary' in the sense that Plato has been accused of being; they did not want to destroy personal freedom or to introduce forms of discipline proper to the school or the camp. They wanted no more than to retain, at the expense of the other classes, the privileges which made them the freest class in central Europe. The same, perhaps, is often true of European settlers in Asia and Africa; they too set a high value on the freedom they enjoy, but without being much concerned that others should also enjoy it. They want to retain their privileges as long as they can, and are too prone to believe that they might even retain them indefinitely if it were not for the cranks and busybodies eager to deprive them of these privileges for the supposed benefit of people not fit to be their equals. The settlers are much more apt than other Europeans to believe that the natives are congenitally incapable of self-government; and they also claim to know the natives better for having lived among them so long.

Some things about the natives, no doubt, they do know better: their habits, their faults, their reactions to how Europeans treat them. It is their interest to know these things, and prejudice does not blind them here. When other Europeans, who make much larger claims on the natives' behalf than they are willing to allow, show themselves ignorant of what is so familiar to them, they pounce on this ignorance and use it to contest the claims. Why listen to the proposals of people so ignorant that they do not even know what the natives are like? Now, the assumption behind this question is only part of the truth.

The settlers often see only what it suits them to see. They are often blind to other qualities which the natives possess; and above all, they do not ask themselves how far the habits and defects so obvious to them are produced by conditions which are only temporary or which their own ascendancy tends to perpetuate. It may be that until the settlers have lost many of their privileges and much of their property, the natives cannot get the education, the standard of living, and even the self-respect, needed to make them capable of self-government. To know what people are like is by no means to know what would become of them under quite different conditions. The first kind of knowledge comes merely from seeing a good deal of them, and the second from history and the comparative study of society and also from political experience. Both kinds of knowledge are needed to solve the problems of any particular country. Yet the people who have the first kind are often no nearer to getting the second; they may, indeed, have strong motives for not getting it or for not applying it properly to the first kind. This is ordinarily the case with European settlers when they are raised high above the natives in wealth and power.

Moreover, they often do not even possess very much of the first kind of knowledge; they often do not even see the natives as they really are, and have only as much understanding of them as they need to be able to use them for their own purposes. This is like the useful knowledge of the shopkeeper who 'understands' his customers or of the officer who 'understands' his men. Neither the shopkeeper nor the officer need penetrate very deep into the workings of their minds; he need do no more than know what to expect of them as purchasers of goods or as soldiers. He can make do with a practical and a superficial understanding. He is interested only in external behaviour, and in no more than a small part of it. Within that compass he can make more accurate predictions than other people; but the understanding of the psychologist or the sociologist is not his.

The settlers feel themselves threatened by the natives in a way that the officials of the alien ruling Power do not. They think they are there to stay, and they hope to pass on their properties (and perhaps also their other privileges) to their children. Even when they allow that the natives cannot be 'kept in their place' forever, they do not care to think of themselves as making way for them; they would like to believe that the natives can make progress indefinitely with no need for the white man to make any great sacrifices. Just as they are more realistic than other Europeans in some ways because their familiarity with the natives is greater, they are less realistic in others because it is more painful to them to contemplate the future. They are, therefore, apt to be both shrewder and more fantastic than the men who have only come to spend their years of public service in the colony. They know the natives as some old-fashioned parents know their children; they know how to keep them in their place, and they mistake this knowledge for understanding of their character. What they often do not know is how to reconcile their own interests with those of the natives, how to make concessions gracefully, how to come to terms at the least cost to themselves with what they cannot in the long run prevent. They are proud of their achievements, which are indeed great, and they believe that for the mother-country to abandon them is a betrayal of civilization. It is easy to sympathize with them. How many would not think as they do, placed as they are? Those in the mother-country who abuse them are perhaps not less narrow-minded than they, and have nothing like the same excuse. Still, though it is easy to sympathize with them, they are often wrong simply because they refuse to admit the obvious: that the maintenance of their position requires the permanent subordination of the natives to them, and that the natives, if they are to be permanently subordinate, cannot realize the aspirations which contact with European civilization has brought to them.

When the settlers are loath to make concessions to the natives and yet cannot do without their labour, they are (for all that they will not admit it) both the enemies and the unwilling proselytizers of the natives. By giving them employment they help them to break away from their old customs and teach them to work (and even sometimes to live) more as Europeans do. It does not suit them that the natives should remain as they were, and it also does not suit them that the process of westernization should go more than a little way. Sincerely though they often deny it, they are impelled by their position to take this attitude towards the natives: 'thus far and no farther'. Many of them find it difficult to make clear what they mean either to others or to themselves. Unless they have been cut off, as the South African Dutch were, from the West during the period when the West was becoming liberal and socialist, they find it hard to insist that what the West most values is suited only to Europeans. They are reluctant to deny categorically that all peoples can make indefinite progress; and so they are often content to say no more than that 'progress' must be slow, and that to hurry it on is to bring disaster. The argument sounds well; indeed, taken in the abstract, it is true. But it is also true that the attempt to slow down 'progress' can lead to disaster. The trouble with the settlers (and why blame them, since it could hardly be otherwise?) is that they too often say that progress must be slow because, in their inmost hearts, they want it to stop at the point that suits themselves. They have an image in their minds of the 'good native', docile, cheerful, honest, not too lazy, and they would like to see all natives in that image. They usually care little for what the native was before he began to be 'civilized', they have not much respect for his folk culture. They are not anthropologists but farmers and industrialists and businessmen; they take it for granted that the native, though better for being civilized, must not be civilized beyond his capacity to assimilate what civilization has to offer. Just what that capacity is, or whether it is limited permanently by heredity or only for the time being by social conditions, they often do not know. They seldom put these questions clearly to themselves; they equivocate and are confused. I speak of the majority without meaning to deny that there are many exceptions.

If this is true, then it is unlikely that the settlers will accept equality with the natives quickly enough to dissolve the tensions between the two groups and enable them to live together harmoniously as members of the same community. If sudden pressure too strong for them to resist forces equality upon them, they will either leave the country or else, if they cling to what is left to them of their properties, risk becoming a demoralized and vindictive class, as several European aristocracies have become. It is surely better to deal firmly and generously with them, giving them the chance to withdraw without too much loss, if withdraw they must, but leaving them in no doubt that the interests of the majority will be preferred to their interests. Though it is a hard decision for a 'mother-country' to take, it will in the long run hurt even the settlers less than they otherwise would be hurt. It still leaves it open to them to stay in the country of their adoption and to play a great part in it if they are willing to pay the price.

(5) Another argument sometimes used to justify delay in granting autonomy or independence to a subject people is that the people, if left to themselves, would fall victims to some aggressive Power or to some movement dangerous to the peace of the world. Sometimes, too,

it is said that the country inhabited by that people is necessary to the security of the ruling Power or of some combination of Powers to which it belongs, so that even its neutrality would weaken that Power and its allies. At one time people who used these arguments spoke openly of the need to maintain the security of 'the empire', meaning that if the ruling Power lost one territory belonging to it, this would weaken its hold on others. Thus British predominance in the Middle East, which involved keeping several countries in a state of half-dependence on Britain, was excused on the ground that it was necessary to keep open Britain's route to India. Even after India and Pakistan got their independence, people spoke of the need to ensure that the routes between the great Commonwealth countries did not fall into the hands of potential enemies. But now that it is clear that what the Commonwealth countries can do for one another is less than what most of them expect the United States to do for them, there is perhaps more talk of the security of the 'free world' than of the Commonwealth; and by the 'free world' is meant all the world not controlled by the Communists. Though this includes many more countries than are allied to the United States, it is often taken for granted that the United States and its major allies are the guardians of the free world.

Apart from concern for empire or Commonwealth or the 'free world', there is also the need felt to ensure that vital natural resources are not lost. Western Europe cannot do without oil from the Middle East, and so any loss of territory or of influence in that area by Britain is put forward as threatening the economic security of Europe by increasing the danger that oil supplies will be stopped. Since the second World War this consideration has counted for more perhaps than any other for Britain's reluctance to withdraw from the Middle East.

Unfortunately for its allies, the United States does not always agree with them about their need to hold on to colonies and concessions in order to prevent strategically important parts of the world from passing under the influence of potential enemies. The Americans are sometimes inclined to believe that trying to hold on to them too long is more likely to have this effect than letting them go easily. This attitude irritates America's allies, and gives them yet another motive for wanting to keep what the Americans would have them abandon: the desire not to be dominated by too powerful an ally. This motive helped to inspire the disastrous Suez adventure, and now makes the French less willing than ever to accept American advice about what they should do in North Africa. Perhaps, too, Britain's policy over Cyprus is to be explained in part (though other considerations now weigh more with her) by the wish to retain a base which would enable her, if necessary, to make her weight felt in the Middle East independently of America. America's principal allies in Europe do not want to break away from the alliance; they believe that their security depends on it more than on anything else. Even the French—except for the Communists and some people on the extreme Right—mostly believe this. Yet the British and the French (though the French more than the British) also resent the overwhelming superiority in arms and wealth of their great ally; and this resentment makes them less willing to make to colonial and other dependent peoples concessions which they fear will diminish their own prestige or military or economic power. They also fear (and this is especially true of the French) that the Americans are using their role of guardians of the 'free world' to supplant British and French influence in Asia and Africa. Some people, indeed, claim to see active in the world an American imperialism falser and more insidious than the Russian because it flourishes at the expense of friends and not of enemies.

We have here some confused arguments and mixed motives. So far, there has not been much evidence that subject peoples, when they get their independence from one Power, tend to fall victims to another or to an international movement dangerous to peace. Rather the contrary. If the old order still obtained, if conquest and domination were not condemned, if freedom and democracy were not praised, if countries lost their colonies only because they were too weak to hold them, then it might well be that poor and weak nations could get independence only to lose it again quickly. But this is not so. Whatever the real motives of the two greatest Powers, both proclaim themselves believers in national independence limited only by international law and by obligations to U.N.O. and to other bodies purporting to treat all nations as equals. Outside Europe the Soviet Union has two small satellites. Communist China is as independent as Nationalist China ever was and much more so than she is now. Friendship with Moscow is in Asia no more a mark of subservience to Russia than friendship with Washington is a mark of subservience to the United States. Russia had special opportunities and special motives, which she does not have in Asia and Africa, for making the smaller Slav states dependent on her. These two great Powers can be played off against

H

one another; and the more suspicious they are of each other, while at the same time being afraid of war, the easier it is to play them off in this way. When the Yugoslav Communists quarrelled with Moscow, the Russians did no more than abuse them and apply economic sanctions against them, thereby giving the Americans the chance to come to their help. The Russians could intervene in Hungary because they contrived to find a Hungarian government willing to invite their intervention and because they had for years kept troops in Hungary. They used force to retain a position they had long held; but even then they hesitated. There is little evidence that they are willing to use the same methods to acquire satellites where they do not yet have them as to keep them where they do. Their hold on their European satellites is, they think, necessary to their security. They will not easily abandon the advantages gained at the end of the last war by their victorious drive into the heart of Germany.

The methods the Russians have used to get and to keep their European satellites are not, of course, the only methods they use to extend their influence at the expense of the West. Their other methods of infiltration and propaganda may be as easily used outside Europe as inside, and perhaps more easily. There are, as I admitted in the first chapter, special causes making easier the spread of Communism in the poorer and politically less sophisticated and organized parts of the world; and the spread of Communism still means (though it may do so much less in the future) the spread of Russian influence. To admit this is not, however, to concede that Communism is less likely to spread if the Powers that have colonies keep hold of them. There may be other reasons why they should keep hold of them, at least for a time, so that they can get independence by stages. But to hold on to them merely to prevent their going Communist does not make good sense. If conditions are such that the colony is already on the verge of Communism, the demand for independence is likely to be so fierce and hatred of 'colonialism' so strong that every action of the ruling Power is suspect to the people or at least to the leaders they follow. However good the intentions of the alien rulers, however sincerely they want to prepare the colony for democracy and to raise the standard of living, they will probably be frustrated by the Communists who will turn everything they do against them. The more the colony is held down by sheer force, the greater the authority of the Communists over the people.

And if the colony is still a long way from becoming Communist, there are better reasons for wanting to bring prosperity and liberal institutions to it than the desire to prevent its falling into Communist hands. If the lead in the struggle for independence is not taken by the Communists, then the victory of the 'rebels', even if it happens in conditions which make the coming of liberal democracy unlikely, will not necessarily hasten the coming of Communism. These, after all, are not the only two alternatives, and there is no good reason for believing that the violent authoritarian nationalism now directed against the West is any more likely to lead to Communism than to democracy. We may dislike this sort of nationalism for what it is in itself and again for being so hot against us, and we may also dislike Communism and fear it. It may come natural to us to lump these objects of our abhorrence together and to speak of them as if they had close affinities. But there is no evidence that they have. Of course, people who hate or mistrust us will try to use our potential enemies against us. Is that a reason for believing that, when our enemies are better known to them, they will prove more congenial than we have been? Why should we believe that Asian and African nationalists who have recently so often got the better of us will be outsmarted by Moscow? Are the narrow and suspicious Communists, with their old-fashioned theories, so much cleverer than we are?

English Conservatives used to excuse Turkish rule over the Balkan peoples on the ground that these peoples, as soon as they were free of the Turks, would become the tools of Tsarist Russia, a Power much more formidable than the Ottoman Empire. The fears of the Con-servatives were mistaken. The liberated peoples were too fond of their liberty to allow new foreign masters to take control of them; they resented Russian interference just as bitterly as they had resented being governed by the Turks. They had much in common with the Russians whom they liked better than they did the Austrians and the Hungarians, without allowing this affection to influence their foreign policies too much. Against the Russians alone they would have been powerless, but they could rely on the support of other Powers. A great Power which uses a nationalist movement to detach colonies or provinces from another Power soon finds that nothing is less enduring than the gratitude of a people who have been helped to gain their free-dom. It is like the gratitude of children to their parents; the more it is demanded, the less it is given. What is more intolerable to a man than that other men should put the weight of their services on his conscience?

If a nationalist movement has already, before independence, fallen under the control of an international body directed by a great Power, then its triumph may mean that the country, when it is liberated, merely gets new foreign masters in place of the old ones. Even that, however, is by no means sure. The local leaders of an international body, when they become leaders of a nationalist movement, soon acquire, if they are at all widely popular, strong feelings which weaken their loyalty to the international body. They may not become exactly patriots; their concern for their country's independence may be at bottom little more than a desire that their own power should be un-trammelled. The motive does not matter; even if it is not patriotism, it has much the same effects. We have only to look at relations between Yugoslavia and Russia since the last war to see how easily Communists, after they have taken control of a popular nationalist movement, can detach themselves from Moscow. The Yugoslav Communist Party was just as drastically purged and made Stalinist before the war as any other Communist party; it was less docile to Moscow than other such parties after 1945 because it enjoyed considerably wider popularity at home and not because it was intellectually more independent or liberal. If there are (as some people claim) considerable thinkers among the Yugoslav Communists, I can only say that I have yet to hear of them. Even Djilas has nothing new to say, though he has shown great courage in speaking out so openly. In Yugoslavia, too, the Com-munists were and still are disliked and feared by most people; and when I say they are popular, I mean only that they are so if we compare them with the Communists in Russia's European satellites. The Communists are, no doubt, also widely popular in China (and perhaps even more widely hated); they are certainly as little subservient to Moscow as the Yugoslav Communists. They give greater support to Moscow partly because they think it their interest to do so and partly because they do not fear Russian domination and are therefore much readier to show respect to the first home of Communist orthodoxy. They feel themselves much nearer to being the true equals of the Russian Communists and are therefore less anxious to prove that equality by open criticism and defiance. They can prove it better by exerting influence in Moscow.

However independent of Moscow a Communist country may want

to appear, it will almost certainly support Russian attacks on western 'imperialism'. It will be apt to be more loudly hostile to 'imperialism' and 'colonialism' than if it were not Communist. But its attitude will also depend on how long it has been recognized as an independent state and on whether or not it is European. Yugoslavia, being now a Communist state, is much louder against 'imperialism' than if she had remained an independent monarchy or had become a parliamentary republic of the western kind; it needed adherence to Communism to make her vociferously opposed to imperialism. Whereas India, so recently dependent, is against 'imperialism' without being Communist; and has sometimes proved more eager even than Red China to condemn or embarrass the 'imperialist' Powers. China, unlike India, was never directly subject to a western Power, and may therefore feel less strongly about the indignities of this subjection. It is only to be expected that subject peoples, when they get independence, should be in favour of other peoples getting it as soon as possible; unless, of course, it happens to be their interest that a particular people should not get it. This is so whether the peoples gaining independence are ruled by Communists or not; and it does not mean that they are willing to make great sacrifices to help others get what they have just obtained.

The enlargement of Communism still means the growth of Russian power. But just how long will it continue to do so? I would not hazard an answer to this question. Yet, clearly, Communism, like every other ideology, as it spreads, becomes more diverse and discordant. The solidarity of the Communist world probably looks greater to outsiders than it is; and might perhaps be smaller in fact if the rest of the world were less noisily hostile to Communism. No doubt, since our principles are opposed to it, we ought to take what steps we can to prevent its spreading; but we need not exaggerate its danger to ourselves. Subject peoples who get independence, even if they take to Communism, will not want to be used by Moscow to increase Russian power; they will probably be more concerned to develop their own countries than to help other peoples struggling for independence, despite their eagerness to express loud sympathy for them.

If independence brings Communism, this is, I think, more to be deplored for the sake of the people concerned than because it adds strength to the Communist part of the world against the free part. Communism takes people further away from freedom than they were before; it brings to them habits and institutions more destructive of the self-respect and respect for others on which freedom thrives than any other system except Nazism. It may be that in the future the Communists, just because they are stronger and feel more secure, will use less ruthless methods than they have done in the past. Their rule may become milder and yet not be less corrosive of the habits and feelings that make for freedom. In the process of having material welfare brought to them by Communist methods, people may lose both the ideals native to them and those acquired from the West. They may cease to want freedom, especially if they have never had much of it and know little of the institutions needed to support it. Perhaps they will be as happy as if they had been westernized. Who can tell, since happiness is not measurable? It is much easier to discover whether people are free than whether they are happy. People accustomed to freedom may be made unhappy by the loss of it; but they might have been happier had they never known it or may become happier when they have forgotten it. Communism is not to be condemned because it makes people unhappy (though it has caused some of the worst suffering known to us) but rather because it helps to make them incapable of freedom. But this condemnation, let us admit it, means nothing except to persons who have learnt to care for freedom.

Colonies and dependent territories may be important militarily or because they produce vital raw materials, so that the ruling or dominant Power is reluctant to abandon them for fear of weakening itself thereby. This fear is often exaggerated or even out of place. If that Power is already the largest consumer of the materials produced there, it is likely to continue being so after independence has been achieved. Commercial ties are not severed by independence, and producers like to keep their old customers. As for the military importance of colonies, it is no longer what it was, since the countries owning most colonies are today more dependent for their security on the United States than on their overseas possessions. In any case, in order not to put obstacles in the way of getting independence quickly, subject peoples are often willing to undertake to lease naval and air bases on their territories. Even if they will not promise them to the Power whose rule they want to put an end to, for fear of seeming still to be dependent, they may be willing to lease them to the Americans or to some international body set up to defend the 'free world'. If they make these concessions, they are more likely to get economic help from the United States and its allies. If all the colonies and dependent states that survive were to become fully independent tomorrow, it is doubtful whether the western Powers would be any less able than they now are to provide for their defence against Russia. And for the weaker among the great western Powers to think that their retaining their colonies helps to maintain their strength as compared with America's is surely a mistake. America, industrially and militarily, is immensely more powerful than they are; they can strengthen themselves against America much more by their prestige among the nations than by trying to keep hold of reluctant colonies. Colonialism of the old-fashioned kind no longer, as I have already tried to explain, carries prestige with it. This is not because men are now more just and humane than they used to be; for there are other and worse forms of oppression which still increase the standing of those who practise them. Of course, oppression is everywhere condemned just as vice is; but then, as we know, some vices make men look formidable or dashing, while others, though they do less harm, make them contemptible. This is partly because fashions change and partly because the vices of the strong acquire some of the prestige of strength. 'Colonialism', even at its worst, is far from being the harshest form of oppression in the world today; it is merely the form most easily attacked.

4

The Arguments Against Continued European Rule Over Subject Peoples

THERE are many arguments used for and against European rule over other peoples, and this essay examines only some of them. In deciding what arguments to consider, I have not asked myself how often they are used or how passionately believed by those who use them. That they are often used will be immediately apparent to the reader; they will all be familiar to him. But my reason for discussing them is that they seem to raise issues which need to be raised if we are to understand what is involved in the recent and rapid westernization of the whole world. If we can make up our minds what we think of these arguments, we have gone a long way to acquiring a definite and reasoned attitude to some of the most difficult and important questions of our time. Economists have gone much more extensively and minutely than before into the special problems of under-developed countries, and there have been many detailed accounts of constitutional and administrative reforms in colonies and dependent or backward states. There have also been excellent studies of the relations between different races. The West has never before paid so much attention to what is happening in Asia and Africa. The broader political and moral issues have not been neglected; they have indeed been raised often and with great fervour. But they have seldom been treated at all systematically; they have been the province of the journalist and the politician, and have been discussed in relation to particular problems. My purpose in this essay is to discuss them more in the abstract, at considerably greater length, and more systematically than men busy with day-to-day affairs have the leisure to do. It is the broadest issues that I care about, and I have selected which arguments to discuss in order to get at these issues as quickly and clearly as possible.

In putting the arguments for and against continued European rule over Asian and African peoples, I have not imagined a model debate between conquerors and their subjects. The arguments for this rule are not arguments which appeal chiefly to Europeans and the arguments against it to the subject peoples. Indeed, we should not expect this; for, as I have often insisted, all these arguments, whoever uses them, rest on moral assumptions first made and elaborated by Europeans, either in Europe itself or overseas. We should expect rather that the arguments against this rule, as well as for it, should have been best put in the countries most familiar with the assumptions on which they rest. This is said without disrespect for the moral beliefs or logical powers of other peoples whose fate it has been to live in a world where the culture of the Europeans is predominant. Not only do all political controversies nowadays rest on assumptions of European origin, but even the systematic study of society and government depends on European methods and ideas. The African knows better than the European what it feels like to be an African; and no doubt behaves in his family and his village with greater tact and understanding than a foreigner could do. But to know how to behave in a particular community is not, as I have also insisted,[1] to understand how that community functions, or how it differs from other communities, or how it is affected by influences external to it, or what needs to be done to secure as smooth a transition as possible from old to new ways. This kind of understanding is not acquired, even by an intelligent man, merely by living in his community; it is acquired by systematic study. As the study of society has been pushed much further by the European peoples than by the others, a man must be educated in the European fashion to have this kind of understanding. To have a grasp of contemporary social and political problems he must have clear in his mind the moral assumptions on which controversies rest and must also be familiar with the terms used to describe political and social processes. Because these assumptions and the current vocabulary of politics and sociology are both European, these problems are better understood by people trained to think as educated Europeans do; and there are still many more such people in Europe and America than in other parts of the world.

This does not mean, necessarily, that the problems of Asia and Africa are better understood by Europeans than by the natives of the

---

1. Political and social problems are extraordinarily complicated, and it is therefore easy, when we are caught up in their intricacies, to lose sight of the obvious.

countries whose problems they are; for of the Europeans educated enough to understand them only a few are interested in Asia or Africa, whereas nearly all Asians or Africans similarly qualified have this interest. But it does mean that many of the arguments against foreign rule used in Asia and Africa are so confused and shoddy as not to be worth discussing in this essay, and that those worth discussing are as much used by Europeans as by the peoples for whose benefit they were invented. The purpose of this essay is emphatically not to examine all arguments which have a wide appeal and therefore presumably also a considerable influence; it is to examine the arguments which raise the really important issues. They are all intellectually respectable arguments, though some are much better grounded than others.

(1) Some critics of colonialism are scornful of the very idea of one people preparing another for self-government. They do not reject the European myth of progress; they do not deny that the peoples of Asia and Africa, or the enterprising and dominant groups among them, now have aspirations which cannot be achieved except by adopting western methods and institutions. Progress, for them as for almost everyone else, means westernization; and if not complete westernization, then at least the establishment of an industrial society which needs to be educated and governed in ways very different from those traditional in Asia and Africa. There must be great changes made in a short time, political and social as much as economic, and they must be changes in many ways similar to those that Europe has already undergone. The critics admit this much, but they will not agree that it is therefore for the European rulers of non-European peoples to decide how these changes are to be made.

A people, they say, must learn by their own efforts to govern themselves; while they are governed by strangers they are shut off from the experience which they need to learn how to govern themselves. Not everything that has to be learnt can be taught; and government, difficult though it is to learn, is among the things that cannot be taught. Good government, as the West understands it, depends on the ability to make just decisions taking into account the interests of a wide variety of groups, the ability of these groups to organize themselves so that they can decide what their interests are and what to ask of government, the ability to carry on many-sided and often protracted negotiations, and the ability to use what means are at your disposal to get your way without overstepping the bounds laid down by law and convention. It involves great resourcefulness and combativeness on the part of those who compete for power or for influence with the powerful, and at the same time considerable self-restraint and public spirit. These are not qualities taught by precept or acquired in the mere process of being governed by people who already have them. They are acquired by practice.

To say this is not to deny that certain kinds of externally imposed discipline are necessary if a people are to become fit to govern themselves by western methods. These methods, even when they are not democratic, require, if they are to be efficiently used, general literacy among the people and also habits of regular work. It will be necessary, perhaps, for a time, to force ignorant and reluctant parents to send their children to school or to use such punishments in factories and mines as are no longer tolerated in the West. When rapid social and economic changes come upon peoples not used to such changes, it is often no good relying on enlightened self-interest and persuasion to get them to adapt their habits to them. With nations as with children, force is sometimes a means of enlightenment. But these forms of discipline, though in themselves not compatible with democracy and yet necessary to create the social conditions which eventually make democracy possible, do not require alien government. They are to be found wherever there is rapid westernization, and there can be rapid westernization (as there was in Japan) without European rule.

All the peoples of Asia and Africa, dependent and independent, have been and still are involved in this tortuous and painful process called westernization. Nobody believes that it can be smooth and easy. Yet the western Powers no longer think it right for themselves to deprive independent peoples of their independence on the mere ground that, by western standards, they are mismanaging their own affairs. Why then should they refuse independence to still dependent peoples on the ground that, if they got what they asked for, they would mismanage their own affairs? What evidence is there that westernization is easier and less painful in backward countries ruled by western Powers than in backward countries independent of them?

Admittedly, the art of government is not learnt by mere trial and error; there is also the imitation of good examples. But a free people may be better at this kind of imitation than a people that are not free. Subjects may resent their masters' lessons, while an independent people are not humiliated by learning from others. They decide what they shall imitate, and can choose more than one model. They can also decide just how much to retain of their ancestral ways. They are willing and therefore quick and intelligent learners.

The Balkan peoples who freed themselves from the Turk took to learning to govern themselves in the western manner. They started doing so only a few generations ago, and they started virtually from nothing; for Ottoman rule was certainly no preparation for what the West calls decent government. By the time that Communism overwhelmed all these peoples except the Greeks, they were still far from well governed. But they had made great progress; they had learnt a great deal. True, they had also discovered some forms of brutality and deceit unknown to the Turks because they involve the misuse of western institutions. But that is part of the usual price of progress. Who will contend that they made less progress, socially and politically, than, say, the Indians or the Algerians who came under effective British and French rule either before or at about the same time as the Balkan peoples threw off the Ottoman yoke? That these Balkan peoples are European by race surely does not affect the matter, for they did not belong, socially and culturally, to the West at the time that they gained their independence of the Porte.

If this is not allowed, if it is insisted that their being European by race made the process of westernization easier for them, there are other examples we can take. Is Japan, which was ruled by the Americans for only a few years, less westernized and less fit for self-government than India, which was ruled by the British for as many generations? Or are the Turks less fit for it than the Pakistanis, whatever criterion of fitness we choose to take? The whole world is much more like Europe, politically, economically and culturally, than it was a hundred years ago; the whole world aspires much more than ever it did to what the Europeans were the first to call desirable. Everyone now admits this, though some (perhaps many) still regret it. But no one who admits it is committed to believing that the 'backward' peoples once or still subject to the Europeans are in a better way to making progress than the others.

This is a powerful but in some ways misleading and even irrelevant argument.

It is true that there are things which have to be learnt and cannot be taught, and that one of them is government. It is, however, only partly true of government; or, to speak more accurately, it is true of some aspects of government though not of all. However well taught a subject people may have been, they are always, when they gain independence, new to the main business of government, which is the making of law and policy. There is never a transition from dependence to complete independence by equal and small steps; there is always at least one great leap forward made. There are some powers that can be transferred gradually, but the most important of all is acquired very quickly or even all at once. This must be so from the very nature of modern government, even under the best possible conditions when the ruling Power and the subject people trust one another. I shall try to explain in a moment why this is so.

But first I must make the obvious point that government is an art and that all forms of art are largely self-taught; that competence comes largely from practice which is either imitation or experiment. If a ruling Power really means to prepare a subject people for self-government, it does not merely impart book-knowledge to them, it does not teach merely by precept. It puts more and more natives into responsible posts, where they learn by experiment and imitation as much as by taking notice of what they are told to do. The more responsible the post, the more the holder of it must learn for himself and the less he can rely on what others have taught him. And in any case, the function of the ruling Power, as it prepares a subject people for self-government, is not only to educate by precept and example; it is also to watch over the process of self-education, stepping in to prevent excessive damage and seeing to it that the learner does not take on too much at a time. This kind of education in government goes on in the ruling country as well as among the subject people; it is needed to carry on traditions of government as well as to create them. The fact that in the ruling country teachers and taught all belong to the same nation or race and in the subject country do not, does not change the essential character of this education, though it may add to its difficulties. There is a need for teaching by precept and deliberate example, and a need for setting limits to self-teaching, as well as for learning by practice and experiment.

The important distinction to make is not between what can be taught and what has to be learnt without teaching; it is between what can be learnt while the ruling Power is still in control and what cannot. It is one thing to train efficient civil servants, soldiers, policemen, and judges, and quite another to prepare a subject people to take over the business of making laws and policy. There can be a gradual permeation of the civil service, the military, and the judiciary by natives, until these services are almost entirely in native hands. But a gradual and smooth transference of power cannot be arranged in the same way in the sphere of law and policy making.

It is, of course, possible to have a legislature which is partly elected and partly appointed, and also to increase by stages the extent to which the executive is responsible to the legislature. In this way the people are put in the way of learning a good deal about how laws are made and policy takes shape. They—or rather their leaders—learn partly by being brought closer to government and partly by taking a subordinate part in it. They learn as spectators and as participants, though probably at this stage more in the first capacity than the second.

Where the legislature is in part elected and in part appointed, the elected part is apt to be either passive or in strenuous conflict with the government. If the government were truly responsible to the elected part, there would be little or nothing gained by also having appointed legislators; for they are appointed, in fact if not in theory, to ensure that the government is not responsible to the people's deputies. The conflict between the government and the elected part of the legislature is by no means like the competition between rival parties in a true parliamentary state, where the rivals take turns in forming governments; it is a conflict between men who are continually in power and men who are brought close to power but are in fact allowed little or no share of it. This conflict, if it does not last too long, is certainly instructive to the people's deputies; they are made close and keen observers of processes which they hope they will soon control. If, however, the conflict is prolonged, it only serves to exasperate the people's deputies who come to believe that authority which is rightfully theirs is being denied to them. They soon feel powerless to meet legal opposition and are tempted to resort to other methods. When the people's deputies become a cohesive majority and the government is at last truly responsible to them, there is a sudden getting of power by persons who have not had it before; and this power is the most important of all, which those who have it must learn to use properly by dint of using it.

Again, if the ruling Power reserves certain powers to itself or to a head of the state which it appoints, otherwise letting the government be responsible to an elected legislature, it creates a situation which cannot last long. For the people's deputies will try to use the powers granted to them to make the government completely responsible to themselves. In this they will either quickly succeed or will be prevented from succeeding by the timely use of the reserved powers. But the use of these powers will almost certainly offend the people's deputies and make them unco-operative, so that the government, if they are to govern effectively, will have perforce to govern irresponsibly. In these days when democracy is cried up everywhere, and the right of self-determination as well, an alien Power must not count on the patience of persons who, because they are popularly elected by their compatriots, believe that they have a better right to govern, or to control the government, than anyone else. Therefore, the passing from alien to native rulers of the greatest power of all, which is the power to make law and policy, is likely to be rapid; or if it is not, will quickly lead to frustration and perhaps even to violence. You cannot give power in small doses at regular intervals, if the giving of the first doses makes those who get them so greedy for the rest that they soon clamour for it and refuse to make proper use of what is already theirs unless everything is conceded to them. Nor is it merely a matter of the appetite for power being increased by the enjoyment of it. Men who have only some of the powers needed to govern their country responsibly feel that, as the full powers are not theirs, they do not really govern; and they are therefore tempted to use what powers they have as weapons to wrest from their alien rulers the powers still not granted to them. They think that by doing this they are putting first things first, even if by their actions they prevent for a time the efficient government of their country.

Thus we may say that in the making of law and policy, though not in the administrative and judicial spheres, power will pass so quickly from alien rulers to natives that the natives, when they get the fullness of it, will have little experience of how to use it; or else that, if the rulers insist that the passage must be slow and gradual, it will not be smooth and may lead, if not always to violence, then to deadlocks that defeat the rulers' purpose. For if their purpose is to ensure that the natives learn to use the supreme power responsibly as it gradually passes to them, they need their willing co-operation, which they are not likely to get. If their purpose is more sinister, if they wish by giving the natives a little power to tempt them to use it irresponsibly so as to have an excuse for taking it away again, they act dangerously. People who have tasted power, even to misuse it, are more bitter and more formidable opponents of alien rule than people who have never known it. It is difficult to share responsibility between foreigners and natives for the general government of a country. What is the gradual transference of supreme power except an attempt to share it and to vary the shares of it from time to time? And what is gained by the attempt unless those called up to share it work together to use it to good purpose?

Where there is a large European settlement this sharing and gradual transference of power is likely to be even more difficult. It could in principle be easier, instead of more difficult, if European settlers and natives worked together, forming mixed political parties. The leaders of these parties would probably, to begin with, be mostly Europeans who would presumably be more ready than natives to work loyally with a still largely irresponsible executive. The tradition of working together once created, it might pass from the first European party leaders to their native successors, making possible a gradual and smooth transference of power. But this consummation, though devoutly to be wished, is most unlikely. Much more probably, parties would be formed on racial lines, and the Europeans would do their utmost to make themselves masters of the legislature. While they believed that the natives were still weak politically, they might venture to challenge the authority of the executive in their own interest; but as soon as they began to be afraid of the natives, they would make their peace with the executive, preferring to be ruled by outsiders of their own race rather than share power with men of other races. If, then, control of the legislature passed from the settlers to the natives, it would probably do so suddenly and in circumstances dangerous to the settlers, making difficult the setting up of a stable parliamentary system or a liberal democracy of some other kind.

We cannot today expect subject peoples to put up for long with the sort of division of powers which the English colonists in America tolerated for several generations, though they always felt the inconveniences of it. The executive power belonged to the governor who was responsible to London for the use he made of it, and who yet could not use it effectively unless he enjoyed the confidence and received grants of money from the colonial legislature. This system was not exactly welcome to the colonists, but they put up with it because it was familiar to them and they had not yet adopted principles which made it seem wrong. Moreover, they were still in those days Englishmen, and they knew that they enjoyed greater liberties than any other colonists and than most of their compatriots in the mother-country.

Though the supreme law- and policy-making power will probably pass quickly from foreign rulers to natives—and in modern conditions probably ought to do so—it does not follow that the transferring of other forms of power must also be rapid. In the administrative and judicial services power can and ought to pass gradually from foreigners to natives. The first natives to enter these services come into them at the bottom; they are subordinates who are in no position to challenge the authority of their superiors. Whatever posts are allotted to them they get the whole authority normally attached to those posts, and can therefore presumably carry out their duties properly. They are in a quite different position from the elected members of a legislature who, in one way or another, are deprived of some of the powers which usually in an independent democratic state belong to people in their position. As they rise in the hierarchy they acquire all the authority they expect to acquire, and they usually (unless they are treated unfairly because they are natives) accept the rules which make ascent gradual.

The foreign ruling Power can also create local governments and give the natives control of them. The authority of such governments is strictly limited, in the West no less than elsewhere. They are known to be subordinate and are expected to act as if they were so; this is generally understood and is quite in the spirit of modern government. Though the holders of local authority may try to make as much of it as they can, they also expect to be controlled from above and even to have their decisions set aside if their superiors judge that they have mis-used their authority. It is much easier to extend gradually an authority which is, both in practice and theory, everywhere limited and subordinate than an authority which is in theory supposed to be supreme. Local governments, as much in independent as in dependent countries, are usually the creatures of the central government; their powers differ from country to country and are in any case often added to and subtracted from. They are, as it were, in perpetual tutelage.[1]

---

1. This was not true in feudal times, but it is now. In speaking of local governments I am not, of course, speaking of the governments of provinces or states in a federal union whose authority is co-ordinate with that of the federal government.

Thus a foreign ruling Power, by allowing natives gradually into the public services, administrative, judicial, and military, and also by creating native local governments and gradually enlarging their authority, can do a great deal to prepare a dependent people for complete self-government, even though the transference of the supreme law- and policy-making power, when the time for it comes, can hardly be smooth unless it is rapid, thus leaving it to the natives to learn for themselves the hardest of all political lessons: how to govern an independent state, and in particular an independent democracy.

Opposition to government, provided it is the right kind, can also be a valuable form of education for self-government and democracy. It is important, even where natives still take no direct part in government, except as state officials and judges or on local bodies, to allow them to form, not only professional, trade, and cultural organizations, but also associations whose declared purpose is to achieve autonomy or independence. Where there are firmly established rights of association, opponents of foreign rule can work openly and legally against it. Though still excluded from power, they put pressure on those who hold it; they watch the activities of government from day to day. They become a force to be reckoned with and often establish contacts of various kinds with holders of office. In this way they learn the art of negotiation. They are, admittedly, not so much rivals as enemies of the government; but they are enemies who carry on the fight as much as possible openly and legally. Even if they also act illegally, which they sometimes do, they usually keep within limits; they abhor violence and cruelty. They have their own methods which the authorities come to know and even to sympathize with, and therefore deal mildly with them. Their work may be partly legal and partly illegal, but their temper is moderate even though their actions are sometimes against the law.

A foreign government, though it may be right in believing that the people subject to it are not yet fit to rule themselves and though it may be strong enough to put down all opponents, ought not in its own interest to put them down; it ought to allow its subjects to create opposition to itself. If it really cares about helping to prepare its subjects for eventual self-government, it ought to allow them to gain what experience they can of organized work for a political purpose, and this purpose, at that stage of their development, must be to put an end to alien rule. Even if the rulers do not care about their subjects' political education for its own sake, they ought to recognize that, conditions in the world being what they now are, they will have to grant independence sooner or later. It is surely their interest, when the time for independence comes, to leave behind them as stable a political system as possible, and not a political chaos leading to a brutal tyranny. If retreat is unavoidable, as it now seems to be, it is surely their interest to retreat before disciplined political bodies which accept what the West understands by decent standards of political conduct rather than before a mere rabble or organizations whose power depends on terror.

Admittedly, violence does not always unfit those who use it for constitutional or democratic government. When rebels (as, for example, the American colonists) have long been used to limited self-government, or when they have had considerable experience of organized opposition to government, and opposition which is mostly open and legal (though perhaps also to some extent illegal), they will be apt to be moderate even in the use of violence; they will hesitate to use methods which make it difficult, after victory is won, to establish mild and constitutional government. But if the rebels have no political experience except what they have gained in organizations working in secret and using any methods, no matter how brutal and treacherous, which they think may bring victory, they become unfit for what the West calls decent government: which, though it is not necessarily democracy or even parliamentary government, does at least entail respect for personal rights and authority exercised according to rules openly proclaimed and effectively enforced.

The Indian Congress Party under the British 'raj', though it took only a limited part in provincial government for a short period and quite often acted illegally, did provide its members with valuable training for government and not only for putting an end to alien rule. It was a vast organization much of whose work was open and legal; it produced leaders of great skill and high character. In the process of helping to put an end to British rule it acquired some of the political virtues of the British; it had to deal with what was, on the whole, a humane and law-respecting foreign government, and was itself humane and usually respectful of the law, though it sometimes disregarded it. Its political ethics were partly British and partly derived from principles developed by Gandhi which, though they owed something to Christian and European thought, were emphatically not

British. Because the party acted mostly in the open, it was its interest to be seen to be loyal to its own principles. Though occasionally it claimed the right to break the laws imposed by the conqueror, it profited greatly from, and probably greatly admired, some of the political virtues of the British: their respect for law and their reluctance to take harsh measures against political enemies.

In the process of opposing the British, the Congress Party acquired some of the experience needed by the rulers of a modern constitutional state. If the Indian nationalists had used the methods of, say, the Mau Mau organization, they would not have acquired that experience. We can say this even if we hold that the Kikuyu are no more to blame for the atrocious methods they used than the white settlers and the men who, in Nairobi and London, govern Kenya. No matter where the blame lies, such methods, if they continue long, destroy the capacity for decent self-government in the people who resort to them. Whatever the excuses to be made for these people, the use of such methods must be put down and put down quickly, not only to protect their victims, but for the sake of the people for whose supposed benefit they are used; because they soon make a social chaos intolerable to everyone and not only to foreigners. These methods, even if they drove the foreigners out, would not bring to the natives a social and political order which would satisfy them, but would merely give power to leaders whom the people would have more cause to fear than to love. No doubt, they would take vengeance on the white man, and this vengeance might give them deep pleasure, though not for long.

That some peoples, never ruled by a western Power, have made as quick 'progress' as others who have known that rule for generations is not really much to the point. We are not discussing whether a western Power would now be justified in imposing its rule on an independent people in order to bring 'progress' to them, for that is no longer a live issue. It is now admitted almost everywhere that it would be wrong for it to do so. Moreover, it would also be dangerous, the state of the world being what it now is. We are asking only what should be done by foreign rulers and subject peoples in countries already dependent, if those peoples are to become fit for self-government; and we have agreed to measure that fitness by the standards discussed in our second chapter. Even if it were true that some 'backward' peoples had made quick 'progress' without benefit of western rule, it would not follow that the best way of encouraging that progress among backward peoples still under western rule would be to give them immediate independence. As I have already argued, we must take care not to confuse the issues, moral and political, involved in two quite different questions: of which the first is, Shall we take control of these people's affairs? and the second, What can we do for them now, we who have already for a long time been in control of their affairs? Among the 'backward' peoples exposed to rapid westernization some have had to cope with their own difficulties while others have been under western rule. It may well be that in the first category there are peoples who have made progress as smoothly as any in the second category. If we allow that it is so, what conclusion should we now draw? That all 'backward' peoples, no matter what their difficulties, should be left incontinently to their own devices? But peoples long subject to foreign rule are, by reason of that subjection, in a different position from peoples who have long been independent. Neither their difficulties nor their advantages are the same.[1] And it may be that the peoples not subject to western rule who have made the greatest progress by western standards have had advantages which the subject peoples did not have even before they fell into subjection to one or other of the western Powers.

Let me take for examples the Balkan peoples and the Japanese. The Balkan peoples, at the time that they threw off the Turkish yoke, had not governed themselves for many centuries. They were almost wholly without political experience except in the management of village affairs and in the Orthodox Church whose autonomy the Porte had long (though not always scrupulously) respected. Yet they had two great advantages: a habit of self-reliance, and a passionate conviction that as Europeans they should partake fully of the blessings of European civilization. Ottoman rule had long been brutal and capricious, but it had also been corrupt and inefficient. The Turk mostly kept away from the villages where he was not safe; even if he held an estate in a Christian province, he did not live on it but in the town, where his rents were brought to him. The Christian peasant saw little of his Muslim superiors, whether they were landlords,

---

1. By 'advantage' I mean here whatever makes 'progress' easier and smoother and by 'difficulty' whatever impedes it or makes it painful. Even if we dislike progress intensely and wish there were societies left in the world that did not aspire to make progress, we can still follow the argument and enquire whether, given the assumptions it rests on, it is convincing.

soldiers or officials. Provided the Turk got his rents and taxes and was not molested, he left the Christian peasant to fend for himself and to live by his ancestral faith and customs. There was a Muslim society lying on top of a Christian society and partly submerging it, depriving it of the light and air it needed for growth, but grafting almost nothing of itself on to it. The Balkan Christians were not oriental, unless we suppose that crudeness and corruption and ignorance were enough to make them so, which is absurd. They were European barbarians eager to become civilized, and they all belonged to the same class, for they were all peasants. Their habits of self-reliance and their equality among themselves made the democratic and libertarian ideals of the West strongly attractive to them. Their peasant culture, rich and varied though it was in its own kind, did not stand in the way of their assimilating western civilization. They were not much torn by conflicting loyalties; they were willing enough to give up ancestral ways to prove themselves good Europeans, as children when they grow up put away what they think is childish. They made remarkable 'progress' in a short time. I do not say that they were always the more attractive for the progress they made or that they did not still have far to go when they fell victims to Communism. But that they made great progress though not subject to western rule cannot be denied.

The Japanese, when they decided to modernize (or in other words to westernize) their country, were already a highly civilized people, and certainly much more civilized than the Balkan Christians at the time of their liberation from the Turk. But the Japanese have this in common with the Balkan peoples: that western institutions and ideas were not forced on them by foreign rulers or by intruders they were too weak to expel. They themselves took the initiative. They took it, not because they aspired to be good Europeans, but because they had a ruling class intelligent enough to understand what was happening in the world outside Japan and strong enough to take timely measures to make their country formidable. They did not make Japan truly democratic or liberal but they did make her an efficient modern state. They made her as fit by western standards for self-government as, say, Prussia had been and a good deal fitter than Russia under the Tsars.

The Japanese were not more civilized than the Indians or intellectually better fitted to take stock of the position of their country in the world; and they were not by culture closer to the Europeans. If anything they were further away. But they had what the Indians did not have at the time that the British conquered them; they had a ruling class strong enough to hold the country firmly together while introducing the most drastic reforms. This was not a cultural but a political advantage. The Europeans went to Asia not to conquer and to rule but to trade, and they became conquerors and rulers only where their trade was too profitable to be abandoned and native rulers were not strong enough to give them the security they needed. Once they became rulers they began, of course, to enrich themselves by other means than trade; but their first motive was to trade profitably and securely. If the Indians had been united and strong enough to do for their country what the Japanese did for theirs, they would never have been conquered. Not because the Europeans would not have been strong enough, militarily, to conquer them, but because they would not have been tempted to the courses which eventually led to conquest. The Japanese, too, before they set about reforming their country, were industrially and militarily weak; they could never have resisted a large-scale European invasion. It was not their external but their internal strength that saved them; they were strong enough to change their institutions and make themselves fit to enter as equals into a community of Powers whose relations, commercial and political, were governed by rules first elaborated in Europe. But the Indians were only welded into a nation strong enough to undertake drastic social and political reforms as a result of being conquered by the British.

It would be rash to say that the Indians are now either more or less fit for self-government than the Japanese. And yet it may be that, in spite of their greater poverty and illiteracy, they have a better chance of establishing an enduring liberal democracy. If they have, it is surely due to their having been ruled for several generations by the European people who have done most to develop democratic and liberal principles and institutions. The educated classes in India are probably the most deeply westernized people in Asia.

(2) It is often said that the Powers owning colonies in Asia and Africa are not really concerned to prepare the peoples subject to them for self-government or democracy. It is admitted that, if they were willing, they could do a great deal to prepare them; but that (it is said) is a matter hardly worth discussing, since in fact they are not willing. True, their very presence among the subject peoples, the kind of trade and industry they introduce among them and the methods they use to

control them, tend to make these peoples more and more western in their habits and ideas, and to that extent closer to being fit to govern themselves decently by western standards. But this is merely an effect of the westernization which cannot be avoided if the foreign ruler is to get as much as he can out of his subjects; it is not the real object of his policy. He is essentially an exploiter, though his methods beget the progress which in the end makes his victims strong enough to drive him out. As soon therefore as they are strong enough, they ought to drive him out. It may be prudent for them to be patient while they are weak, but they are fools if they act in the belief that their foreign masters care seriously for their good, except to the extent that any intelligent master cares for his servant's good when he sees that he has more to gain than to lose by doing so. He cares for it not for the servant's sake but his own, and thwarts his servant's aspirations whenever they conflict with his own good.

Foreign rulers may now be wise enough to understand that the peoples subject to them are caught up in social processes which will in the end make them ungovernable by foreigners; they may admit that they will have eventually to grant independence to them. But their purpose is always to hold on to their colonies as long as they get more out of them than it costs them to maintain their hold on them. They make concessions only when they must, and always with reluctance. They are seldom concerned about what may happen to their subjects after they get independence, and are usually quite willing to sacrifice their future good for the sake of some present benefit to themselves. The political theorist, sitting within the four walls of his room, may amuse himself by showing that the enduring interests of the ruling Power are in harmony with the enduring interests of the subject people. He may even be right. But his being so helps nobody, for nobody takes notice of him. Nations and groups seldom see more than a little way ahead. The interests of foreign rulers and their subjects, as they themselves see them at any time, are mostly opposed to one another; and that is what really matters.

Even granted that the men who actually rule a colony are long-sighted and have good intentions, what chance is there of their doing what their wisdom inclines them to do? They are exposed to all kinds of pressure which prevent or delay their giving effect to their good intentions. There are people in the 'home country' who have invested money in the colony, and will raise a clamour if anything is done which seems to endanger their investments; there are military men and other patriots who insist that the colony is strategically important and must not be abandoned; there are millions of voters who still take pride in the empire and do not like to see any part of it lost. These people may be short-sighted or plain foolish; or they may be concerned only with their own interests and blind to other things. In politics it is the short views and the narrow views that count, and the successful politician is usually the man who can satisfy or neutralize as many groups as possible for the time being. It is useless complaining about the lack of foresight of public men, especially in modern democracies. They are not less intelligent than other people, but it takes all the ability they have to accommodate temporarily the many interests they cannot afford to neglect. And the men who actually rule the colonies are subordinate to the men whose prime concern is to appease special interests at home.

This argument that foreign rulers cannot be trusted to prepare subject peoples for self-government clearly has a great deal of truth in it. And yet it is not wholly true. Certainly, we ought not to expect much altruism in public life; for public men are, in a sense, the prisoners of the groups and classes for whom they speak, and on whose approval their power depends; and groups—as Rousseau noticed—are usually more selfish and more obstinate than individuals. Indeed, the unselfishness of individuals can sometimes strengthen 'corporate selfishness' if they devote themselves too exclusively to the group they serve. The structure of authority and the conditions of keeping it are such that the actual rulers of a subject people, wise and unselfish though they may be as individuals, must in practice prefer the interests of the home country to those of the colony; for they are, after all, the servants of the home country and not of the colony, and therefore serve interests foreign to the people they rule.

Without rejecting this doctrine of corporate selfishness, we can question some of the conclusions drawn from it. The ruling country has not a single corporate interest or bundle of mutually compatible interests in the colony. Only a few people in the ruling country have any real say in the government of the colony and only a few groups have interests there; the 'ruling people' as a whole are usually not much concerned to keep the colony in subjection except to the extent that they take pride in their country's power over foreigners—which they nowadays do much less than they used to. The burden of empire rests on few shoulders and its direct and visible benefits do not go to the great majority—though no doubt more people share the benefits than the burdens. Burdens and visible benefits belong mostly to privileged groups in the ruling country.

But these groups have domestic enemies whose principles usually condemn 'imperialism' as much as aristocracy or the rule of the wealthy. Socialism and hostility to empire usually go together, especially in the early stages. Later on, after the radicals have won their great victories and the imperial country has become democratic and equalitarian, the leaders of the socialist parties may come to change their minds. When they take office, they take over the responsibilities of the men who ruled before them; they begin to think of themselves less as spokesmen for the working classes and more as spokesmen for their country. They see virtues and advantages in what used to be suspect to them, and faults in what they admired and expressed sympathy for. They are, as the saying goes, 'sobered by office'; they take greater care what they say and sometimes draw unexpected conclusions from the principles they proclaimed before they got office. Still, they do not repudiate those principles and are in many ways bound by them; they see virtues in the empire which they used not to see, but their declared and still sincere purpose is to prepare the subject peoples for self-government. They have, as public men, nothing to gain by repudiating that purpose; especially as time, which has brought power to them, has also changed conditions in the world and the colonies, so that it is now no longer possible to rule subject peoples as they once were ruled. Public opinion in the West, and not least among the nations owning colonies, has been one of the strongest forces making for the grant of independence to subject peoples; though of course this public opinion has been reinforced by the desire to be less vulnerable to Communist propaganda.

The more cohesive a nation and the more its public men in their political conflicts abide by constitutional rules, the more likely it is that the victories of the radicals will moderate the attitude of the conservatives. They may fight hard to prevent the victories, but once they have happened, they accept their consequences both at home and in the colonies. That is partly why the British, who have had a much larger empire to lose than the French, have found it so much easier to reconcile themselves to the loss of it.

The Powers that own colonies, knowing that they must lose them, have a clear interest in parting with them amicably, which they cannot do, conditions being what they now are, unless they make up their minds to part with them in the fairly near future. If the British have made their minds up to this more easily than the French, it is not because they are more understanding and generous towards other peoples or more long-sighted; it is because political parties in Britain have learnt to get on better with one another, and can therefore consider more calmly what they must do to reduce their national commitments to suit their diminished position in the world.[1]

Nevertheless, it is true that even the most long-headed and benevolent foreign Power needs to be badgered by its subjects if it is to be induced to grant independence to them. It will never treat them as a good parent treats his child, urging it to greater and greater self-reliance no matter how apathetic it may be. It is not enough to wait for independence or to ask for it politely; and there is no set time for a subject people to come of age. If independence is to be got, there must be a hard fight made for it, unless the ruling Power withdraws from sheer weakness as the Romans did from Britain. But a country thus abandoned is usually not fit for independence and soon falls an easy prey to other conquerors. By fighting for independence a people prepare themselves morally for it. The question is, how shall they fight? Now that the Powers having colonies are in retreat, the peoples subject to them should seriously consider whether the methods they use to hasten that retreat will prevent their getting the sort of country they want after independence is achieved. If they care for constitutional and humane government, and still more if they care for freedom and democracy, it should matter enormously to them what methods they use.

In the countries that own colonies most people now admit that all colonies will soon be self-governing, and will be either completely independent or else associated with the mother-country in some form of federal union. Even the conservatives in France admit this, except for Algeria, where there are close on a million European settlers. They do not deny that the Algerian Muslims must soon have the same political rights as the settlers, and are only puzzled how they can be given them without breaking the close ties between Algeria and France

---

1. This is also why British governments have been stronger and better able to control the men ruling dependent territories in their name.

which they think it would be a betrayal of the settlers to allow to be broken. Everywhere it is conceded that colonies and dependencies must soon either get complete independence or else be associated with the countries now ruling them on terms which they have freely accepted. The great difficulty is to decide just how they are to get independence or on just what terms they are to be associated with their former rulers. Unfortunately, even where everyone, or nearly everyone, agrees in principle, whenever specific proposals are made, there are always some vociferous groups who feel that their interests are threatened. It is mostly because of these groups, who often have great influence, that the ruling Power is sometimes reluctant to promise complete independence, preferring to grant a wide autonomy within some form of federal union. This autonomy may be as much in the interest of a subject people as complete independence would be, or even more so; and yet it may be rejected because any kind of association, on however equal terms, with their former rulers seems a mark of inferiority to people used to being treated as inferiors. This fear, on the one side, and on the other, the pressure of special interests in the ruling country (interests often much more conciliatory in the principles they profess than in their reactions to concrete proposals), add greatly to the danger that a colony will be lost in anger and blood.

Twenty years ago people were still divided about whether or not colonies ought to get independence or autonomy in the foreseeable future. Nowadays, they mostly agree that they will get it, whether they ought to or not. It is astonishing what difficulties still remain even when there is general agreement about what is imminent. Both 'hosts' and 'guests' know that they must part, and yet the parting is painful, because they do not know how to do what they know they must do.

Those who care for freedom and democracy, both in the ruling country and in the colony, have a clear interest in working together against the groups who, though they no longer deny the inevitable, still recoil from it, and also against the extremer nationalists in the colony. But the greater burden must rest on the friends of democracy in the ruling country. They belong to a country long independent and respected, and ought therefore to be less intimidated by nationalism in others than even the most liberal persons in a colony struggling for independence. Psychologically and politically, it is easier for them than for those who think like them in the colony to take the initiative.

They are less likely to be denounced as traitors in their own country or to suffer if they are so denounced; they can defend themselves more easily against their accusers and perhaps even turn the tables on them. It is above all for them to press for a settlement with the subject people, whether the settlement provides for new and looser ties or for complete separation. It matters less perhaps what the settlement is than that it should be reached by parties who can still trust and respect one another after it is made. Better a friendly parting, even though premature, than a parting in blood; better independence for a people not yet fit for self-government than trying to keep them in subjection by a *prolonged* and massive use of force.

Not that the use of force by foreign rulers against nationalists is always wrong. If the nationalists are more feared than trusted by the people, if they use atrocious methods, then they ought to be put down quickly. But the blows of authority at rebellion ought to be sharp and quick. There are some victories not worth winning unless they are won quickly and with apparent ease. The war is hardly worth waging, unless the foreign rulers can turn the people against the terrorists. If the people doubt their victory or good intentions, they become hopeless and apathetic and allow the terrorists to use and bully them. The longer the struggle lasts, the more difficult for the foreign rulers to find any group or party enjoying the people's confidence willing to make a settlement with them. If they cannot put the rebels down quickly, they must at least quickly confine them within narrow limits away from the main centres of population; they cannot afford a struggle which is both long and widespread, for it will destroy their moral authority. It is then not much use inflicting many more casualties on the rebels than they inflict on you, for in those conditions rebellion may actually flourish on casualties. The first duty of any government, foreign or native, is to maintain domestic peace or restore it when it is troubled; and if it cannot do that quickly, it will not for long impress its subjects with the size of the armies it can put in the field and the number of rebels it can kill. And the rebels, brutal, nasty, and hated though they may be, will none the less acquire in the end the prestige which always comes to those who successfully defy established authority year after year.

The best policy for subject peoples in their dealings with western governments is neither to trust them too much nor to despair of them altogether. If they care for freedom and democracy, they should admit that these governments, partly inadvertently and partly with intention, have done much to prepare them for democratic and liberal government, and may yet do more. If they can create large and well-disciplined bodies able to put pressure on their rulers without resorting to violence, they will be the better off for it in the end. They will not appear the less formidable for their discipline and moderation. On the contrary, it will seem safer to make concessions to them, if not more dangerous to refuse them. They may take longer to get independence, but they will get it under circumstances making it easier to establish constitutional government and eventually a liberal democracy.

They should not, of course, rule out the use of force. If they cannot make further progress towards independence (or towards any other settlement short of independence which seems desirable to them) except by using force, then they ought to use it. Force resorted to as an *ultima ratio* by disciplined bodies which have tried in vain to reach their ends by other methods and have considerable experience of legal opposition is much less likely than sheer terrorism to lead to authoritarian government after independence is achieved. No doubt, however it is achieved, the first governments are likely to be so imperfectly liberal and democratic that some people will refuse to call them so. Much of the experience needed to make liberal democracy a success is only to be had after independence. But at least there will be a good chance that the people can get that experience; as there is, for instance, today in India.

But the largest responsibility for the character of the struggle which leads to independence (or to some other settlement desired by the subject people) must lie with the ruling Power, with the men at home or in the colony directly concerned in its government and also with the political leaders generally. If the ruling Power allows legal opposition and allows it to grow stronger with the passing of time, if it makes provision for beating an orderly retreat, then it makes it much more likely that the subject people when they get independence will be fit for decent self-government and will be well on the way to becoming a liberal democracy. No people can be fit for self-government or democracy unless they are eager to have them, and if they are eager, they will struggle hard to get them even against the best-intentioned and most humane foreign rulers. No people can be spoon-fed to liberty; they must fight for it, though not necessarily with arms. And yet they can also be trained for it. These two things, the fighting and the training, are not incompatible; they go together. But not all kinds of fighting are compatible with good training. Some provide it or allow it, while others prevent it.

The defeat of France in Europe and of Britain in the Far East during the last war and the quick emergence of the United States and the Soviet Union as by far the greatest Powers have made the difficulties of countries having colonies much greater than they were. The chances are that nowadays they will have to abandon their colonies before they are fit for self-government; or rather, before they have reached that stage in their social and political evolution when they can make further progress best if they are left to themselves. For, as we have seen, the later stages of education for self-government and democracy are stages of self-education; the 'leading-strings' are off, though the nation is not yet by western standards politically mature but must become so by learning from its own experience. Owing to the second World War independence must now in most cases come prematurely.

This has led some people to say that, if there had been no second World War, colonies would have got their independence by easier stages and under conditions more propitious to freedom and democracy. But this is by no means certain. The two World Wars, and especially the second, have greatly changed the attitude of all peoples to the subjection of some peoples by others. This change and the diminished importance in the world of the imperial Powers have certainly enabled the colonies to move towards independence at an astonishing, perhaps even dangerous, speed. But if the change had not happened and the imperial Powers had still bulked as large in the world as they used to do before 1914, the movement towards independence might have been dangerously slow. The dangers that come of too quick movement are very much present to us now; so that we give no thought to what the dangers might have been if the movement had been too slow, or ask ourselves whether, if it had not been accelerated by the two wars, it would have been fast enough. This hypothetical question cannot now be answered. It is, however, worth putting, for it reminds us that there are dangers and dangers, and that those that face us now are not necessarily the worst. Powerful nations, liberal though they may be in their domestic policies, are always reluctant to loosen their hold on subject peoples, even when they admit that they must and ought eventually to do so. It is true, after all, that they are not to be trusted altogether but must also be hustled. The peoples subject to them were too weak before 1914 to hustle them much. The balance was then tilted too far against those peoples and is now perhaps tilted too far in their favour. But not, I suspect, as much as many apologists of empire think; for the difficulties of the imperial Powers have been due not only to their diminished position and the world's changed attitude to imperialism; they have also been due to their undecidedness and lack of imagination. In some ways they have been remarkably generous; but they have not been consistent in their attitudes, and this has served to increase mistrust of them.

On the whole, since the last war, the intentions of the imperial Powers have been better than their actions. They have allowed themselves to be too easily offended by the attacks made on them, forgetting that the nationalists who make it their business to goad and hustle them are often more extreme in their words than in their acts. The Powers make some concessions and then find that the people who profit from them do not take them in the proper spirit but use them to try to extort further concessions; they are offended by this ingratitude and incontinently decide to take a stiffer attitude. These shifts of policy, since they have no clear connection with changes in the objective situation, are taken for proofs of hypocrisy: the concessions were evidently made in bad faith with the intention of withdrawing or neutralizing them at the first opportunity. The 'imperialists' give with one hand because they must, but with the other they seek always to take back what they have given. They are mistrusted for their duplicity and despised for their weakness, not only by the subject peoples but by other nations as well. If they had been more consistent and more predictable, they might have made fewer concessions and yet earned a better reputation for justice and for sympathy with the aspirations of 'backward' peoples. It is foolish to be firm from injured pride. While the mood is on you, you refuse to give way, though it may be reasonable that you should, and then later, when the mood passes, you see how much your pride has cost you and you suddenly give way, feeling foolish and looking it. Nobody deserves to be trusted merely for his good intentions if he has not sense and patience enough to make his intentions clear, which he can do only if he acts consistently.

If the peoples of Asia and Africa are at all as the Balkan peoples once were in their attitude to the western Powers, they probably expect better and wiser conduct from them than they are accustomed to find among themselves. I speak, of course, of political and not private conduct. They expect it, though usually without admitting that they do. Therefore, when they find it is not so, they are both indignant and contemptuous. They do not exactly say to themselves: How intolerable it is that these people should be no better than we are! They say rather: This is what they are always accusing us of doing, and now look, this is precisely what they are doing themselves! When they see the western Powers behaving politically as they often do themselves, they accuse them of hypocrisy; for the claim of the West to superiority includes, in their eyes, the claim that the West does not behave like this. Selfishness they expect from all nations and arrogance from the strong. But they expect the strong to be wise and con- sistent and reliable; they expect them not to be capricious, they expect them to know what they are doing. They even expect them not to be too much put out by the passions, the treacheries, and the insults of their weaker neighbours. The strong, after all, can afford to live better than the weak, morally as well as materially. When the world finds in them the faults of the weak, it quickly ceases to trust and respect them.

(3) Some people, though they care for freedom and democracy, like to be practical and hard-headed and are made angry by what they think is untimely advocacy of them. Let us, they say, put first things first; for before people can put a value on democracy, they must first be adequately fed, clothed, and housed. They must have some measure of security and good living. Therefore, first get rid of poverty and illiteracy, and then set about establishing liberty of conscience and democracy. The poor and the ignorant, if they are to be raised out of their squalor, must be bullied. More ruthless methods than the colonial Powers now dare use, or can expect to use successfully, must be used if the peoples of Asia and Africa are to be lifted out of their present condition to a level of material well-being and social discipline at which it makes sense to talk to them of freedom of thought, of the right to choose one's own career, of the right to take part in deciding who shall govern. These drastic methods can, in practice, be used successfully only by a dedicated native minority; for they alone can acquire over their fellow countrymen the moral authority which makes it possible to achieve by these methods the ends which justify their use. This minority need not be Communist; but whether it is Communist or

K

not, it will in fact be hotly nationalist and intolerant of opposition. We must not be soft-headed in our faith in democracy; we must admit the obvious, that where the material and social conditions of democracy do not exist, they cannot be created by gentle methods. But the western Powers are morally committed to using such methods, and are therefore at a great disadvantage. They do not, of course, always use gentle methods; they are not seldom angered or frightened into brutality. But when they do use harsh methods there is a falling off from their own principles; they are condemned by the world and by many people at home. They cannot be consistently harsh for years on end; or if they can be, it is to put down rebellion rather than to lift whole peoples quickly out of squalor and ignorance. Their instinct is to let sleeping dogs lie; they are foreigners who came in the first place to make profits, and if they now have more generous ambitions, they are still reluctant to do anything that might stir the people up against them. They are keepers of the peace and not disturbers of it; their harshness is punitive rather than corrective; they are not close enough to their subjects to feel passionately about them. As strangers and masters, whether harsh or benevolent, they are remote; they are not possessive and fanatical lovers who can mould the object of their love to suit their will. What the Chinese Communist Party is doing in China no foreign rulers could do or would even want to do. And yet it must be done if the Chinese are ever to live well enough materially to care for freedom or democracy; if ever they are to get the social discipline and education which they must have if they are to learn how to work the institutions which make freedom and responsible govern- ment possible in the large and highly intricate modern industrial society.

We can reject this argument without insisting that the western Powers have always put first things first, and without denying that freedom and democracy are not to be achieved in large industrial societies except by getting rid of illiteracy and the extremer forms of poverty. Only in small self-sufficing communities can the institutions which preserve freedom and make government responsible to the governed be so simple that even the unlettered can work them. But it does not follow from this that a people, in order to get freedom and democracy, must first devote all their energies to getting rid of illiteracy and poverty, using whatever political methods enable them to do this the most quickly. The recipe, *first* raise productivity and material well-being and abolish illiteracy, doing whatever needs to be done to these ends, and *afterwards* set about establishing freedom and democracy, though specious, is bad.

The peoples who now have freedom and democracy did not always have them; not freedom in the forms which it now takes in the West. They did not always have liberty of conscience, the right to choose their careers, the right to elect their governments and to criticize them. When they learnt to value these rights and to work the institutions which make them effective, they were already among the most prosperous and literate peoples in the world. The English, the Dutch, the French, the Americans—the peoples with the longest record of devotion to freedom or democracy or both together—have long been and are still among the richest and the most widely educated peoples. But they are also peoples who never used drastic methods to make themselves prosperous and literate, who never felt the need to catch up in a hurry with peoples much more 'advanced' than themselves. They did not owe their prosperity to the long-sighted and severe action of authoritarian governments; they owed it to the enterprise of their upper and middle classes. These classes, when they first arose, did not enjoy as much freedom as they were to know later, but they were already freer than other classes; and as they grew more prosperous and cultivated, their idea of freedom was refined. In their endeavours to realize that idea, they helped to create the institutions of the modern liberal state. Liberal democracy, as the West now understands it, is largely the enjoyment by all of some of the freedoms [1] which were once the privilege of the prosperous and the educated. Though the same causes that strengthened these privileged classes also made possible the emergence of the strong modern state, these privileges were not so much created by the state as wrested from it. That the state needed to be strong for many of these privileges to be securely enjoyed does not affect the point I am making. Much of what we today understand by freedom was impossible in the Middle Ages because the state was weak, and yet the state can clearly become strong without creating this freedom. The western state did not first grow strong and then create this freedom; the strengthening of the state and the enlargement of freedom were processes that went on together. This was true, at least, of

---

1. Of *some* of the freedoms but not of all. Clearly, not all the privileges of a minority can be enjoyed by all the people, for some of them (especially some property rights) can only in practice be enjoyed by a minority if they are denied to the rest of the people.

the English-speaking countries, and even, though less so, of France. For the revolutionary movement in France, though it sometimes drove the country into the arms of a dictator, did serve, on the whole, both to increase the liberties of Frenchmen and to strengthen the state. Let us not confuse longevity with strength; the old monarchy in France, as a tax-gathering institution, was more inefficient than any French republic, and when it tried hesitantly to reform the country and itself, it quickly collapsed.

I am not suggesting that other people can become wealthy and literate and free in the same way as the English and Americans, nor yet that, failing this way, there is no other. I confine myself to saying that history gives us no example of a nation that first grew prosperous and acquired a strong centralized government and then afterwards became free and democratic. It is not true of the Greeks or the Romans or the Dutch or the English or the Swiss or the Americans; of any of the peoples who have cared most for freedom or democracy, or have enjoyed them the most securely. It is not true even of the French, whose 'absolute' monarchy, even in its prime, was more liberal than either the oriental monarchies or the modern authoritarian state.

The methods we use in pursuing our ends affect us; they change our characters and preferences. Rulers who use cruel methods to create prosperity and literacy, even though they want them because they are conditions of freedom, soon lose the taste for freedom. They drive and trick the people out of their old habits, they hurry and stampede them, and in the process of moulding them to their will come to despise them. They come to despise them as individuals though they may praise and admire them in the mass; for it is out of the mass that they create the social order which, in their opinion, crowns and justifies their actions. They are proud of their people, proud of what they can do with them, of what they can accomplish in their name, but are without respect and without pity for them as individuals. The pleasure they take in them is aesthetic, like a sculptor's pleasure in the qualities of the stone he uses. What wonderful stone it is, for see what wonderful shapes can be hammered and carved out of it!

It is not possible, of course, to use democratic methods with a people unfit for democracy. But it is possible to deal with them in ways that do not destroy their self-respect and self-reliance, building upon whatever notions of freedom and voluntary public service are already acceptable to them. These are, no doubt, slower methods, but they have two great advantages: they cause less suffering, and they create more trustful relations between rulers and ruled. The quickest methods have not only bad psychological effects, breeding arrogance in those that do the bullying and servility in those that get bullied; they also require the setting up of institutions which preclude democracy and freedom: a single authoritarian party pervading all other organizations in the state, courts of law which never venture to protect the citizen against the government, administrative departments insensitive to public opinion, an intrusive police force acting in secret and with the power to hold trials and impose penalties without reference to the ordinary and open courts.

These institutions are dangerous to freedom in a way that the institutions of a primitive or backward society are not; for primitive institutions tend to disappear as society makes 'progress', whereas these institutions are both causes and effects of 'progress'. They do not prevent a people becoming prosperous, literate, and powerful; they actually help them become so more quickly than they might otherwise have done. They also create vested interests, new groups tenacious of power and privilege in place of the old ones, and with incomparably greater prestige and self-confidence on account of the stupendous achievements placed to their credit. They receive the supreme tribute of fear, which of all tributes adds most to the apparent stature of the men who receive it.

These institutions are also dangerous to freedom for another reason. They are not, like the institutions of the old monarchies in Europe, frankly undemocratic, or like more primitive institutions, obviously unsuited to modern industrial society. The claim is made for them that they are democratic because the groups that use them like to think of themselves as spokesmen of the people. These groups altogether reject the old-fashioned idea that rulers are responsible only to God for how they treat their subjects, and yet will not admit that they are imposing their own preferences on the people. They seldom put themselves forward as creatures superior to the people who know better than they do what is good for them.[1] On the contrary, they usually

---

1. In this respect the Communists and Nationalists in 'backward' countries differ from the Nazis and Fascists in Europe who openly reject democracy. About the Nazi or Fascist there is often something of the buffoon or the guttersnipe, of the man who thumbs his nose at culture and decency, as there hardly ever is about the Communist or about the Nationalist from a backward country.

claim to be popular, treating their own enemies as enemies of the people; they claim to be interpreters of the people's will and keepers of their conscience. How seriously they take this claim, it is difficult to say. Probably quite seriously; for though they are cynical, they are probably also credulous. Cynicism and credulity quite often go together.

Whether or not they deceive themselves, they certainly deceive others. The peoples they rule usually know very little about democracy and personal freedom, and still less about the institutions needed to realize them. What men understand by freedom in primitive and illiterate communities is not liberty of conscience or a man's right to choose a career according to his ability; for these are quite difficult and sophisticated notions. If they do not appear so to us, it is only because we are already familiar with them. Still more difficult to understand are the processes, legal and governmental, needed to make good these rights. Even in the West most people do not understand these processes, but many do and the others take them on trust. Though they might not venture to explain them, they would soon notice their absence. But backward peoples are not familiar either with the rights or with the processes; they know only that some things which they cared for deeply are disappearing and that they are now called upon to admire and to praise other things. They are told to do certain things, and are also told that when they do them they are taking an important part in something excellent called democracy; and many of them are disposed to believe what they are told. If there are sceptics among them (as doubtless there are), they probably conclude, not that what they are told is democracy is not so, but that democracy is not much good. Why should they conclude otherwise? They have not known anything else called democracy to compare it with what they now have; they have not received lessons about it except from their present rulers. What else can the sceptics say except, 'so this is democracy and this the new freedom! We were better off when we still lived like our ancestors.' But in time there will be no one left to remember the old ways, and no historians will attempt to reconstruct their image as they were. There will be only vague traditions about them and distorted accounts, and they will be officially condemned. The people will mostly take for genuine what is offered to them as freedom and democracy, even though many may not like it.

We are sometimes warned not to assume that the only institutions making for freedom and democracy are those which have been evolved in the West. The advice is good, taken in the abstract, though it is sometimes given when it is not relevant. It may well be that western institutions are not the only ones allowing of democracy and freedom in large industrial societies. After all, western institutions differ greatly from country to country, and we cannot decide that they make up between them the whole range of differences compatible with liberal democracy. If the warning is given merely to deter us from concluding that institutions unlike those we are in the habit of calling democratic are undemocratic, it is well found. But it is sometimes given with a different purpose, to suggest that it is somehow narrow and pedantic to question other people's right to call their institutions democratic, no matter what those institutions are.

Now, if the point at issue were merely a verbal one, it would be pedantic to raise this question; for it would then be enough to show that these other people use the word 'democratic' in a different sense from ours. But this is often quite untrue. When these other people (say, the Russians) call their institutions 'democratic', they often mean to say that they serve to make the rulers of Soviet Russia responsible to the Russian people. This is a statement of fact which we are fully entitled to deny, and we cannot reasonably deny it unless we are prepared to show that Soviet institutions do not make the government responsible to the people. It is impertinent to say that only western methods and institutions can ensure that governments are responsible to the governed or can preserve freedom, but it is not impertinent to argue that many of the methods used in the last few decades to bring prosperity and literacy quickly to 'backward' peoples have so affected their minds and institutions that they are today even further than they used to be from democracy and freedom. Nor is it impertinent to argue that the use of these methods soon makes government more concerned to increase the industrial and military power of the state than to raise the people's standard of living, and more intent upon training their subjects to be docile and useful than upon teaching them to think for themselves. But the apologists for these methods, after pointing out that poverty and ignorance are great obstacles in the way of freedom and truly popular government, then go on to say that by the use of these methods prosperity is brought much more quickly to the people and illiteracy got rid of. If, then, without even troubling to consider the actual machinery of government in detail, we can show that these methods have enriched the state much more than the citizen, and that, despite universal and free education, the people are no more apt than they used to be to think for themselves about public matters, we have already gone some way towards destroying the case made by these apologists.

There may be other processes than those known to the West making possible democracy and freedom in large industrial societies. No one should deny it. But the fact remains that, so far, only in the West have such processes emerged. I say 'emerged' rather than 'been discovered' because political institutions are not ordinarily contrived in order to realize ideas clearly understood beforehand. Institutions and ideas develop together, not always in step with one another but always intimately connected in all kinds of ways. It has taken centuries for the liberal and democratic institutions of the West to become what they are, and despite their variety, they are essentially alike. It is improbable that other parts of the world, politically less experienced, will produce in the near future institutions as democratic and liberal as they are but very different from them. Certainly, there is no sign of their doing so. Whenever large industrial societies have not adopted or have failed to use successfully the democratic institutions of the West they have always resorted to authoritarian methods. Not, however, to the authoritarian methods of the past, which are not suited to industrial societies, but to methods which are, as often as not, devices originally democratic now put to undemocratic uses—the political party, the trade union, the general election. Of course these devices change character when they are put to new uses; they do not, like mechanical tools, operate in the same way whatever the purpose they are used for. The political party and the trade union work quite differently in Communist countries from the way they work in the West. It is easy enough for the student of politics to understand how they work and the purposes for which they are used. They are not new instruments of democracy unknown to the West; they are western instruments originally used to make government responsible to the people, now transformed to make the people docile to government. Apart from these instruments there are others—for instance, the political police—borrowed not from the democratic West but from the old authoritarian monarchies of central and eastern Europe. These instruments have also been adapted to new uses; or perhaps I should say, less to new uses than to much more extended use. They too have been in many ways transformed. There has therefore been in recent times genuine political innovation outside the West; for to transform is to innovate. But most of this innovation has not been propitious to democracy and freedom. Quite the contrary.

Even these innovations, though not western, are nearly all European. The non-European peoples in changing their institutions have been almost entirely imitative. They have sought to make 'progress', which has meant little more than that they have tried to get what the Europeans were the first to think desirable; and it is therefore natural that they should have adopted European methods. They have in practice two alternatives: to use western methods and move 'forward' more slowly than they might otherwise do, or to use authoritarian methods and move 'forward' more quickly. But the 'forward' movement is not really as simple as it looks; it is not a movement towards one goal or towards several goals so related to each other that to move towards some is necessarily also to move towards the others. The authoritarian methods may lead more quickly to a higher national income, to full literacy and good technical education, to military power and international prestige, but they lead away from rather than towards personal freedom and responsible government. Western methods lead, though more slowly, to what the other methods lead to, but they lead to other goals as well, goals less easily seen but not less essential to the idea of progress or less precious to eyes that have learnt to recognize them. It is hardly practicable first to use the quick methods to get what they bring, and then afterwards the slow methods to get what is not to be had by the quick ones; because the quick methods create habits and ambitions which prevent the use of the slow ones.

We need not go as far as Rousseau did when he said that Peter the Great by his reforms had put the Russians forever out of the way of getting freedom; we need not say that peoples who have learnt to be servile to government can never afterwards learn to be free. It is the most arbitrary pessimism to say that in the lives of nations there are false turnings from which there is no coming back, as if nations were individuals with an allotted span of life and a fore-known cycle of growth and decay. Yet there are false turnings, even for nations; there are some methods much more painful and much less likely to succeed than others. If your goal is freedom and in your hurry to create the material conditions of freedom you use methods that weaken self-reliance and self-respect, you are not likely to get what you want. Indeed, after a time, you are likely to cease caring about it, though you may still go on saying that it is your goal. And this, if it is not hypocrisy, is at least self-deception.

(4) These arguments in reply to those who say, 'Aim first at the material conditions of freedom, using the quickest methods, whatever they may be, and then afterwards set about establishing freedom', will carry weight, even if they are true, only with people who really care for freedom. I can imagine an objector saying, 'You have yourself admitted that the use of these methods weakens the love of freedom both in the rulers who use them and in their subjects. What does it matter if they still go on speaking as if they cared for freedom, paying lip-service to it? If they really do not care for it, your arguments mean nothing to them, though their still speaking as if they did care may enable you to amuse yourself by pointing out that they are going the wrong way about trying to get what they say they want. Your arguments are therefore, as Burke might say, "fit only for the schools" and of not much practical interest.'

I can imagine the objector continuing, 'You have also admitted that freedom is among the less understood of the ideas incorporated in the European myth of progress. Backward peoples wanting to make "progress" are in fact much keener on other things than on freedom. They want independence and wealth and knowledge and power more than personal freedom. This being so, their self-respect depends rather on their getting these things than on their getting what the West understands by freedom. If they still feel inferior to the western peoples, it is because they are weaker, poorer, and more ignorant. To remedy these defects, they are willing to make great sacrifices; or, if they are not exactly willing, are disposed to be grateful to rulers who force these sacrifices on them as soon as they see what they bring. The citizens of powerful and independent states are treated much more considerately and respectfully by foreigners than people who belong to weak and dependent countries. The pride that individuals can take in the greatness or independence of their country also serves to give them self-confidence and self-respect. What is more humiliating than being ruled by foreigners, and being treated by them as inferiors in your own country? Surely, it matters more, if men who have been made to feel inferior are to regain self-respect, that their country should be independent than that they should have the rights which constitute individual freedom in the West? And you ought to admit that self-respect matters more than freedom as the western liberal understands it, for without self-respect a man is frustrated and deeply unhappy, whereas he can have self-respect without being what the western liberal would call free.'

There is great force in this argument, though I do not accept it altogether. It is certainly true that persons who are treated as inferiors because they belong to a particular nation or community or profession are more eager to raise the status of the group they belong to than to be free to think and act for themselves. Italy was 'greater' under Mussolini (or for a time appeared to be so) than she had been before 1922, and many Italians thought the freedom dear to the liberals well lost for the sake of this greatness. The Yugoslavs under Tito are less free than they used to be between the two wars, which does not prevent many of them being glad that their country now bulks larger in international affairs. If Europeans can feel like this, how much more must coloured peoples do so, who have been subjected to much greater humiliations and have been less affected by liberal ideas! Even the English, who pride themselves on their freedom, are sometimes offended at no longer being treated with the respect they were accustomed to not so long ago when England's power was so much greater. The desire to be respected by others is much simpler and more common than the desire for liberty of conscience and for the chance to live up to your own ideals, which is the heart of freedom as the western liberal understands it. To the liberal, lack of freedom may bring with it diminished self-respect; a threat to his freedom is a threat to his dignity, and if he is deprived of freedom, he can retain his self-respect only by fighting to regain his freedom. But with others it may not be so; it may be enough for their self-respect that they should be treated respectfully by others.

There are several comments to be made here. The harsh methods that quickly bring independence or make a backward country strong and formidable to its neighbours not only preclude freedom as the western liberal understands it; they also destroy older forms of security and privacy, forms which are just as much understood and valued by the peasant in a backward country as by the sophisticated Westerner. They are just as much forms of freedom as the freedom of thought and opportunity for 'self-realization' precious to the liberal, and the self-respect of the peasant does to a large extent depend on them. Unless the modern state is democratic and liberal, the citizen is almost powerless before it; he is not only prevented from acquiring forms of freedom unknown to backward societies and perhaps meaningless to him, but is also deprived of other forms which mean as much to him as to anyone. In a backward society man is tied down by ancestral customs which also tie the hands of authority; he knows his place and others know it too. He must do what is expected of him and has no acknowledged right to criticize or to try to remove the bonds that hold him; but the social order that restricts him restricts others also. Government preserves that order and does not subvert it, so that men feel that they are bound, not by the will of other men, but by something superior to the will of any man. In this order which does not change, or changes so slowly that change is not noticed, there is a kind of equality between men, an equal submission to fate. There is also more authority within the family or kinship group and less outside, so that power sits closer to the individual and attends more quickly to his needs and moods.

Freedom as we find it in the West is more than a positive ideal, it also compensates the citizen for the excessive authority of the modern subversive state, the state which is perpetually busy changing the social order, creating new rights and new duties. If the citizen is not to be the victim, the plaything, of authority, he needs the right to criticize and to call authority to account as he never needed it before. He may not be aware that he needs it, and may not know what to do to get it; but this ignorance is no proof that the need is not there. Modern industrial society, restless and changing, is perhaps oppressive or frustrating in ways that more primitive and stable societies were not. And it may be that the antidote to this oppression is freedom as the West knows it.

A man's pride in the group he belongs to may add to his self-respect but may also be a substitute for it. Certainly, a man who is ashamed of his country or community or profession is less likely than another to have self-respect and self-confidence. Patriotism and personal dignity often go together, as they did in the Roman or the Victorian Englishman. But patriotism can also be a collective boasting to cover up a sense of inferiority. It is by no means certain that independence of itself increases the respect in which one people are held by others. They may get independence and still find themselves as much despised as ever, and able to take no greater pride in their country to increase their self-respect. Or if they are already independent but backward, they may by harsh methods preclusive of freedom add quickly to their wealth and power without adding much to their prestige among the nations. History shows that it can be so and offers many examples.

Among the small nations of central and south-eastern Europe long ruled by foreigners, some achieved independence or a large measure of autonomy several generations before the others. The Ottoman Empire would have fallen to pieces more quickly than it did but for the efforts to hold it together made by Britain, long the blindest and the least generous of the western Powers in her attitude to the smaller Slav peoples.[1] Still, it did fall to pieces more easily than the much better governed and more prosperous Habsburg Empire. The Greeks and the Slavs subject to the Turk got independence or autonomy earlier than the Slavs subject to Vienna and Budapest. Since Ottoman rule was incomparably worse than Habsburg rule, it was a good thing for them that they did so. But they did not find that independence or autonomy added anything to their repute in Europe—and they were unknown elsewhere. From being the victims of the Turk entitled to the sympathy of the other Christian nations, they became the most incompetent, corrupt, and untrustworthy of self-governing peoples. They were certainly no more respected, as nations or as individuals, than the Slavs in the Habsburg Empire still subject to the foreigner. As a matter of fact, despite their many shortcomings, they were making progress; they were growing wealthier, were becoming better educated, and were learning to work a political and judicial machinery, borrowed from the West, to make government responsible to the people and to protect individual rights. But they were not making progress faster than the still subject peoples, and were held in lower esteem. They were accounted less civilized. To make progress at all they had to get free of the Turks, whereas the Slavs subject to the Habsburg could make progress without getting independence, and perhaps gained rather than lost prestige in the eyes of Europe from being incorporated in one of the great empires. If they had succeeded in getting real autonomy inside the empire they would have been looked upon by others (and probably by themselves also) as much better off than the Balkan Slavs; and thus it would have been, even if their autonomy had fallen far short of independence, even if their

---

1. Except when Gladstone was Prime Minister. Later, when the will to independence of these peoples was proved, Britain changed her mind.

rights of self-government had been as limited as those of the Virginians or New Yorkers in the United States.

It may be objected that this example of the Slav nations is scarcely relevant when we are considering coloured peoples. The Slavs in the Habsburg Empire had only to acquire certain capacities and to conform to certain standards to be as 'acceptable' socially and politically as other people; they might be refused national autonomy, but their rights and social prestige as individuals were as great and secure as anyone else's provided they had the wealth and education to maintain them. The Magyars, who hated Slav nationalism more than the Austrians did, were very willing to accept a Slav as an equal and a compatriot if only he would behave appropriately; just as willing as the English were to accept an Irishman. The educated Croat, if he felt inferior to the educated Magyar and resented feeling so, did so only because he insisted on being a Croat nationalist when he might quite easily have become a patriotic Hungarian proud of his Croatian ancestry. Few Hungarians minded his being a Croat if only he were willing to be a Hungarian as well, or minded even his concern to preserve the Croatian language and culture so long as he did not repudiate things Hungarian. But no such compromise is offered to the coloured man ruled by Europeans; he is treated as an inferior merely on account of his colour, no matter how educated and well qualified he may be. The Europeans in practice refuse him equality whatever he may do to deserve it, and he is therefore condemned to perpetual inferiority while he lives in their society and under their government. To feel equal to them as a person, to regain his self-respect, he needs, as no white man does, to belong to a community quite independent of them. Since they will associate with him only as an inferior, he must dissociate himself from them to assert his equality. National independence is more important to him than responsible government and the individual freedom dear to the liberal; and he ought to try to get that independence even if he uses methods which, from the liberal's point of view, retard his progress.

I agree that it matters more that coloured peoples subject to the Europeans should get independence, or at the least a large measure of autonomy, than that white peoples similarly placed should do so; it matters more that they should be masters in their own country because it is so much more difficult for them to rise to full social equality with Europeans unless they are so. But it does not follow that the sooner they get independence, the better. If they get it before they are capable of efficient government (not to speak, for the moment, of democracy and freedom), they may sink into such corruption and squalor that they are more despised than they would have been had they continued under European rule. And where there is corruption and squalor there is usually oppression as well. The people will be under the heel of a brutal and corrupt minority, with nothing to comfort them except the thought that their oppressors have skins of the same colour as their own. If their country is naturally poor, they will be left to themselves and have few foreigners among them to treat them with contempt; but if it is rich, foreigners will come to exploit their resources and will be allowed by their corrupt rulers to make what profits they please provided the rulers get their share. And so, despite their country's nominal independence, they will still have among them foreigners behaving as if they were superior beings. Unless their native government is efficient, their country will be truly independent only as long as it is not worth the foreigner's while to interfere with it; and this kind of independence, as it goes with corruption, oppression, and weakness, does not preserve them from contempt or add to their self-respect. True, the foreigners who despise them keep away from them, and that is some consolation.

The attitude of the European active in governing coloured peoples is different now from what it used to be. It is the European settler, and perhaps even the European businessman, rather than the European official, who treats the native as an inferior; and even the businessman does so much less than he used to do, for he, like most other Europeans, has been sobered and humbled by recent events. He too has seen what 'civilized' Europe has been capable of during the last generation. If he has any sense, he sets a greater store than ever on the European values desecrated by European dictators, but he also sees how precarious is even Europe's hold on them. The educated European is also perhaps more modest and understanding than he was because he has learnt something of psychology and sociology. Freud has reduced his pride more than Darwin did, offering to show him what he is like now and not his remote ancestry. Only the European settler has interests which can scarcely be defended unless the native is kept subordinate to him, and therefore cannot afford to treat the native as an equal however well qualified he may be. Of course, the white man is still arrogant, for old habits die hard, and the coloured man is still apt to see insults where none are intended. Relations between coloured and white people are still much more difficult than relations among white people, and are likely long to remain so. But they are, I suspect, least difficult where the white man is merely engaged in government and is not trying to establish a community of his own in the colony he governs.

I have argued that national independence or a large autonomy, necessary though it may be to enhance the self-respect of coloured peoples, is not enough. There must also be efficient government. But clearly, efficient government need not be liberal and democratic, and indeed need not even be gentle. Why, then, should not a subject people get independence (and thus enhance their prestige among nations and their self-respect) as soon as they are capable of efficient government, no matter how illiberal or undemocratic or ruthless it may be? Why should not the native Communists or some nationalist group, no less bold and confident and capable of strong government, seize power? If what the natives want is national independence and the sense of being the equals of the Europeans, if they care more for this than for freedom and democracy or constitutional government or gentle treatment, why should they not get it this way, if it is the most likely and the quickest? What reason has so far been given against it except that the citizen of the modern state may need the freedom of the liberal as his ancestors did not need it to offset his sense of powerlessness at the hands of government? It was only said that he *may* need it, as if the matter were doubtful, as indeed it is; for how can we be sure that governments have not the means today of making their subjects happy in their docility? And even if the need exists, is it greater than the coloured man's need for the self-respect which independence and efficient native government bring?

I should answer these questions by saying that in the modern world, if government is both efficient and gentle, it is likely to respect the freedom precious to the liberal and also to be moving towards democracy; and that the people have little to gain from its not being gentle unless it makes their country more formidable to others. In the old days, before industrialism and general literacy, government could be efficient and gentle without being liberal or having leanings to democracy; it could preserve order and respect custom and popular beliefs without being required to submit to criticism or to allow freedom of thought or to make provision for free elections. But relations between governments and their subjects are now much more varied and active, both where there is democracy and where there is not. People expect incomparably more from their governments than they did; they make enormous demands on them. Governments must either allow most of these demands to arise independently of their wishes, being content to do no more than compete with others in forming public opinion, and must then do their best to satisfy these demands as equitably as they can, or else they must seek to control popular demand. To put the matter more simply—and perhaps too simply, though the gist of it is there—they must either try to do what the people ask of them or else must try to create the impression that the people want them to do what it suits them to do. If they embark on the second course, they must in practice be willing to use harsh methods, though it may be their interest to deny that they are doing so. In the family or circle of friends a clever woman (and sometimes even a man) can by mere gentleness get others to want what it suits her (or him) that they should want. Such feats have often been celebrated in fiction and are also to be met with in real life; but governments must use rougher methods. If, however, they keep to the first course, and are determined to be gentle, I do not see how, under modern conditions, they can long do so without becoming liberal and democratic; that is to say, without creating and learning to work efficiently the machinery, judicial, electoral, and administrative, which preserves the rights of the individual and makes government responsible to the governed. In the literate industrial society, all classes and groups, if they are left to themselves, become politically articulate; they learn how to organize to put pressure on government, they find spokesmen to formulate their demands and to negotiate on their behalf. If they are allowed to do this, they expect government to take notice of their demands, and are satisfied only if they believe that government is dealing justly with them, weighing their demands against the demands of other groups and making fair compromises. But if the government will not allow these groups to find their own voices, it must somehow contrive to speak for them all or create the illusion that it does so; it must organize them, or so permeate the organizations they form, that it can decide, within broad limits (though never completely), what they demand. It cannot decide completely, for the simple reason that what people can be induced to demand always depends considerably on needs which government does not create. The systematic and

L

all-pervasive control of public opinion and effective political demand in an intricate and universally literate industrial society is extraordinarily difficult and elaborate; it is not a crude business fit for simple-minded bullies, it is subtle and flexible. But it is not gentle; it requires the use of harsh methods against the recalcitrant, it is often dirty and cruel. The industrial society, if it is to be efficient, requires everyone to be able to read and write, and a large minority to be highly trained, technically and administratively; it requires greater initiative, greater powers of decision from a large number of people; it requires intelligent discipline and not the blind following of custom and routine. Whether it is democratic and liberal or not, it requires intelligent discipline if it is to be really efficient. If, however, it is undemocratic and illiberal, it also requires perfect docility in some spheres as well as intelligence and initiative in others.

Liberals are, I think, inclined to exaggerate the difficulty of meeting both these requirements, as if it were impossible to discourage initiative and curiosity in some directions without at the same time inhibiting it in others; as if intelligence, to go really far in any direction, needed to be given free play in all. This is perhaps a liberal illusion. Even in the freest society, people who are remarkably intelligent about some things are quite unintelligent about others. The natural scientist who never thinks for himself about society and government is not likely for that reason to be any less open-minded and imaginative as a scientist. A few problems are enough to keep even the brightest intelligence busy for a life-time. The intelligent, no less than the stupid, enjoy praise and fear censure, and can be induced to exercise their powers in some directions rather than others. If authority discourages independent thought in the social studies, it can still encourage it in the natural sciences without risk that the natural scientist will establish principles dangerous to political orthodoxy; for these two kinds of study are in any case independent of one another, in the sense that the laws discovered by the sociologist or economist or political theorist are not derived from, or reducible to, the laws discovered by the natural scientist. Of course, these two sets of laws, if they are true, must be compatible with one another, since they both refer to events happening in the same universe, but each kind of study is autonomous. It is true that natural scientists sometimes seek diversion by moving out of the sphere of their competence, and sometimes even expect to be taken seriously when they do so, not just as intelligent citizens, but as possessors of a special wisdom due to science. It is also true that social and political theorists have in the past affected to derive their conclusions about what society is and what it should be from theories of the universe which have owed a good deal to science as well as to theology. But these are aberrations. The natural sciences do not tell us how society functions nor what is socially desirable, though they give us information we need to help solve a great many practical social problems; and the natural sciences can probably flourish just as freely in an authoritarian as in a free society. To the extent, therefore, that wealth and power and efficiency depend on these sciences, authoritarian societies need be no worse off than free ones.

When orthodox doctrine (that is to say, opinion supported by power) was essentially theological, and theology made statements about the world which natural science could prove to be false, orthodoxy and science were often at war; so that where orthodoxy was triumphant science was discouraged, and along with science the technical progress which depends on it. But now that orthodoxy is essentially social theory, there need be no conflict between orthodoxy and natural science, though there will be conflict between it and the social studies. In the Soviet Union, for instance, physicists, chemists, and even biologists [1] may put forward what hypotheses they please; it is historians, sociologists, economists, and political theorists who may not do so. It is only to the extent that efficiency and power depend on the use of knowledge supplied by the social studies that a modern authoritarian society is really at a disadvantage compared with a free society.

How pleasant it would be to believe that this disadvantage is really great; pleasant not only for the lover of freedom but also for anyone concerned for the prestige of the social studies! The social studies have certainly made great progress; no one who has been engaged in them at all seriously would deny it. But they have not made the same kind of progress as the natural sciences; they have not produced a large body of principles accepted by most people whose competence is acknowledged. Their findings are both vaguer and more controversial, it is more disputed both what the principles assert or imply and whether

---

1. I have not forgotten the Lysenko controversy. But, then, it was not necessary for the defence of Marxist–Leninist orthodoxy that Stalin should adopt the opinions of Lysenko.

they are true. No doubt, there are always controversies among physicists or chemists or biologists, but there are also much wider areas of agreement between them. Not only that, for scientists know more precisely than students of society just to what extent they disagree.

The knowledge that the social studies aim at producing is as much needed for practical efficiency as the knowledge produced by the natural sciences; the administrator or educator needs it just as much as the engineer or manufacturer or farmer or medical practitioner needs physics or chemistry or the biological sciences. What is more, his thinking about the practical matters he deals with is as much influenced by the social studies as is the thinking of the engineer or the doctor by the natural sciences. In a sophisticated society, wherever there is practice, there is also theory; and the theory does not have to be scientific or beyond controversy in order to affect the practice. In a modern industrial society, authoritarian or free, the influence of social theory on government and education will certainly be great; and I refer here not to speculation about what is desirable but to theories about what actually happens or is likely to happen if conditions are changed. However, if in a free society these theories are still confused and inadequate, and there is no wide area of agreement among the experts, they do not give that society much of a practical advantage over an authoritarian society. Efficiency is the ability to achieve as economically as possible the ends you desire, no matter what those ends may be. There is, I think, little evidence that authoritarian societies are less efficient than free ones merely because they do not allow independent thinking in the social studies.

Nevertheless, I abide by the assertion that the social studies have made great progress in the free societies of the West. They have not yet produced a body of knowledge which can be used for practical purposes as effectively as scientific knowledge can, and in any case there is not the same agreement about what purposes that knowledge should be used for. The practical problems that natural science helps to solve—as, for instance, how to produce machines to move through the air faster than sound or how to destroy disease-carrying pests without also destroying forms of life useful to man—are usually easy to define; but not the problems that need for their solution such knowledge as the social studies seek to acquire. We are still often at cross purposes when we discuss what ought to be done about social problems, let alone when we argue about what facts are relevant and what explanations are likely to be true. And yet more has been done in the West than anywhere else to produce and to test plausible explanations of man's social behaviour. Given agreement about what social aims to pursue, the relevant information to be obtained in the West is more plentiful and better established. But before it can add much to social efficiency, there must be agreement about what is socially desirable, and also those who make policy must know where to look for and how to use such relevant information as there is. In authoritarian societies, the main causes of inefficiency are ignorance and the brutal use of inappropriate methods; in free societies they are action at cross purposes, timidity, and not knowing how to get and to use inadequate knowledge allowing for its inadequacy. Authoritarian government is often reckless and by its recklessness causes great suffering, but it also to some extent makes up for this recklessness by its boldness. It is more prodigal of the people's energies but also forces them to exert themselves more. I speak, of course, of this type of government as we find it today, when it is mostly revolutionary, nationalist, and fanatical, as well as authoritarian, and not of the old-fashioned types.

Even if it were true that to forbid independent thought in some directions discourages it in others as well, this might not of itself put authoritarian societies at a serious disadvantage compared with free ones. Admitting, for the moment, that the freer atmosphere in the West encourages speculation in the natural sciences, and that great advances in scientific theory are for this reason more likely in the West than in the Soviet Union,[1] this need not give the West any advantage, economic or military, over the Soviet Union. It is one thing to put forward hypotheses which profoundly alter our picture of the world, and another to make large and quick use of them for some practical purpose. The first half of this century has seen revolutionary advances in several of the natural sciences. Most of these advances were made in western Europe, but it is America and Russia that have used them the most extensively to add to their wealth and power. The world gains immensely (or loses, if their discoveries are misused) from the

1. There are many other things, besides lack of freedom, which could explain the comparative weakness of pure science in Russia: for example, the preoccupation with the practical of a backward country exerting itself to make material progress quickly, the absence of universities with a long tradition of respect for clear, rigorous and original thought.

speculative intelligence of the greatest scientists, but a country need not produce any such scientists to be able to take the fullest practical advantage of what they do; it is enough that it should be industrially developed and should produce plentifully men who are good organizers or who have the kind of intelligence (which is far short of genius) which enables them to work out the practical implications of the great discoveries. It is only recently that America has rivalled Germany or England in her contributions to pure science, and yet she has been the richest country for several generations. Wealth and power depend more on the capacity to *use* than to *produce* good ideas.

The modern authoritarian state is as much alive as the liberal state to the advantages of the natural sciences, even if its atmosphere is less propitious to original scientific thought; and it is well able to use scientific knowledge to increase wealth and power. Nazi Germany, wedded to a doctrine of racial superiority, did not allow full freedom of thought to the student of human physiology and psychology, but the Communist state is not obscurantist where the natural sciences are concerned. The dialectical philosophy tied to its social and political theory is so amorphous that no conclusion reached by natural science can be said to contradict it, and all that the Communist requires of the scientist is that he should speak respectfully of that philosophy if he speaks of it at all. It is as easy as making obeisance to the flag. The Communist in power is obscurantist only with the social studies. Of course, in principle, this could put him at a disadvantage even in the pursuit of wealth and power, because the knowledge accumulated by the social studies can be used to make that pursuit more effective. If the Communist is not yet at a serious disadvantage, it is because the social studies, though more open-minded and imaginative and rigorous in free than in Communist societies, do not yet offer clear and firm conclusions to be used by makers of policy, and also because in free societies, more even than in Communist ones, there are differences of opinion about social objectives. In the West people are confused by the profusion of theories offered to them, even though many of these theories, taken separately, are more lucid, more carefully thought out, and better supported by the evidence than Marxism. The Communist, interpreting the world in terms of his opaque and often wretchedly inadequate theory, is sometimes blind to what stares him in the face and makes great blunders. But his immediate objectives, though he sometimes makes abrupt changes, are usually for the time being set clearly before him; if he fails to achieve them in one way, he tries another, quickly persuading himself that his later course is as much in keeping with Marxist orthodoxy as his earlier, if not more.

Still, though putting impediments in the way of free thought in some directions need not discourage it in others or lower its quality, it must involve much suffering. It is not possible, merely by offering rewards, to encourage the free play of intelligence in some directions and at the same time to confine it in others. Your physicists and chemists may be no less excellent in their spheres because you deny freedom to those who wish to study society and government. But if your society is sophisticated, if it is not held together merely by custom and routine and traditional beliefs, if it is dynamic and reforming, if it encourages curiosity and initiative in many directions, it cannot discourage them in others, except painfully. Intelligence is not like water to be guided easily into whatever channels are prepared for it. Once people get used to doubting received opinions, to planning their lives and not just living as custom requires them to, and once they get used to sustained and rigorous thinking, intellectual curiosity moves them in all directions. True, it does not move the same people in them all, but it moves some in each. The man whose bent of mind makes him a good physicist will probably not need to be kept within bounds in the sphere of politics, for he is unlikely to be tempted into that sphere. But others as imaginative, as apt for hard thinking as he is, will be tempted. Not only tempted but allowed to move in; for the authoritarian state needs social and political theorists as guardians and interpreters of orthodoxy. And the theorists need to be intelligent, for they must guard the doctrine in a society where intelligence, in many fields, must be encouraged. The modern authoritarian state cannot treat its corpus of orthodox doctrine as if it were received from God and beyond human understanding, though mysteriously not beyond human belief; and if it is to be efficient and powerful must encourage clear, systematic and independent thought in many directions. It cannot help but create habits of mind which make the defence of orthodoxy difficult and painful—difficult for the defenders and painful for their victims.[1] The policing of thought is nowadays a much vaster

---

1. And sometimes painful also to the defenders, even the sadists among them. If you want faith without doubts, it is surely best to keep away from the doubters, which you cannot do if you actively defend the faith. True, the more you fight, the more devoted

undertaking than it used to be, though it may also be easier because the modern state has the resources needed to undertake it. But that is the only sense in which it is easier, for it requires immense efforts and inflicts great suffering.

What could make this suffering worth while? Some may say: 'Because by means of it authoritarian government can more quickly make society prosperous and the state formidable to other states, and so add to the sense of importance and the self-respect of the citizens.' I want to consider this answer to the question because it is probably the answer that weighs most with coloured peoples struggling for independence in order (so they hope) to escape the inferiorities and the contempt which now so gall them. I shall admit (less because I believe that it must be so always than because my argument does not require me to deny it) that harsh authoritarian government can increase a backward country's wealth and power more quickly than the kind of government that prepares a people for democracy—which kind I shall call predemocratic. This can be admitted without also admitting that authoritarian government is more efficient than predemocratic, in the sense that, for a given effort, it produces a larger result.[1] Predemocratic government will also strive to increase the nation's wealth and power, but its other aims will preclude its using the most drastic methods; methods which do not produce a larger result for a given effort but rather bully the people into making a much greater effort than they would otherwise have made. Clearly, the quickest methods need not be the least wasteful.

It is a mistake to suppose that a country by rapidly increasing its wealth and power necessarily makes itself more formidable, or even that if it does so, it enhances its international prestige. If its neighbours are immensely more wealthy and powerful than itself, a very considerable increase in its wealth and power may not make it any more formidable to them than it was before. Even if we take the cynical view and say that men behave more respectfully to those they fear than to those they approve of, it does not follow that the best way to gain their respect is by adding quickly to your strength. You may be able to

---

you are to the cause you fight for, closing your mind to what is strongest in the enemy's argument; but with the enemy always at your door, the effort to keep it shut must be painful.

1. In any case, since authoritarian and other states have only some ends in common, they cannot be compared in respect of efficiency except in limited areas.

add very greatly to it without becoming dangerous to them. And even if you succeed in becoming dangerous to your immediate neighbours, you may still remain weak compared with the most powerful persons, whose contemptuous treatment of yourself moved you in the first place to try to add rapidly to your strength, using the most drastic methods. Even in a world where the strong are treated with greater deference than the considerate and the well-behaved, it might pay you better, if you want to avoid contempt, to improve your manners than to add some inches to your muscles. For who is more contemptible than the would-be strong man not strong enough to sustain his role?

Backward peoples all over the world have been much impressed by the example of Russia; they have been impressed even when they have disliked Communism. The methods used by the Russian Communists to make their country strong could be used in other countries by nationalists. At least most of them could, for they are not methods peculiarly appropriate to believers in Marxism. But what these peoples often forget is that these methods may not do for them what they have done for Russia, even if they use them skilfully and add greatly to their country's wealth and military power. Russia's natural resources are immense, and the same methods used in a country which is smaller and naturally poorer could not raise it to Russia's level. Russia's prestige rests, more entirely than any other country's, on wealth and power rapidly acquired. But Russia's prodigious effort made her one of the world's two greatest Powers; she added enormously and quickly to her wealth and military strength and thereby made the world fear her. Another country might make what was for its size as prodigious an effort, and perhaps within a generation multiply its wealth and military strength as many times, and yet do no more than raise itself from the status of a sixth- to a fourth-rate Power. It might, by so doing, make itself more formidable to some countries than it was before, but not to others. It might be less trusted and less sought after as an ally, and its citizens might be despised for their servility to government. Russian methods have caused Russia to be hated by many people, but Russia has also inspired fear and admiration which more than make up to her for the hatred. Another country, smaller and naturally poorer than she is, using the same methods might come to be equally hated and yet nowhere near equally feared and admired. Perhaps China, by using these methods, may in time (and perhaps soon) make herself a world Power stronger than any except the Soviet

Union and the United States. India has scarcely the natural resources to do it, and is more likely to gain international respect by skilful diplomacy and decent conduct than by trying to raise industrial production quickly or to build up a great army. Of course, she needs to raise her industrial production to achieve her other purposes: to raise the standard of living and education, to provide a wider choice of careers, to help eliminate what remains of the old caste system, and to strengthen democracy. The quicker she raises production the better, provided she does not use methods which prevent her achieving her other purposes. For even if she sets great store by the world's attitude to her, she has nothing to gain and something to lose by using such methods.

All the Communist states use much the same methods as the Soviet Union to make themselves industrially and militarily strong, and yet only China is more formidable and respected today than she was before she became Communist and began to use such methods. Among the smaller Communist states Yugoslavia alone enjoys greater prestige than she used to do, and she owes it, not to her industrial wealth or military power, but to her position between the two great alliances and to her skill in engaging the sympathy of the 'uncommitted' states. Actually, since Belgrade's breach with Moscow, Yugoslavia has been the least brutally governed of Communist countries and also one of the less successful in raising industrial production. It might be argued that the other small Communist states, if they were free of Moscow but still went on using their present methods, would count for more internationally than they do now. True, but they would owe their greater importance to being free of Moscow rather than to using these methods, however effective they might be in raising production and military power. For today, militarily, the smaller states count for almost nothing.

The real interest of the smaller Powers is that there should be a world order strong enough to deter the great Powers from bullying them, and they do nothing to strengthen that order merely by adding to their own wealth and armaments. If (outside the Communist part of the world) it is today rather more dangerous for the great Powers to bully them than it used to be, this, as I have several times pointed out, is not due to their being wealthier and stronger. The great Powers never outmatched the others more overwhelmingly than they do now. If the smaller Powers are better treated, this is due to the relations between great Powers being different from what they were and also (and just as much) to its gradually being brought home to all Powers, great and small, that if they go on behaving in the future as they have done in the past mankind will be destroyed. We live now in a world where the weak still fear the strong, and the strong still fear one another, but also where the strong, as never before, fear themselves, lest by a blunder they let loose a catastrophe as fatal to them as to the weakest of their neighbours. When the greatest Powers have grown so formidable that they hardly dare move for fear of knocking against one another, what have small countries to gain by trying to be formidable? Why should they use drastic and painful methods to add quickly to their industry and armaments? Or even, if they are still subject to the foreigner, to get independence before they are ready to govern themselves, not only efficiently, but gently and considerately?[1]

Sometimes an effect is taken for a cause. Some of the coloured peoples are more truculent in their behaviour towards the western Powers than they used to be, and those Powers take greater account than they did of the coloured peoples and their aspirations. But are the coloured peoples better treated because they are truculent or can they afford to be truculent because the West has changed its attitude to them? Surely their truculence is much more an effect than a cause of the better treatment. No doubt, the truculence, if it is nicely calculated, brings quick results; it induces some western Power or other to make concessions it might otherwise not make. But the truculence is effective because the West is conscience-stricken and lacking in self-confidence as it used not to be before 1914. Nasser, who rules one of the weakest countries in the world, has been truculent with conspicuous success. If he were as great a nuisance to the Russians as he has been to the British, and if Egypt were in a part of the world which Russia was accustomed to dominate, he might have armies incomparably tougher and better equipped than he now has and yet be conquered in a day. That is not to say that he is to be blamed for his truculence, though it may be that if the British had been cleverer he would not have been tempted to be truculent. However, the point remains that there was no need for him to make Egypt industrially and militarily strong to

1. If they pile up arms to get an advantage over their small neighbours they may gain nothing by it; for the great Powers hostile to them will arm those neighbours. Today the influence of lesser Powers depends less on their being militarily stronger than their neighbours than on their ability to play on the fears and hopes of the great Powers.

enable him to be truculent with success; no need for him in his domestic policies to use Russian or other pitiless methods to enable him to make his country count for more internationally. As a matter of fact, as dictators go, he has been a humane ruler, and if the western Powers had helped him solve his country's economic and social problems, they might have diverted his energies into channels less irritating to themselves and more useful to the Egyptians. Nasser would still have been an Arab nationalist, and we, not being his enemies, would not have had our eyes closed by anger to what seems plain sense: that we have no interests that run counter to Arab nationalism, since the Arabs cannot afford not to sell us their oil or to forgo the dues paid by our ships passing through the Suez canal.[1]

How sad it is that so many of our sins should come to roost after we have begun to mend our ways! The Europeans have greatly improved their manners towards the coloured peoples; they are much less arrogant now than they have ever been. But the coloured peoples, just because they are making 'progress', are more sensitive than they used to be, more apt to see insults where none are meant and more deeply offended by what insults come their way. If they were not so eager to make 'progress' (which means, in effect, to become more like the Europeans) they would perhaps be much less offended by European behaviour towards them. This is only natural, for the more we want to imitate other people (even though we will not admit the desire), the more their disdain hurts us. It is the same within nations as between them. The peasant who cares nothing for his superiors is beyond the reach of their contempt; if he takes no offence, it is not from humility but from indifference. Indeed, he often despises his superiors as much as they despise him, and hides his contempt only because it pays him to do so. Even his flattery is sometimes a form of contempt; he expects educated and rich fools to be taken in by it, believing that he himself

---

1. We are, however, in honour bound not to allow the Arab states to destroy Israel. Perhaps it is a pity that the Jews returned to Palestine and Israel was created; but that is now past history, and we have to stand by the consequences of our own actions. It may be said that this commitment must necessarily have set the Arabs against us. I doubt it. If, after the war, when Allied prestige was high, it had been made plain to the Arabs that the Allies meant to create and to defend a self-governing Jewish state in Palestine, the Arabs, then much less truculent than they are now, would probably have bowed to the inevitable; it was probably want of decision in the western Powers that tempted them to try to settle the question by force, thus creating an atmosphere which made it a matter of honour to them never to accept a Jewish state in their midst.

would never fall into so simple a trap. Only when he begins to rise socially does he become vulnerable to the contempt of his superiors. That some coloured peoples are highly civilized while the peasant is not makes no difference here, for the peasant too has his *mores* and his culture, and becomes more vulnerable to contempt as he loses faith in them. The closer the coloured peoples come to us, the more careful we need to be in order not to offend them.

N.B. Miss Perham reminds me that much that I say in this chapter about the Europeans in Asia and Africa does not apply to the Portuguese, whose relations with the coloured peoples subject to their rule have been unusually smooth and pleasant.

5

The Nature of the Problem

A. The General Purpose of the Essay

IT would be quite beyond the scope of an essay of this kind to suggest any plan of action for granting self-government to dependent peoples. Circumstances differ from place to place, and the general situation changes from decade to decade, and therefore it is hazardous to lay down in advance an order of progress towards a set goal. It would be presumptuous, even for someone far better informed than the author of this essay, to say, 'Do this and then that'. It is for practical men to decide practical matters and the student and theorist can say little more to the practical man than, 'Consider these things before you make up your mind!'

The purpose of this essay is only to discuss some of the broad issues involved in the disputes between ruling and dependent peoples in the hope of promoting clearer thinking about them. It does not tell people what to aim at; it attempts no more than to make clearer what is involved in their declared aims, to explain how these aims are often misunderstood by those who pursue them, to consider how they are related to one another, and what methods are to be avoided in the pursuit of them. It says, for instance: 'If you want democracy (that is to say, not merely its outward trappings, but governments truly responsible to the governed) and freedom (that is to say, the right of free enquiry and the opportunity to make the best of your life according to your own notions of what is good), then, when it is a question of a subject people getting self-government, look out for certain dangers.'

Not everyone who wants self-government for a subject people also wants democracy and freedom. I admit that capacity for self-government is not the same thing as capacity for democracy and freedom, and in my second chapter I define three senses of capacity for self-government which fall short of this last capacity: the ability to afford to modern trade and industry the security they need; the ability to afford security of person and constitutional government; and the ability to produce native rulers strong enough to respect international law. I try to explain how these three senses arose as a result of the emergence of strong centralized governments in western Europe and the intrusion of the Europeans into Asia and Africa, how they are related to one another, and how they differ. But I do not attempt to describe in detail the institutions which make possible fitness for self-government in any of these senses, nor the sentiments and habits which support these institutions. Even when I discuss the fourth sense of fitness for self-government, which is the ability to work the institutions that make democracy and freedom effective, I do not say much about the institutions; for they have often been described, and there is no need to add one more to the many descriptions already published. I limit myself to discussing two capacities which must, in my opinion, be widespread in a people before they can have effective democracy and freedom in the modern world. One of these two capacities I have called 'political sophistication', and the other is the ability to produce at all levels of society organized bodies to formulate group interests and to promote them effectively. I try to explain how political sophistication differs from the kind of understanding which the academic student of society and government aims at and from the skill of the practical politician, and yet how it is closely related to them both. I try also to show why the ability to formulate group interests and promote them by negotiation, though it is confined to a minority of the people, must be found in all classes and sections of the population, if there is to be effective democracy; that is to say, if government is to be quickly responsive to a large variety of popular demands, which are popular, not because those on whose behalf they are made always understand them, but because they accept the persons who make them as their spokesmen. In other words, I try to show that, for a people to be 'politically articulate', it is only necessary that some of them should be able to formulate and negotiate 'popular' demands, but that this *élite* must be drawn from all classes and must not be organized into, or controlled by, any one body, if they are not to manipulate or dominate the people whose spokesman they claim to be.

I thought it right to discuss at some length political sophistication and the ability to formulate and negotiate popular demands, because these are matters usually neglected or else treated so much in passing to other things that the treatment is not enlightening. For example, we are often told that democracy and freedom cannot flourish unless people are tolerant. This is true enough; but the question is, tolerant in just what way? For there is a good deal of tolerance, as well as intolerance, in all societies; and I rather doubt whether the democratic peoples are, in a general way, more tolerant than the others. They are, for instance, often very much given to snobbery, which is a form of intolerance; they are given to it, no doubt, in spite of their democracy and not because of it. The English, who are politically among the most successfully democratic peoples, have a very marked difficulty in understanding and allowing for feelings different from their own. Peoples who have tried democracy and failed to work it are sometimes very tolerant, as the Italians were before Mussolini's time. I suspect that an impartial person who had lived among both peoples might say that the Italians are more tolerant of those unlike themselves than the English are, partly because they have quicker sympathies and partly because they are more sceptical. Certainly, if fanatics get power more easily in some countries than others, it is not always because the people generally are more given to fanaticism or to a rigid and unforgiving morality; it is rather because the political system works in a way which gives fanatics a better chance of seizing power. Indifference, hopelessness, anger born of frustration, lack of precision in political goals and of skill in negotiation: these are the things that give fanatics their opportunities. And they come less from intolerance than from lack of what I have called political sophistication and the widespread ability to formulate clear demands and to transact political business. People are immoderate or unstable politically largely because they do not know what demands they can reasonably make on government or what to do to get government to attend to their demands. They are quickly overborne and made angry because, politically, they are unbusinesslike, and are therefore apt to fall easy victims to bullies, swindlers, and fanatics.

I take it for granted that most people (or the leading groups among them) now want to make 'progress', and that 'progress' is conceived in European terms. There may still be hundreds of millions in Asia and Africa to whom progress means nothing or even who, whatever their notions of it, dislike it intensely; but they have little political influence. They are politically negligible, which means no more than this, that we need take little account of their wishes when we are trying to explain how the world is changing and is likely to change. They may be the wisest of mankind, for what they dislike and want to stop may lead to destruction or to anxieties and restlessness which are among the worst forms of unhappiness; but they are in their wisdom (or lack of it) powerless. To stop 'progress' they would have to use the instruments which 'progress' brings with it; for whatever we may think of 'progress', it certainly brings power. Progress is not inevitable in the sense that it will go on forever without leading to catastrophe, or in the sense that men are bound to be happier or wiser or better on account of it, or in the sense that it would happen whatever men did; but it probably is inevitable in the sense that those who are against it cannot now stop it because of its very nature it adds to the power of those who are for it.

To make what is now commonly understood as 'progress' is to increase and extend scientific knowledge and the power to control one's environment, natural and social. Everyone would agree that in this sense the Soviet Union has made very great progress in the last thirty years. But the making of progress is also commonly understood as coming nearer to democracy and freedom, and there are great differences of opinion about whether or not the Soviet Union has made progress in this latter sense. It is generally conceded that to make the second kind of progress it is also necessary to make the first. Rousseau would not have conceded it, but the great majority of social and political writers do so now. In any case, there is now no making our way to the simple society which Rousseau thought was the only proper home of democracy.[1] If we are to have democracy at all, we must have it in the very highly complicated industrial society which produces immense wealth and at the same time depends on general literacy and on widely dispersed technical skills and scientific knowledge. Though I do not agree with Rousseau, I certainly believe that the first kind of progress, though it must be made if the second kind is to be possible, can be made as easily in ways that hinder as that help the second kind. I have tried in the course of this essay to explain why it is so; why some methods used to extend knowledge and to

---

1. Rousseau's simple society is small and uncomplicated, but it is not like any of the primitive societies that social anthropologists study. The conception of it is sophisticated. To create it we should have to get rid of much that we now have, but we should not return to anything known to our ancestors.

M

th are preclusive of freedom and of government truly
the people.

ried to consider the granting of self-government as it
both the 'ruling nations' and the peoples subject to them. For
though, strictly speaking, no nation governs another, since the men
who actually rule a subject people are only very indirectly and partially
responsible to the people in the ruling country, how they rule and their
ultimate purposes are very deeply influenced by the political and social
philosophies of that country. The ruling peoples—at least those of
them possessing the largest empires—have in fact come nearer than
most peoples to getting freedom and democracy for themselves, and
have also been pioneers in science and industry. They now say that
they want to bring freedom and democracy to the peoples subject to
them. They realize as well as anyone does that these things are not
now to be had securely except where there is general literacy and widespread technical skill and scientific knowledge, and also considerable
wealth; and they have rather less simple and more adequate ideas than
most peoples about how these two sides of 'progress', the 'moral' and
the 'material', are related to one another. They are at least as interested
in bringing moral as material progress to their subjects; for they have
nothing to gain by increasing their wealth and skill and allowing them
to achieve independence as undemocratic and illiberal states. It may be
that, if they could order the world to please themselves, they would
keep their subjects in perpetual bondage; but this they know they cannot do, and therefore, since their subjects will get either independence
or equality with themselves in some kind of union between them, it is
clearly their interest that their subjects should adopt their moral and
political ideals. The ruling peoples now admit that this is their interest;
and if they do not pursue it vigorously and with clear eyes, it is
because there are special interests that go counter to it and old resent-
ments that obscure it.

The subject peoples may also be attracted by the moral and political
ideals of the West as well as by science and industry and the wealth
that comes with progress. Certainly, they are likely to say they are, and
even to believe it, since these ideals are as much involved as science and
industry in what is commonly understood by progress. But, as we
have seen, some aspects of progress are much more readily understood than others, and it is also often supposed that the more readily
understood must come *before* the others. Therefore the subject peoples

are in practice often more concerned to make progress in science and industry than in other ways. I have tried to explain how this rather simple-minded concern to get 'first things first' may put people out of the way of getting what they think comes afterwards, and may even cause them to cease to want it, which can happen without their even knowing that it has happened. Because their original conceptions of freedom and democracy were hazy and inadequate, they easily lose hold of them while they pursue other things. They may even accept the Communist account of them, and so come to think of freedom and democracy as better realized in Russia than in the West; they may do this partly because the Communist account is attractive to people impatient to make quick progress, and partly because the western account (which is the more difficult to grasp of the two) comes to them from peoples whom they distrust. Besides, moral and political ideals are not understood fully in the abstract; we come close to an entire spiritual possession of them only in the process of discovering how to make them actual; they come to maturity in our thoughts and feelings as we learn to realize them in society. If we use methods preclusive of them to get their supposed material conditions, we weaken their hold on us. This is true of all peoples, 'backward' or 'advanced'.

The peoples that have gone furthest towards realizing freedom and democracy and have sown the seeds of desire for them the most widely are also the peoples who have created the largest empires and are regarded by their subjects as oppressors. If they had not taught their subjects to desire what first seemed valuable to them, they would not now be so regarded. But 'oppressors' who preach freedom and democracy are easily taken for hypocrites; and this is how the western peoples are apt to appear in Asia and Africa. That is the simple and not altogether false view; for in the past these peoples have been hard and predatory and hypocritical, and are so even today, though much less so. It is therefore difficult for the subject peoples to bring themselves to admit, not only that their actual or recent masters know more about freedom and democracy than most peoples, but are also better able and more willing to help other peoples achieve them. More able, no doubt, than willing; and yet also willing because, now that 'colonialism' is obviously on the decline, the more there are liberal and democratic states outside the West, the more secure western civilization. It is not primarily a question of the balance of power or wealth between authoritarian and democratic states but rather that the rejection of western values by peoples lately subject to the West is a moral defeat for the West, and therefore disheartening.

B. Two Spectres that Haunt the West

One is Communism and the other is the hatred of the 'coloured' for the 'white' peoples; and I call them spectres less to suggest that they are not there when they appear to be than because I believe that we fear them too much or for the wrong reasons.

(1) *Communism.* Communism has hastened the decline of the great colonial empires, and this the liberal democrat need not deplore. But it has also caused panic among the western Powers; so that their policies towards their dependencies, and towards the 'backward' peoples generally, is too much determined by military considerations. They are eager to retain strategic bases or sources of raw materials, or to build up alliances against the Soviet Union. If they can retain these bases and have access to these raw materials without making enemies of the peoples who live where these things are, so much the better; for they then feel the more secure for doing so without offence to others. Nuclear weapons probably make most of these bases much less useful than they once were, but their maintenance, if it costs only money and not the good-will of small nations, does not do much harm. The Powers that have the bases, if they have long had them, do not add appreciably to the danger of war merely by retaining them, for the world is used to their having them and takes little notice of it, if otherwise they behave without giving provocation. But the making of unnecessary alliances or the setting up unnecessarily of new bases is not so easily excused, not even when they are sincerely meant to be only defensive; for they cannot but seem a threat to the country they are supposed to deter. To treat a country which in fact does not contemplate military aggression as if it did so is a mistake; and it is also a mistake, even when the country does contemplate aggression, to erect barriers against it too feeble to deter it. These things are doubly mistakes when they lead, as they too often do, to the support in small or backward countries of unpopular governments or of groups having little domestic influence or prestige but thought to be well disposed to the West.

Since Communism is not primarily a military danger, it is not wise to behave as if it were. The more the West supports unpopular governments or groups, the more it exasperates the popular groups into trying to get help from the enemies of the West. The backward peoples, having long had to endure interference from the great Powers, try to assert themselves by playing these Powers off against one another. It is only natural that they should do so. I do not suggest that the western Powers ought always to try to win over the popular groups, as if the supreme object of imperial and foreign policy were to make as many powerful friends as possible. I suggest only that, where they do support unpopular groups against more popular ones, they should do so for some better reason than the desire to set up barriers against Communism. For barriers set up in this way are usually ineffective. Either Communism is militarily aggressive, in which case these barriers are mostly too weak to deter it, or it is not, in which case they are not only out of place but are likely to add to the real danger which is not military. A better reason for supporting some groups against others is that they are more likely, if they can gain in popularity and eventually get power, to establish the kind of government which prepares the way for democracy and freedom. When the western Powers in their dealings with their colonies and dependencies or with other backward peoples oppose the more popular groups, they should do so rather from concern for their own ideals than from fear of the Communists. I am not arguing that it is in principle always wrong to support the less against the more popular groups in a country in order to obstruct some other country supposed to be dangerous; but the danger must be great and the obstruction effective.

After the first World War the French decided to get themselves allies against Germany in eastern Europe, and to do this they thought it wise to support some national groups against others in two of the states successor to the Habsburg Empire. In Czechoslovakia they supported the Czechs and in Yugoslavia the Serbs against the other nationalities, and so helped to create two unitary where there might have been two federal states. The Czechs and the Serbs were friendly to France, and the French counted on them to keep the countries they dominated firmly on the French side against Germany if ever that country were to threaten the European order established by the peace treaties. Though the Serbs and the Czechs were the largest, and perhaps also politically the most vigorous, of the national groups in their respective countries, the French miscalculated. While Germany was weak, the Czechs and Serbs maintained their ascendancy, but as soon as she became strong and threatening, the German danger served to disrupt rather than to unite the peoples of Czechoslovakia and Yugoslavia. Admittedly, these two countries, even if they had been federal and cohesive states, would have been too weak to resist a German invasion; but at least the first would have given Hitler less excuse for interfering in its domestic affairs, and the second would not have drifted into civil war after being conquered by Germany.[1] A stable and cohesive state is usually a considerable obstacle to the ambitions of other states, even when it is much weaker militarily than they are. In a part of the world in which several great Powers are interested, none resorts to quite naked aggression; it does not attack a small state merely because it is small, but looks for some better excuse. Germany found it in the enmity of the Sudeten Germans against Prague, and Italy in the enmity of the Croats against Belgrade. It was much more to France's interest that Czechoslovakia and Yugoslavia should be stable and cohesive states than that they should be her allies; but this the French did not see. If this is true of France and the countries east and south-east of Germany between the two wars, it is even more true of the western Powers and the countries which they fear might be invaded by Russia or China; for the Czechs and the Serbs were stronger in their regions than the groups devoted to the West in the regions of Asia 'threatened' by the two great Communist Powers.

I believe that, even if we leave out of account the military factor, we are still apt to exaggerate the danger of Communism, and to be driven by fear to act in ways which increase rather than reduce that danger. Granted that the democracy and freedom which the Communist Party does not seek to provide (though it pretends to do so) are less attractive to many 'backward' peoples than general literacy, and science and industry, and the wealth and power they bring; and granted also (though this is by no means certain) that these more attractive things are more quickly provided by the kind of methods which the Communists use than by any that liberals and democrats could approve, there still remains one great objection to Communism —which may be a strong objection even in the eyes of people who care nothing for democracy. The men and women who apply Communist

---

1. It may be objected that Hitler would have attacked Czechoslovakia anyway. True, but his apologists in the West would have been harder put to it to excuse him. But the objection does not touch my main point, which is that France gained nothing by helping to create a Czechoslovakia dominated by the Czechs.

methods may enjoy doing so, and may willingly put up with a hard discipline for the pleasure of being hard to others or of serving a cause they believe in; but the people who have the methods applied to them have more to suffer and less to compensate them. The truth is that Communist methods, especially during the early and the cruel years, are bitterly disliked even by the backward peoples, except by the dedicated and the ambitious among them; for while that period lasts there is only the suffering to be endured, and its fruits not yet there except in the imagination of the faithful. In no country in the world have the Communists enjoyed the support of anything like the greater part of the people at the time that they got power.[1] They either seized power, prompted by the Kremlin and in the shadow of the Red Army, as in Poland, Czechoslovakia, East Germany, Hungary, Rumania, and Bulgaria, or else they came by it in times of confusion in countries where other organized bodies were weak and few in number or else under a cloud, as in Russia, China, and Yugoslavia. I confess that there is much less sure evidence as to how they got power in Albania, but in spite of this gap in my knowledge, I shall still risk the generalization that everywhere they have owed their political victories more to the weakness and disintegration of other groups than to their own strength and popularity.

The western Powers in their colonies and in all backward countries where their influence is great ought to encourage the formation of popular organizations, whether parties or trade unions or other bodies, and ought to take care that by their behaviour towards them they do not drive them into the hands of the Communist Party or some other body as intolerant and tightly disciplined; they ought to encourage a wide diversity of such bodies, not on the principle *divide et impera*, but because this diversity, the longer it lasts, the more it makes a people fit for constitutional and democratic government. They ought also to resign themselves to the idea that, in many parts of the world, truly popular organizations are likely to be hostile to them; or if not hostile, then suspicious. If these bodies work together to get independence or to lessen western influence, it is not really, in the long run, against the interest of the West that they should do so, provided they still remain diverse and do not resort to certain methods. If, however, they work

---

1. Except perhaps in Indo-China; though I suspect that even there the French had more enemies than the Communists had friends.

together for *all* purposes, and not merely for independence, they become virtually one body and therefore do not prepare the people effectively for democracy.

The Congress Party in India existed in order to fight the British, and yet has been the most powerful defender of western ideals, moral and political, in Asia; a far from perfect defender, and yet more effective than any other. To call it a *bulwark* against Communism is to use perhaps the wrong word; it has not yet had to repel any strong challenge from the Communists. It has rather played the part (though with much greater gentleness and humanity) which they would like to play; it has so far forestalled rather than repelled them, though it may have great difficulties with them later. The trouble with it is that it is too large and too little responsive to minor currents of opinion which, taken in the aggregate, are important. If India is to have stable democracy, the Congress Party must make more room for other parties and must learn to be content with less power than it now has. A vast democracy needs large parties, but it needs more than one, if the people are to have a real say in choosing their governments, and if pressure groups are to be able to make their weight felt without being oppressive or oppressed. If the Labour Party were the only party in Britain, and if the trade unions had the voting strength inside it which they now have, Britain might really be (what some diehards like to say it is) at the mercy of the trade unions; but the trade unions have in practice to be moderate if they want their party to win elections, which it cannot do unless it seeks to do justice to other interests besides those spoken for by the trade unions.

The image of Communism as a flood which threatens to cover the world, and which must soon do so unless we hasten to stop it, putting in its way anything we can lay our hands on, regardless of what it is, anything which seems to serve in the emergency, is quite untrue to the facts. 'All hands against Communism!' What a foolish panic cry it is! All hands, no matter how feeble, or how dirty, or how ready to commit crimes as vile as the ones that make Communism loathsome to us? Support King X and President Y because they are staunch enemies of Communism still just strong enough, with our support, to keep in power! But there is no emergency, no imminent danger of Communism sweeping the whole world, or even the whole of it except the old bastions of democracy and liberty in the West. There is, of course, a danger of war, and one of the ways of increasing that danger is to behave as if there were an emergency when there is none. Modern war destroys Communists as totally and impartially as lovers of freedom, and Communists have therefore as much cause to fear it. This panic thinking, even when it does not add to the risk of war, causes us to do things which in the end are more profitable to the Communists than to ourselves. Our last-minute interventions and abrupt changes of policy are visible to everyone, whereas the intentions and manoeuvres which we attribute to the Communists and give as excuses for our actions are either figments created by our fears or else are not seen by the peoples offended by what we do.

The world is not really the safer from Communism the more backward countries and former colonies are ruled by governments friendly to the West; it is the safer from Communism the more these countries have strong and popular governments able and willing to preserve their independence. As the peoples of Asia and Africa are now suspicious mostly of the western Powers, and sometimes even hate them, the chances are that the native governments best able to preserve their independence against Communism will not be friendly to the West. This is perhaps an unwelcome truth but we ought to face it. And really, I do not see why it should be unwelcome to us. Why should it matter to us that they should be friendly, provided they are stable and effective and jealous of their country's independence? If we hope for more than that from them (as I think we mostly do), it ought to be that they should be liberal and democratic rather than merely friendly to us. If they are all these things and friendly too, we must count that one blessing the more to us; but these other things ought to matter to us as their friendliness does not.

The Communist Party enjoys the widest popular support in France and Italy, where it is for its size strikingly ineffective. In these two countries people are free to vote as they please, and they please to vote Communist in large numbers. The support which the Communists appear to have in the countries they rule we cannot know to be genuine, but we can assume that it is so in France and Italy. Why, then, is the Communist Party so ineffective where it is the most widely popular? Because there are many other organized bodies quite independent of it. They oppose each other in many things, but they have at least one interest in common: not to allow the Communists to get power, for if they do, they will either destroy these other bodies or reduce them to subservience. Though the Communist Party is the largest and the best disciplined, though its rivals are also rivals of one another, and are often variable and fissile, the forces opposed to the Communist Party are stronger than the forces at its disposal. Not only do these rivals diminish the power and influence of the Communist Party by not allowing it to take part in government; they also weaken it by affecting the quality of the support it receives. It cannot rely on the unlimited support of its followers because there are other parties they could turn to if, for some reason or other, they felt like turning against the Communist Party. And not only that; for the electors who vote Communist in France and Italy, though mostly loyal enough to their party at elections, are very far indeed from giving it the kind of support it would like to have. To ask someone to vote for you is to ask him to take a little trouble and no risk on your behalf. But to ask him to go on strike or to use violence to help you get power or achieve some other purpose, is to ask him to make a real sacrifice or to take a considerable risk, and that is a different matter. There are other parties in France and Italy besides the Communist Party willing to help the classes from whom that party gets most of its support. The 'bourgeois' democratic state has in fact done a great deal for the industrial worker and the peasant, who have no pressing need to make sacrifices and take risks in order to destroy it. They may want more than they have been given, and may vote for the Communist Party in the hope of getting it, and yet what they expect of the party and what the party expects of them may not be congruous. They may even be subtle enough to believe that the Communist Party is more useful to them as a spur to others than it would be if it got power. There are many motives for voting for a party, and what else a voter will do for it besides giving his vote depends on his motives and not on his vote. The Communist Party is popular in France and Italy. But what is the quality of the devotion to it? Just how far are its followers willing to do what its leaders would have them do? Just how much more do the leaders intend than they are willing to disclose to their followers? Of the leaders and their followers, which have the greater illusions about the others? We do not know enough to be able to give definite answers to these questions; but we do know that the Communist Party, in the countries where it has gained the widest popularity under conditions which make it reasonable to suppose that the popularity is genuine, has been remarkably ineffective.

There is no good reason to believe that Communism is more

attractive to 'backward' and politically unsophisticated peoples in the throes of westernization than to more 'advanced' peoples. One of the countries where the Communist Party is the most popular is reckoned among the most 'advanced' of all countries, and yet there are other countries, no less 'advanced', where the party enjoys almost no popular support. We can say only that the Communist Party tends to have a much greater chance of getting power in 'backward' than in 'advanced' countries. I have tried to explain why this is so, partly because the explanation serves to throw light on what makes a people fit for mild and constitutional government and for democracy, and partly because it helps to show what should be done to lessen the Communist danger in backward and dependent countries. If the explanation is correct, then it may increase rather than lessen the danger to mobilize against it any and every group which is hostile to Communism or devoted to the West, regardless of what else it may be; and it will be far from enough to help increase industrial production or raise the standard of living.

A country is not the less likely to fall into Communist hands because it has doubled or trebled its production of steel or wheat or oil in ten years, or even because its workers are considerably better paid than they used to be, unless there has been political progress to keep pace with the economic. As wealth increases, so too do people's expectations. What then keeps them loyal to a political system which is not repressive is less that their standard of living rises than the belief that they have a reasonable chance of getting what they reasonably demand.[1] They do not expect all their dreams to come true but they do expect justice; or, in other words, they expect that an effort will be made to give them what they feel they are entitled to, which is by no means whatever they may happen to want. Everywhere people distinguish what they consider they are entitled to from their mere desires. If a people are to be satisfied with a political system, it must be possible for bodies to be created to formulate their demands and to put pressure on government to meet those demands; and if they do not get all that is asked for on their behalf, it must not seem to them that

---

1. Even in a Communist country, industrialization creates tensions which would be dangerous to the regime if the regime were not repressive. A Communist government does not need the present loyalty of most of its subjects, though it may hope to get it later; whereas, a government using methods which promote freedom does need their present loyalty, even when they are still unable to work democratic institutions.

their interests have been sacrificed to other people's but that a just compromise has been made. They must feel that their interests are being adequately cared for; and, as I have been at some pains to show, in order to feel this they need not be able to define their interests themselves. It is enough that they should trust the men who speak and negotiate on their behalf, and that these men in their turn should feel that they are able to speak and negotiate effectively. When these conditions hold, we can say that a people are 'politically articulate'. It is when a people come to expect much more from government than they used to do and are not yet politically articulate (and this is the condition of most 'backward' peoples today) that they are most in danger of falling victims to Communism. Not that Communism is then overwhelmingly attractive to them, for it is usually far from being so; but they are then so confused, so angry, so lost, that lovers of strong methods have their best chance to trick and bully their way to power. Therefore, to make a people safe from Communism, it is above all necessary to make them politically articulate. Unfortunately, they cannot be made so by the simple device of giving power to people who have distinguished themselves by their hatred for Communism or by their love for the West.

The western Powers are too prone to act as if any advance made towards Russia, or any help received from her, by an Asian or African people were a victory for Communism. To receive help from Moscow is not necessarily to be in Moscow's clutches. Especially is it not so if there is also help to be got from other sources. The more the great Powers compete with one another in helping the poorer countries economically, the better for those countries. For though, as we have seen, they need to do much more than make material progress if they are to get constitutional government and perhaps also democracy,[1] they do need to make that kind of progress as well. As a country becomes industrial and literate it is exposed to new political dangers and also gets opportunities unknown before. What we choose to call 'dangers' and what 'opportunities', depends, of course, on our sense of values. We call the risk of Communism a danger and the chance of democracy an opportunity, and we hope that, eventually, most of the

---

1. I remind the reader of my argument in Chapter 4 that constitutional government, though it does not logically entail democracy, is not likely to survive in modern conditions unless it is or soon becomes democratic.

peoples of Asia and Africa will think as we do. But a country's material progress, merely because Russia has a hand in it, does not necessarily bring the 'danger' without also bringing the 'opportunity'. It all depends on circumstances. Economic help from Moscow might enable a government to consolidate its position and strengthen itself against *all* foreign interference, and this might make the eventual coming of democracy easier rather than more difficult. We hope that this may happen when we give the help, even when we give it without laying down political conditions. Why, then, should we suppose that it cannot happen when the help comes from Moscow? Because Moscow never gives, and is not likely to give, help unconditionally? But why should we believe this? If we are willing to give help to backward countries unconditionally in the hope that this will prevent their falling into Communist hands, why should Moscow not be willing to do the same to prevent their falling too much under our influence? When the wealthy nations are rivals, it is then that the poor nations have their best chance of getting generous and unconditional help.

The western Powers, in large parts of Asia and nearly all Africa, still behave as if they expected to have a monopoly of external influence there. They admit in principle the right of the peoples in those regions to keep their independence, if they already have it, or to get it eventually, if they cannot in the meantime be persuaded to accept equality of national status and a measure of self-government short of complete independence. But they are most reluctant that, as a result of their withdrawal, others should acquire as much influence as they have in these regions. For example, they admit that they can no longer have over the Arab peoples the kind of ascendancy which the British acquired when the Ottoman Empire fell; and yet they are as eager as ever they were to keep the Russians out. It is as if they were saying, 'Let there be less influence from outside in the Middle East than there used to be, since it must be so, but let whatever influence there is still be ours.' They treat the 'backward' peoples rather as parents or teachers sometimes treat children who are growing up: the children can no longer be treated as they used to be, but let an outsider acquire an interest in them, and the interest is at once denounced as evil. And not only as evil, but as large and fast growing. There is still a possessiveness in the attitude of the western Powers to the peoples of Asia and Africa which lingers on after their right to independence has been admitted. If a 'backward' people are helped or influenced by the

Russians or are friendly to them, they at once appear to many circles in the West as being well on the way to being under Moscow's thumb.

Let us in the West, if we can, keep a sense of proportion. No doubt, Moscow is not full of good intentions. The Russians have already forced Communism on several reluctant peoples. But these peoples are mostly in eastern and central Europe, where the Russians had special opportunities at the end of the war. They have not the same opportunities in Asia and Africa; nor the same interests, for their security does not depend on their dominating any parts of Asia or Africa as they think it depends on their keeping their hold on what they acquired in Europe since 1939. In Asia and Africa the western Powers had between them for several generations a virtual monopoly of foreign influence, and now they are losing it. For a time Japan was a threat to them, but America defeated Japan and became for a few years the dominant Power in the Far East. If she quickly lost that position, it was not to Russia that she lost it; for the Russians do not dominate Red China. Russian influence in Peking is now greater than the influence of the western Powers, but Russia is also subject to influence from Peking. The rest of Asia, except Indonesia, is still much more under western than Russian influence, and exerts rather less pressure on the West than China does on Russia. Our influence in Asia and Africa will probably decline even more, and in any case, as all the 'backward' peoples gain independence, will change character; it may even be, if relations between them and us become happier, that our influence over them will decline less than their influence over us will grow.

In our dealings with the peoples of Asia and Africa we have special disadvantages. It is against us that they have had to struggle for their independence; it is our arrogance that they have deeply resented. The Russians have one great advantage lacking to us: they are the supreme example of a backward nation which by stupendous efforts has quickly raised itself to being the dreaded rival of the West. Not until Nazi Germany had defeated France and controlled all that she wanted of Europe, except Russia and England, did she succeed in frightening America as Russia has done. The Germans, in any case, were not a backward nation; they belonged to western civilization, and their threat to it was an internal threat. The Russians appear more as outsiders, and their challenge to the West weakens it in its dealings with Asian and African peoples.

But we also have advantages that the Russians do not have. We have greater experience in dealing with Asians and Africans; we have our liberal and democratic ideals which, though they are misunderstood by many, are also understood by some who are still powerful, especially in India and the other states successor to the British Empire. We have more to give and to lend to the needy than the Russians have. Above all, the peoples of Asia and Africa know us; they have seen us at our worst and sometimes also at our best. There is no fear of future disillusionment; the non-European peoples probably think rather worse of us than we deserve. Though the Russians are not likely to behave in Asia as they did in Yugoslavia, where they destroyed in three years a good will rooted in centuries of friendship and 'racial' sympathy, they are almost unknown there. They are not the least arrogant and impertinent among European peoples, and Communist manners are seldom tolerable except to fellow Communists, and not always to them.

We also exaggerate the threat of Communism because we over-estimate the inclination of Communists to stick together. At the moment the Chinese Communists, faced with great difficulties at home, attach great importance to the defence of orthodoxy. They are busy making enormous changes regardless of the feelings and sufferings of millions of their fellow countrymen; they are still in the pitiless and most exacting stage in their self-imposed task of making China 'socialist' and industrially powerful, and therefore feel the need to be inflexible and to justify their being so. They are jealous of the integrity of their faith, and want nothing to happen which decreases the authority of Communist doctrine. That doctrine is not being used against them by the Russians to try to dominate them, as it was against the Yugoslav Communists; it is being used by them to coerce their own people. Hence their rigorous orthodoxy and their loyalty to Moscow, the first home of Communist orthodoxy. But they are more than loyal, they are also demanding; they use their great influence in Moscow to make the Russians doctrinally more inflexible than it might otherwise pay them to be. They are, for the time being, the 'ultras' of the Communist movement, 'more royalist than the king'.

If, however, the Chinese Communists succeed in consolidating their power, they may care much less for maintaining all over the world a single rigorous orthodoxy. The 'heroic', the pitiless phase is now already over in Russia, and as new issues arise among people growing in literacy and sophistication, it becomes more difficult to use the old wholesale and brutal methods of maintaining discipline, and the doctrine, if it is to retain its hold on men's minds, must be interpreted with greater subtlety. This is certainly not a move towards what we understand by freedom and democracy, but it is a move from a harder and simpler to a milder and subtler form of dictatorship. When the 'heroic' phase ends in China there will probably be the same kind of move made there. But the two countries and peoples are nevertheless very unlike, and the new issues arising in a more 'advanced' China will probably not be the same as those now arising in Russia. The two countries, as they develop, will not pass through precisely the same phases, with China always some distance behind Russia; and when the 'heroic' phase is over in China as well as in Russia, there may not be the same pressure put by one country on the other to maintain a rigid orthodoxy all over the Communist part of the world.[1]

It is not explicit doctrines shared in common but common organization and common loyalties that hold people together over a long period of time. While there are several Communist states and no structure over them strong enough to keep them united, their community of faith will not long suffice to do so. Communist states, as much as any others, have divergent interests; and the only way in which communities having divergent interests can present a permanently united front to the world is to establish a larger community within which they can reconcile their interests peacefully, and which can give them a sense of common identity and common loyalties. Even community of faith, to be long preserved, requires a single 'church'; that is, if the one faith is really alive, with power to move men to great achievements. But the Communist peoples have neither one state nor one effective church;[2] and there is no sign at present of their acquiring either.

We do not need so much to exert ourselves *against* Communism as *for* our own ideals. If all Asia and Africa were to go Communist, I

1. Rigorous orthodoxy can serve the rulers of a Communist state in two ways: as an excuse for exacting great sacrifices from their own people, and as an excuse for trying to dominate other states sharing the same faith. The rulers of Russia have used it for both purposes. But now that there are two independent Communist great Powers, the temptation to use it for the second purpose may be smaller; for neither of the Powers will allow it to be used for that purpose against itself, and the chances are that they will not long agree about the sort of discipline to be imposed on the lesser Powers.

2. By a 'church' I mean, in this context, any organized body whose avowed purpose is to maintain and give expression to a common faith. In this sense, the Comintern and the Cominform may be called churches, though neither was truly international.

doubt whether the West would be much less secure than it is now. The example of Asia and Africa is not, I think, likely to be catching in Europe and North America, where people are not accustomed to follow leads given in other parts of the world. Militarily and industrially, 'free' Europe and North America are, and are likely long to remain, as powerful and wealthy as the rest of the world put together. The destructiveness of war is now so great that war against Russia alone is to be feared as much as war against a grand alliance led by Russia; for when one country can do the injury that either Russia or American can now do, it cannot much matter to other countries how much more it adds to its armaments or what allies it acquires. Or it can matter only if these additions enable it to ward off blows as destructive as the ones it can give. If Russia by acquiring allies in Asia and Africa merely puts herself in the position of striking twice as many blows at America as America can strike at her, when perhaps a tenth of the number would suffice to destroy either country, she gains nothing militarily and is no more dangerous to America (or to any allies for whose sake America would go to war with Russia) than she was before. Only if Russia, by acquiring these allies, could make herself much less vulnerable to America than America was to her, would she gain any serious military advantage; but there is no reason to suppose that she could do so. Of course, if Russia and America always refrained from going to war with one another, they could still fight each other, as it were by proxy, by provoking wars between their allies or satellites. In this way each could strive to gain the mastery of Asia and Africa, or to prevent the other from doing so. But these limited wars, whatever their outcome, would not lessen the security of 'free' Europe and North America, provided Russia remained as vulnerable to America as America to Russia, and America were willing to go to war with Russia to defend these regions. Given the present destructiveness of war between the two greatest Powers, the military security of the West would not be seriously diminished if all Asia and Africa were to go Communist.[1] And the West is perhaps as likely to get into war with Russia following a badly conceived attempt to prevent the 'backward' parts of the world turning Communist as because they have actually turned.

---

1. The loss of oil from the Middle East could be made good by sending American oil to Europe, though this would involve rationing.

N

Nevertheless, we ought to try, if we can, to make freedom and democracy realities outside the West. We ought to do it partly because we have by our own past actions implanted the desire for them in other peoples, and partly because the effort helps to keep alive in us our own ideals. We are already deeply involved in the affairs of many parts of Asia and Africa, and how we disengage ourselves from those regions must affect their future. We cannot behave as if we had never been there and by our presence started an immense social and political revolution. If we allow these regions where we have been so long active to go Communist or authoritarian by default, it must be dispiriting to us. That parts of the world we have never touched should care nothing for our ideals need not matter to us, but that peoples whom we have disturbed and controlled and made ourselves responsible for should reject them may serve to weaken our own faith in them. We may feel a kind of moral isolation which is debilitating even though we are not militarily any less secure than we were before.

There is, of course, no question of our forcing democracy and freedom, as we understand them, on other peoples, for these are things which of their very nature cannot be imposed by force.

(2) *Racial Hatreds*. The division of the world into 'white' and 'coloured' peoples is merely a result of European conquests and the spread of European civilization. If the Bantu were overwhelmingly the wealthiest and most powerful 'race', the world might be divided into the 'black' and the 'pale' peoples, the Chinese and Indians being reckoned with the Europeans among the 'pale' peoples. There is no deeper difference between 'white' and 'coloured' peoples than between different types of coloured peoples. This is as true of cultural as of physical differences between them. Indeed, the Chinese and the Indians have culturally more in common with the Europeans than they have with the negroes of Africa. All this is obvious enough, but it bears repeating, as the obvious so often does, because it goes counter to our favourite prejudices.

The 'fellow-feeling' among coloured peoples comes of their all feeling themselves to be victims of the Europeans, pushed around by them and despised. Colour prejudice arises just as easily between 'coloured' peoples as between the 'whites' and them. If it has arisen less often in recent centuries, it is because there has been less occasion for it to do so; the coloured peoples have intruded upon each other less than the Europeans have intruded upon them. True, they have recently been brought together in many parts of the world, but usually in countries dominated by the Europeans, who have treated them all as inferiors. And yet, in countries where there are several 'coloured' peoples all disdained by the Europeans, the colour prejudice between them is often as deep as the prejudice which divides them from the Europeans. It is as deep but not as prominent. They fear, hate, and despise one another as much as the Europeans fear, hate, and despise them, or they the Europeans. But these feelings between them are, for the moment, politically less important than the feelings that divide them from the Europeans, and are therefore less discussed. Also, the coloured peoples do sometimes work together against the Europeans, and when they do, are apt to speak more pleasantly of one another than of the common enemy. How far their words express their true feelings is another matter. Clearly, they have common interests against the Europeans, and equally clearly they have interests against each other. If the first interests are now more prominent than the second, it may not be because they are more important in themselves but rather because nothing can be done about the others until something has been done about them. The coloured peoples in relation to one another may be placed rather like the western Powers and Russia during the last war, whose mutual distrust and dislike were not less than their distrust and dislike for the Germans, but who had first to defeat the Germans before they could come to grips with each other.

European domination, while it has brought the coloured peoples closer together in some ways, has in others brought them closer to the Europeans. India, before the British conquered her, was socially and culturally as different from China as she was from Europe. If her economy was more similar to China's than to Britain's, it was because Britain, at the time she conquered India, was already, in agriculture, commerce, and industry, the most 'advanced' country in Europe, and her methods of production were changing more rapidly than they had ever done before. The economy of mediaeval Britain was probably no more unlike India's economy than India's was unlike China's. And, of course, since the British conquest, not only India's economy, but her social and political system have become more like Britain's, as India has slowly acquired more and more the character of a modern industrial state. There have been equally great changes in China which has also been profoundly affected by European ideas and techniques; but these changes, in some ways like the ones that India has undergone, are in other ways quite different. China, unlike India, was never ruled directly by Europeans, and she has now gone Communist; she was almost as deeply disturbed by western intrusion as India, but was never able to absorb as much of western culture and institutions. Thus, India, socially and culturally no more distant from Europe than from China three centuries ago, is today a good deal closer. The spread of western civilization has, no doubt, made all peoples more alike than they used to be; but it has not made the 'coloured' peoples more like each other than they are like the Europeans. It has, however, given them all certain feelings towards the Europeans; feelings which sometimes incline them to believe that the division between 'coloured' and 'white' peoples is the most important of all.

The difference in colour is an outward symbol of other differences: 'white' peoples have ruled 'coloured' peoples but not the other way about; the 'white' peoples are generally much richer than the 'coloured', and have usually moved a good deal further in those directions which the world agrees to call 'progress'; the 'white' peoples have more living space than the others. China, with a population of six hundred millions, is smaller than Canada with only fifteen millions, and has as great a proportion of uncultivable land and fewer natural resources. Australia is two and a half times as big as India, and has less than one-fortieth of her population. The coloured peoples are the poor peoples, the cramped peoples, the still subject or only recently liberated peoples; they are the peoples who have been taught by the Europeans to want things which they may not have space enough or wealth enough to get.

This division between the 'white' and 'coloured' peoples will probably matter more in the future than the division between the Communist and the liberal [1] countries. At the moment, 'coloured' against 'white' means in practice pretty much 'coloured' against the West; for when coloured peoples think of white peoples as oppressive and racially prejudiced, it is the English, the French, the Dutch, and the Americans they have in mind rather than the peoples of central and eastern Europe. They even think of Communism as an ally of the

---

1. I say 'liberal' rather than 'free' because free often means independent, and also because it is sometimes used (especially in America) to mean non-Communist, as in 'free world'; and I say 'liberal' rather than 'democratic' because the Communist countries also claim to be democratic.

coloured peoples against the West, which for the present it is to some extent. The Communists are enemies of the West, and are therefore very willing to use for their own purposes the resentment of the coloured peoples against the West. True liberals are, of course, just as sincere as the Communists in denouncing colour prejudice, but they cannot as easily take the kind of action which persuades coloured peoples of their sincerity; they are more cautious, more fearful of the consequences of too drastic action. They want to move slowly; they do not want to use the hatred of the 'oppressed' for their 'oppressors' to destroy parliamentary or other democratic institutions but rather to use those institutions to put an end to oppression. They do not want to make irreconcilable enemies of peoples who do not think as they do, for to do this is (they think) to strike at the roots of democracy; they want rather to destroy prejudice than to win spectacular victories over the prejudiced. They therefore preach patience to the victims of prejudice, who often resent the preaching and set them down for hypocrites. Colour prejudice is a serious problem only for the liberal peoples of European stock, and so the Communists can take full advantage of it. The Communists may believe in racial equality just as sincerely as in other things, and just as sincerely as the liberal believes in it, and yet take bolder action in pursuit of it without damage to the other things they believe in; and even if they cared for it much less than for other things, and much less than the liberal cares for it, it might still be good politics for them to press for it loudly and recklessly.[1]

When all the coloured peoples have been independent [2] for some

---

1. There are coloured peoples in the Soviet Union, but the outside world knows almost nothing of their fate. They have been treated by the Russians much more cruelly than the British or the French have treated any of their subjects in our century; 'progress' has been forced on them without regard for their feelings, and with scant respect for their native cultures. Positions of authority over them have either been given to Russians or to natives who have become 'reliable' Communists; which means, in effect, to natives who have adopted the manners and beliefs of Russian Communists. But there has been little 'colour' prejudice; the native who is recognized as having become a 'reliable' Communist is accepted as an equal by Russian Communists, though there is, I understand, a tendency to believe that a Great Russian is more likely than other people to make a reliable Communist.

2. Some of them may choose not to be completely independent, being content with autonomy within a federal union which also includes white peoples. This might be, for many coloured peoples, the wiser choice; but I doubt whether it will often be made. People who have been treated as inferiors must have a strong desire to dissociate themselves from the peoples who have so treated them, especially when congenital inferiority has

considerable time—that is, for time enough (which is not much time) for new tensions to appear deep enough to make old memories dim— they may not feel about the West as they do now. Of course, their governments may try to relieve the tensions by raising up feeling against the foreigner, and the foreigner most apt for the role of enemy may still be the old 'imperialist', but he may also be the coloured man just across the frontier. Or the governments of coloured nations, unable or unwilling to become democratic, may slide or rush into dictatorship, and may have so much more in common with the Soviet Union than with the liberal states, that dislike and envy of the white man are still almost entirely against the West; but equally the dictator-ships may come to blows with domestic Communists and therefore be more friendly to the liberal than to the Communist great Powers. Or most of the coloured peoples may go Communist, and may come to think of Communism as the cause of the poorer nations against the richer, and may look upon the western peoples with as much mistrust and resentment as they do now; but equally their Communism may come to divide them in new ways rather than to unite them against the liberal West. Just as the Christian churches have often been more concerned with their differences from one another than with what separated them all from Islam, so it may be with the Communist states. It is part of the Communist faith that 'proletarian' states should work together, and that irreconcilable conflicts are impossible between them. But that does not prevent conflicts arising, and whether or not the parties to them can effect a reconciliation depends more on the political methods they are accustomed to (and the political tempera-ment which goes with the methods) than on community of faith. When two Communist and self-styled 'proletarian' states quarrel and cannot reach a compromise, what is each of them likely to conclude? Either that, Marxist doctrine notwithstanding, irreconcilable conflicts can arise between two genuinely proletarian states, or that the other state is not genuinely proletarian? What conclusions did Red Russia

---

been imputed to them. The essence of colour prejudice is this, that the person who feels it wants to treat the coloured person, no matter how intelligent and well behaved he may be, as inferior to himself. It is this attitude that seems unforgivable to those who suffer from it. The African can say to the European: 'You have taught me that superiority rests, not in colour, but in qualities acquired by education and self-discipline, and yet, even when I acquire these qualities, you still treat me as inferior to yourself. This is intolerable!'

people educated enough to limit the size of their families, or must she lower her birth rate before she can seriously raise her standard of living? It is certainly in the early stages of industrialization and the spread of literacy that a 'backward' country is most in danger of moving to Communism or some other form of authoritarianism rather than to democracy. Not because it is growing poorer, not because population is growing faster than production, but rather because people are coming to expect much more than they used to expect, and more than can be given to them. Wealth may grow considerably and yet more slowly than demand for what wealth brings.

And yet, for all we know, a country the size of India and with natural resources as great might, even with a population larger than India's, be able to have material prosperity enough to make liberal democracy secure. A standard of living much lower than what the British or the Dutch now enjoy might be enough for the purpose, provided the people get the right kind of education, willingly spending a large part of their national income on it. The British and the Dutch could afford to spend several times as much as they do on education if they learned to do without other things on which they now spend a great deal of money, and their education might teach them not to want these expensive things or to prefer other cheaper things to them. India might conceivably learn to be a relatively poor but nevertheless highly educated and liberal democracy with a population half again as big as she has now. She might contrive to be a literate, industrial, equalitarian, and freedom-loving society, and yet not chase mammon as we do in the West. It would be impertinent to say it could not be done merely because we have not done it or felt the need to attempt it.

It might, however, be a very difficult thing to do. What most impresses the 'backward' peoples about the West is the fast rising standard of living and the immense power of the state. It is their poverty as individuals and the weakness and straitened means of the states they belong to which contribute most to making these peoples feel inferior to the West. To catch up with the West means for them, as much as anything else, to become rich and powerful like the great western nations. It would need extraordinary wisdom and self-restraint, a quite unusual understanding of the limited opportunities given them by nature and history, for them to be content with being much poorer than the western peoples provided only that they are well enough off to have educated and free self-governing societies. If they find themselves without a chance of becoming anywhere near as rich and powerful as the nations whose 'superiority' has in the past borne most heavily on them, there may be created tensions so deep as to prevent their achieving democracy. That is to say, it may be that countries whose natural resources are in themselves enough to give them the material conditions of democracy, will not achieve democracy because of their too strenuous efforts to keep up with countries naturally much richer than they are, and because of the passions generated by a sense of their own comparative poverty and weakness. If they could strive for democracy without having other countries set material standards beyond their reach, they might achieve it without too much difficulty; but as it is, the chance is greater that they will be deflected from their course by the ambition to rank as high as possible among the Powers. Feeling their deficiency in natural resources and living space they may make demands on the wealthy white nations which those nations will almost certainly reject; and if they feel too weak to press their demands against the wealthy and the strong, they may be driven to aggression upon one another.

If the coloured nations, with few exceptions, find themselves permanently very much poorer than the white nations, they may feel themselves victims of injustice; they may claim a larger and fairer share of fertile land and other natural resources. Whether or not they dare press this claim against the wealthy nations, they will feel bitter resentment towards them. If they do, they will perhaps feel it as much against Russia as against the western nations. Indeed, they may feel it more against Russia than against the already heavily populated countries of western Europe. The 'haves' will still be white nations and the 'have-nots' coloured nations; but the 'haves' will be the Soviet Union and the United States, Canada and Australia, and no longer Britain and France and Holland. The envy and resentment of the coloured peoples will perhaps soon be directed less at the old 'imperialist' peoples than at the white peoples who have tried to win favour by denouncing 'imperialism'.

What can be done to allay this resentment and to relieve the tensions, domestic and international, which it leads to, and which are likely to prevent or retard the secure establishment among coloured peoples of democracy and freedom? It is not to be expected that the wealthy nations will open their frontiers to immigrants from the poor nations, unless they are of the same racial stock. The Negroes in the

United States are only a tenth of the population, and yet their presence has created social problems so acute that it will take generations to solve them. Men are rightly afraid of mixing the races in the same political communities; they have seen what this mixing leads to, what passions it generates, what injustices, and what conditions destructive of freedom and lowering to human dignity. They have seen what it leads to, not perhaps always, but so often that the experiment is too dangerous to be worth trying. It may be that a time will come when the races will mix freely, when they will intermarry; but that time has not yet come. Nor can we expect the wealthy white nations thinly spread over vast territories to evacuate large parts of them to make more room for the coloured nations whose countries are too densely populated. Self-sacrifice of that kind has not yet been seen in the world, and is not to be hoped for. Millions of Germans have made room for Poles and Czechs east of the Oder and the Neisse and in the Sudetenland, and thousands of Arabs have made room for Jews in Palestine; but they have not done it of their own free will. The wealthy nations with space to spare are also the powerful nations, and there is little hope of their making room for anyone. At least not in the near future, and the problem is urgent.

The only suggestion so far made which there is any hope may be accepted by wealthy nations too strong to be coerced is that natural resources should be shared more equally. If India, whose deposits of iron ore are relatively small, could rely on being able to develop an iron and steel industry of the same order of magnitude as the great western Powers, if she could become almost as highly industrialized for her population as, say, Germany is, it would not much matter to her (as it does not matter to Britain) if she had not land enough to produce all the food needed to feed her people much better than they are now fed. She could import foodstuffs and pay for them with her exports. She would not want charity indefinitely; she would not want countries richer than herself to send her food and finished products out of their superfluous stocks. She would not want to be partly 'kept' as poor relations are by rich ones; she would not want the products of other people's labour to be given to her for nothing. But natural resources are not products of labour, apart from the cost of extracting and transporting them, which cost India would no doubt be willing to bear. What she needs, in order to be put much more on a footing of equality with countries at present immensely richer than she is, is as good a legal right to receive certain basic raw materials which she does not produce as the countries which do produce them, and to pay no more for them than it costs to extract and transport them. No doubt, for some time to come, she also needs to borrow capital and the services of foreign experts and technicians; but these are passing needs. The one permanent need, if there is to be much greater equality than there now is between the coloured and the white nations, without mass immigration of coloured persons into the Americas, Australia, and the Soviet Union, and without a drastic shift in international frontiers to allow the coloured peoples to establish new nations as the Europeans have done since the sixteenth century, is to make provision for the fair distribution, *as a matter of legal right*, of basic raw materials. It is not enough that the countries lacking these materials should wait upon the good will of the countries which have them; they must be able to rely on getting them. Agreements for a limited period of years between the naturally rich and the naturally poor countries are not enough for the purpose; there must be an international agency permanently established to secure this fair distribution. But it is unlikely that the Soviet Union would work with the western Powers to make such an agency a success; or rather, it probably would not want to work with them until the agency had proved a success and it began to look as if the West were beginning to win the poorer nations over. Therefore, it is unlikely that, to begin with, the agency could work as part of the United Nations Organization. But there is, as I hope to show later, another alternative.

If India and other economically backward nations not already in the Communist camp were to become securely established liberal democracies, and if it were made possible for them to grow wealthier in conditions not altogether less favourable to the pursuit of wealth than those which the West has known, there need be no lasting and bitter enmity between the coloured and the white peoples. Once these backward nations have become fairly prosperous and truly free and democratic, the idea of a perpetual competition between nations in the pursuit of wealth and power may become distasteful to them. This is the more likely to happen, the more has been done internationally to enable them to raise their material standards. They may then not mind being considerably poorer than the wealthiest nations provided they can live comfortably and securely, as befits free and educated men. Just what that implies depends on current notions of what is comfortable and fitting; and these notions can be quite modest and still allow of a full and civilized life. They are already more modest in Western Europe than in North America, though the West Europeans enjoy the benefits, cultural, political, and moral, of western civilization every bit as fully as the North Americans. Having so recently possessed the largest empire that ever was, the British are still apt to be jealous of America's being now so much more powerful and important than their own country, but they do not in the least mind the Americans enjoying a much higher standard of living. The French, angry though they have been with American policy inside Europe and outside, mind it still less. What Frenchman would not rather be comfortably off in his own country than rich in the United States?

Provided they have security enough to be able to live comfortably and decently by whatever standards they have made their own, most people care little or nothing that foreigners are better off than they are. They are less jealous of foreigners as consumers of wealth than of the power and prestige of foreign states. It is the power of America and not the high living of Americans that makes us feel small. True, America is powerful because she is rich; but true also, that the more nations learn to work together, the less the weaker among them are made to feel small by the power of the stronger.

C. Liberal and Authoritarian States

I have said so much about the danger of Communism being exaggerated that I now feel the need to make sure that I am not misunderstood. I do not believe that the Communist Powers think of war as a means of spreading their doctrine all over the world, and I do believe that the more Communism does spread the less united the Communist states will be. The Communists have never glorified war, and are no less alive than we are to what war must do to mankind in this nuclear age. By their actions they have sometimes increased the danger of war, but I do not believe that they have done so more than the western Powers in the last twelve years. They have every now and then tried something on to see how far they could go with impunity, but have always either drawn back quickly or refrained from further provocation when they felt they were on the brink of war. They did the first in Persia soon after the war, and the second in Berlin at the time of the air-lift. Their recent intervention in Hungary was more destructive than the British and French attack on Egypt, and was perhaps also less excusable, because the Hungarians never provoked and insulted them as Nasser did the two western Powers,[1] but it did not involve a greater risk of war. On the contrary, it involved almost no risk, since there was no reason to believe that America and her allies would intervene to save Hungary. The Communist Powers have sometimes risked war when they have moved tentatively forward to test the reactions of the West, and the West has risked it when it has been exasperated into taking ill-considered action. I should say that, on balance, the intemperate actions of the West have been rather easier to excuse and rather more dangerous than the provocative actions of the two chief Communist Powers. If only Russia's provocations are taken into account, the advantage in prudence would be even more with the Communist Powers and the advantage in excuse even more with the West; for China's intervention in Korea was more excusable and more dangerous than Russia's in Hungary.

Having said all this, I hasten to add that nevertheless the Communist Powers stand more in the way of good international relations than the liberal Powers. Avoiding war is one thing, contributing to harmony among the nations is another. Women, we are told, are less given to striking their husbands than men are to striking their wives. I am not sure that this is true, but even if it is, it does not follow that wives contribute more than husbands to domestic harmony. I think there are good reasons for believing that under present conditions liberal states are apt to be less competitive and more conciliatory than authoritarian states. This was not so always, but it is so, I believe, in the contemporary world.

The modern state, whether it is liberal or authoritarian, is much more enterprising than any state was in the past; it provides education and many other services, and it controls, more or less closely, the nation's economy. The old despotisms and narrow aristocracies were incomparably less obtrusive than the modern state; they defended privilege and maintained order, they collected taxes and regulated trade, but were not given to reform and experiment on a vast scale. Often, from sheer weakness or complacency, they were uncom-

---

1. The Hungarians never tried to make trouble for the Russians inside the Soviet Union as Nasser has tried to make trouble for the French in French Africa, especially in Algeria where there are a million Europeans; and for the British wherever they have interests in the Middle East. But if Hungary had become independent and neutral, it would have been a blow to Soviet prestige.

petitive and peace-loving, leaving others alone in the hope of not being disturbed themselves. Some of the most despotic states have been among the most peaceful. The more liberal states, being wealthier, were sometimes less peaceful. They were aggressive because they were looking for trade or new fields for investment; and yet they attacked, not strong and well-organized states, but weak ones. They moved, as it were, into a political jungle; into parts of the world without effective government as they understood it. The greatest of all empires was created by a freedom-loving European people never strong enough to dominate Europe. In Europe, since the fifteenth century, the English, militarily, have always been on the defensive. All the countries that have sought to dominate Europe, to bring into subjection countries about as 'advanced' and efficiently governed as themselves, and belonging to the same community of nations, have been absolute monarchies or dictatorships. The more or less liberal states, England and Holland since the seventeenth century, France since the great Napoleon's fall, the United States expanding at the expense of Mexico, have been aggressive only against countries much poorer and more weakly governed than themselves. 'Nations of shopkeepers' want large returns on a small outlay even in war, and all these countries, while they were creating their empires or extending their frontiers, were much nearer being such nations than were the central monarchies and Tsarist Russia. Of course, absolute monarchies have also enlarged their dominions by attacking much weaker and more backward peoples; Spain did it in the sixteenth century and Russia in the nineteenth. I do not deny that absolute monarchies as well as liberal states have been aggressive on the cheap; I say only that the liberal states, though they have been imperialist, have not tried to subjugate their 'equals', or even countries much smaller or poorer than themselves but efficiently governed. They have wanted secure trade, and have set about conquering other countries where there has not been a political order strong enough to make trade secure or where they would not otherwise have been able to make as profitable a use of local resources. After they have moved in, they have been heartless and predatory, as the English sometimes were in the early days of their conquest of India or the Americans in their dealings with the Red Indians or the Belgians and French in Africa. A people can value their own liberties highly for a long time before they learn to deal humanely with peoples much weaker than they are. In the past, autocracies have often been more peace-loving, and sometimes also more humane, than liberal states; but they have also often been more aggressive and cruel, and they alone have tried to subjugate peoples who were their 'equals' by European standards.

Imperialism is on the decline, and one of the reasons for this decline is that the liberal peoples have pushed their own principles further than they once did. At one time the liberties on which they prided themselves were in practice confined to the well-to-do and educated, to the upper classes; but they have since made an effort to extend them to all classes, and have made a deep social revolution in order to do so. With this concern for the 'backward' classes in their own countries has gone a concern for the 'backward' peoples ruled by them. Imperialism is dying, and there is no reason to believe that the liberal states (which are now democratic and partly socialist as well as liberal) will now try to do what they never attempted in the past: to gain world hegemony.

As the liberal state becomes democratic, it undertakes many more duties than in the past; it is more, and more diversely, enterprising. But the duties it undertakes are nearly all justified on the ground that they make for the freedom or the well-being of the citizen. It is part of the philosophy of the liberal state that public duties arise from private rights. What is supposed to matter above everything else is that the individual should have certain opportunities; and if one social or economic system is preferred to another, it is because it enlarges these opportunities or gives them to more people. Of course, in all political communities, liberal or otherwise, the citizens and the government are concerned with more than private ends and private rights, and with public ends for other reasons than because they contribute to private ones. Everywhere the citizen cares for more than himself and his fellow-citizens as private persons; everywhere he cares to some extent for his community for its own sake, as an 'end in itself'. That is to say, he wants it to be one sort of community rather than another, not only because he believes that its being so would contribute more to the happiness and good qualities of individuals, but merely because he likes it best that way. The man who would dearly love to see England as she was when he was young will be tempted to argue that Englishmen were happier then than they are now, and perhaps even that they were better, but he will love the old England of his memory as much for being the sort of community it was as for the happiness and good qualities it encouraged in individuals. After all, his memory is imperfect and his knowledge, even at its freshest, of the old England was only partial. What good evidence has he that Englishmen really were happier and better when he was young? He wants to say that they were so largely because his image of the old England attracts him more than his image of the new; he wants to justify in terms of personal happiness and merit a preference which he has largely on other grounds. No one is a complete individualist in the sense that the Benthamite Utilitarians imagined they were; nobody prefers one social or political system to others only because he believes that it does more good to individuals, whether he thinks of this good as only happiness or as other things besides.

This is true and important, and is also what liberals are too much inclined to forget, especially when they repeat the rather obscure sentence that 'the state exists for the sake of the citizens, and not the citizens for the sake of the state'. Still, in the liberal state, the private ends and private opportunities of ordinary citizens do count for much more than in the authoritarian state. Public policy is more often and more elaborately justified on the ground that it does this or that for the individual man and woman. Even if the justification is mistaken, or is only thought of as an excuse after the policy has been adopted on other grounds, the need to make it is strongly felt.

The modern authoritarian state (unlike many old ones) is quite as enterprising as the most active liberal and democratic state; quite as much intent on transforming society. But it is, for obvious reasons, less concerned to improve the lot of the citizen, and more concerned to achieve some kind of social or political order desired for its own sake.[1] I do not mean just that the authoritarian state is less concerned to give the citizen what he wants than what his rulers have decided is good for him. That is certainly true, but that in itself would not make the authoritarian state less concerned than the liberal state for the citizen as a person. The authoritarian state cares less than the liberal state for the citizen, not because it tries to force on him what it takes to be good for him, whether he likes it or not, but because it cares more for the

---

1. This is so even when the rulers of the state profess that nothing matters ultimately except the good of individuals. The communist society which Marx imagined is as 'individualistic' as any society could be; whereas Communist governments in fact care less than others for what the private citizen wants or aspires to.

social and political order which includes him than for him. No doubt, it is not indifferent to him, and in any case often improves his lot even when it is more concerned to do something else. If it raises productivity and the national income, it probably also raises the real incomes of most citizens. It creates its social and political order not out of bricks but out of men; it must consider the nature of the living materials it uses; it must know something of their wants and feelings if it is to know what can and what cannot be done with them. Moreover, the 'it' I speak of, which is the government, consists also of men with the ordinary human needs for affection, admiration, and understanding. The modern authoritarian state wants more than to use men for its own purpose; it also wants to make them, as far as possible, sharers in those purposes. Sharers, not as taking a real part in deciding what the purposes shall be, but sharers as being eager to work for their attainment. The authoritarian state exhorts the citizen to serve society, and must therefore continually place before him social goals, seeking to make them attractive to him. The citizen will be told that by working to reach these goals he is also working for himself; and in a way, the more he comes to believe what he is told, the truer it will be. For the more it comes to matter to him that the goals should be reached, the more he will be able to find happiness in working for them. Still, that does not ensure that the goals were chosen by those who had the power to choose primarily in order to make the citizen happy or free or anything else, nor yet that the citizen in making them his own is primarily concerned for the happiness or good of his fellow-citizens. There are public goods which are not sums of private good [1] or means to private good, and both ruler and citizen can easily come to prefer them to all other things except their own good and the good of

---

1. By a 'private good' I mean some desirable quality or condition of the individual, like courage or kindness or happiness; and by a public good some desirable condition of society. If we call a society happy, we can mean only that its members are so; but if we call it 'well-ordered' or 'socialist', we are not speaking of its members, taken individually, but of a whole system of relations between them. Communists (and even Fascists) often say that they prefer one system to another because it makes for the happiness or freedom (or both) of individuals. But the methods they use to get and keep power make them in the end care more for the system established by these methods than for happiness or freedom, though they still continue to say (and even to believe) that they value the system because it brings, or will bring, happiness or freedom. That is what makes the system a 'distortion'; it is different from what it would be if it really made for happiness or freedom, while the persons in power seek (consciously or unconsciously) to close everyone's eyes to this difference.

the few persons dear to them. There are public goods of this kind in both authoritarian and liberal states; but in authoritarian states—and especially today—they are much more important than in liberal states.

The less the public ends pursued by government are in keeping with the private ends of the citizens, or, in other words, the more citizens are required to make sacrifices for the community as a social order valued for its own sake, the more persistently and excitingly these public ends must be presented to them. This is perhaps most easily done by inducing them to think of their community as in competition with others. Hence the modern authoritarian state, precisely because it requires so much from its citizens which does not help them get what they want for themselves or even what could plausibly be held to be good for them, whether they want it or not, is much more competitive than the liberal state. It is perpetually comparing itself with other states, measuring itself up against them. It sets targets for itself, and these targets are important to it more as things to be striven for than for what they bring to individuals. As long ago as Louis XVIII's reign, Bazard, the more humourless and strenuous and austere of the two 'Fathers' of the socialist sect founded in the name of Saint-Simon, spoke of the society of the future as having 'science for its theology and industry for its cult'. Today we have such societies whose priests, instead of psalms, recite statistics. It matters less to them that men should live well than that production per head should be greater each year than the year before, and greater in their country and in countries adhering to their creed or camp than elsewhere.

Competition, of course, is not aggression, and need not lead to it. The authoritarian state striving hard to catch up with and to surpass other states, to raise productivity or literacy or something else, to score more heavily, to have better statistics than its neighbours, is not therefore the more prone to war. It is busy achieving what war must destroy. Even soldiers and armaments can be amassed without any desire to use them destructively. The tall, well-drilled, well-polished soldiers of Frederick William I were too smart and expensive to risk the blood and dirt of the battle-field. But the authoritarian state, though not more prone to war in these days when war achieves nothing and destroys everything, is more suspicious than the liberal state, less ready to make concessions, less willing to think in terms of a world community of diverse states. Afraid though it may be of war and careful to avoid it, it cannot help thinking of other states as potential enemies, especially if they repudiate the doctrines which it holds sacred. No doubt, liberal states are also competitive and suspicious; it is a matter of degree. But they are apt to be less so. They can exact much smaller sacrifices for public ends not clearly related to private goods, and they can expect as much criticism as co-operation from their citizens. The citizen of the free state is closer than the citizen of the authoritarian state to being a citizen of the world; he is more inclined to look upon government as existing for his benefit and the benefit of others like himself, and less inclined to look upon it as entitled to his services to ensure that his country makes a better showing when compared with others.

Competition between independent states is different from competition between individuals or lesser communities. Competition between individuals or communities within the state is subject to law, and is therefore kept within bounds by something more than fear of violence and hope of advantage; it is also kept in bounds by public policy. The rivals belong to the same larger community and have much the same values. But the citizen of the authoritarian state knows very little of states rival to his own; he is called upon to make sacrifices to keep up with or out-distance something which exists for him chiefly in the image presented to him by his rulers. A man's personal or business rivals are known to him and are perhaps even friends, or else are, as members of the same class or profession or community, persons for whom he can feel sympathy. There is ordinarily no one whose power depends on maintaining and exacerbating these personal rivalries, for public authority exists to keep them in check; they arise naturally as men seek to make a living and a career for themselves and nobody makes it his business to create them. But the rulers of modern authoritarian states, to strengthen their hold on the loyalty of their subjects, teach them to look upon rival states as alien and hostile. All rulers are at times tempted to do this, but in liberal states they are subject to criticism, and in the old-fashioned quiescent despotisms (which are nearly all passed away) the temptation is much smaller because rulers require so much less of their subjects. The modern authoritarian state is revolutionary; it seeks to impose discipline in order to achieve vast aims. Even when it rejects war as an instrument of policy, its temper is military; it mobilizes its citizens for the service of the community and tries to keep their loyalty always at fever pitch. It probably asks too much of them and exhausts them morally; for what deadens a man more, taking from him gaiety and humour and curiosity and the sense of possessing his own soul, than perpetual and strident loyalties artificially kept alive? But that is another matter, which I must not discuss here.

D. Warnings and Suggestions

(1) I have said that it would be beyond the scope of this essay to put forward a detailed programme of positive action. What the essay seeks to do, apart from raising and disentangling the broader relevant issues, is to give a number of warnings, which it may now be useful to summarize. Some are addressed to the Powers ruling dependent peoples, and some to peoples who are still struggling for independence, or who have recently got it. All the warnings assume that constitutional government and liberal democracy [1] are desirable, and that the first cannot, under modern conditions, last for long unless it leads on to the second.

To ruling Powers:

(*i*) Take care that in putting down some forms of opposition to your rule, forms which may help to prepare the peoples subject to you for constitutional government and liberal democracy, you do not drive them to other forms of opposition which help do the opposite. Opposition to your rule should be diverse, widespread, and predominantly legal, increasing the people's political sophistication and their capacity to organize peacefully and effectively for political purposes.

(*ii*) Remember that, though some forms of power (administrative, judicial, and police) can be transferred gradually, and others (local government) can be gradually enlarged, the most important form of all, which is the making of law and policy for the entire nation claiming self-government, must in practice be transferred rapidly.

(*iii*) Take care that when you come to leave, another form of 'alien' rule does not replace your own; that some tribes or communities do not come to dominate others. You owe it to your subjects to see to it

---

1. I would as soon leave out the adjective 'liberal', for I do not believe that democracy can be genuine except where the rights of individuals, as the liberal understands them, are respected. But because there now exist regimes calling themselves 'people's democracies' I feel the need to take this precaution for fear of being misunderstood.

that those who claim to speak for them, and on that ground to take over power from you, really do speak for them.

(*iv*) Beware of the European settlers. Even when they admit that concessions must be made to the natives, they are bent on retaining their superiority, their 'acquired rights', which are usually so large that they cannot be retained if the natives are to realize the aspirations which your rule and influence have created in them. The settlers are entitled to your sympathy and to compensation from you for any sacrifices which you require of them, but they have no right to expect you to protect their privileges indefinitely, and in any case it may not long be in your power to protect them.

(*v*) Do not bother too much about strategic bases and access to vital raw materials. Methods of carrying on war are changing so rapidly that your bases are probably not as important as you think, or not likely long to remain important. As for raw materials, if you need them and can afford to pay for them, the countries that produce them will probably be as eager to sell them to you are you are to buy them.

(*vi*) Do not try to hold on to a colony or dependency *at any cost*, even if it is still, by your standards, very far from fit for self-government. If you find that you have to use force extensively and over a long period of time to put down rebellion, the chances are that, however excellent your intentions, it is already out of your power to do much to help prepare your subjects for self-government; and in any case the cost of maintaining your rule will exceed any profit that you can make, so that the colony or dependency must be a source of impoverishment to you.

To Peoples still struggling for Independence or who have recently achieved it:

(*i*) If you value personal freedom and democracy as well as national independence, do not allow the need to maintain a united front against the ruling power to be used as an excuse for intimidation. Above all, do not allow terrorists to take control of your nationalist movement. This does not always necessarily mean, *Be prudent*; it may also mean, *Be bold*. Nor does it mean, *Never use force*. It means rather, *Let your united front consist of willing partners*, and *Use force when other methods do not serve your purpose.*

(*ii*) Remember that, if 'colonialism' is on the decline, this is due much more to the spread of liberal and socialist ideas among the Europeans than to any increase in your strength. The nations of European stock, economically and militarily, are immensely more powerful than they were when you were conquered; and your strength against them lies chiefly in the fact that your subjection is against their principles. No doubt, they have not, from being selfish, suddenly become unselfish; but the groups among them interested in keeping and exploiting colonies are weaker, while other groups with different interests are stronger. It is your good fortune that you are on their conscience. If they had the temperament of a Mao-Tse-Tung or a Colonel Nasser, you would not stand a chance against them.

(*iii*) Do not suppose that because liberal democracy, to be effective in the large nation state, requires general literacy, widespread technical education, and a fairly high standard of living, you should begin by trying to improve literacy, technical education, and material conditions by all means in your power in order to get freedom and democracy the more quickly. Since time is on your side, because colonialism is on the decline, do not, in your hurry to get independence and literacy and material prosperity, jeopardize your chance of getting what you still hope for after you have got them.

(*iv*) If you want your people to be treated as equals by the Europeans and especially by the western nations whose claims to superiority have probably been the most galling to you and have caused you to set so much store by this equal treatment, do not imagine that you can achieve your purpose merely by getting national independence. You can achieve it only if your people, being independent, behave respectably by western standards, both within their frontiers and towards other peoples, or if they make themselves formidable to the western nations. But there are only two or three countries placed as the Soviet Union is, with natural resources enough to make themselves really formidable to the West while setting western standards at defiance. Moreover, these standards, as they relate to behaviour between independent nations, though western in origin, are no more in the interest of the western than of other nations; and it is doubtful whether even the greatest Powers can afford to neglect them to-day. Therefore, by all means raise productivity to increase the well-being of your people, but do not raise it to make your country more formidable to others;

and do not use methods calling for excessive sacrifices and austere discipline from one or two generations for the sake of posterity. Great sacrifices and austere discipline are for self-dedicated persons, and not for entire nations, except in an emergency.

(*v*) Remember that the peoples whose 'imperialism' or 'colonialism' you condemn are also the peoples who gave to the world the principles which give point to your condemnation, and that the Russians, who now join you in this condemnation, of all the great European peoples care for these principles least. It is among the 'imperialist' peoples that there is probably the deepest understanding of your predicament and the truest sympathy with your aspirations. This understanding is confined to small groups but they have considerable influence, and the sympathy is widespread if not always ready.

(*vi*) Beware of your resentment against the white peoples, for though it is natural and excusable, it may do more harm to you than to them. If you were, by your actions, to unite them against you, you would be lost, for they are still (and are likely long to remain) immensely more wealthy and more powerful than all the peoples of Asia and Africa put together. If the world were to be divided into the 'white' against the 'coloured' peoples, it is the coloured who would be the more in danger.

(2) There is one rather more concrete suggestion which is not, I hope, out of place even in an essay of this kind; an essay which deals in a general way with a vast and intricate problem. It may already be too late to carry it out, for the best time for it would have been soon after the second World War when the prestige of the western Powers was at its highest. I assume that 'colonialism' is ending quickly, that the western Powers are concerned that liberal democracy should spread, and that the still subject and emancipated peoples (or rather the political leaders whom they trust) want to establish it in their own countries, even though they may want other things more.

Britain, France, Holland, and Belgium, being liberal democracies which own or recently have owned colonies, together with the United States, and all other countries which have been colonies of any of these four Powers and are now independent states and also liberal democracies, should form an International Authority to which the countries still administering colonies should be responsible for how they administer them. This Authority should have two main purposes: to see to it that all the states members of it and their dependencies get the vital raw materials and the credits they need to maintain and develop their economies, and to help prepare the still dependent peoples for independence or for autonomy on equal terms with other peoples within some federal union. I shall say no more about the first of these purposes, in spite of the importance I attribute to it, because I am not an economist; and about the second, I shall say only this, that the Authority should enquire into the circumstances of each colony and prepare, together with the country administering it, a scheme for its gradual emancipation. I am less concerned to suggest what precisely the Authority should do to carry out these two purposes than to point out how much all the peoples who care for freedom and democracy would stand to gain by its activities if they were really effective.

The Authority would bring the liberal and democratic peoples to-gether regardless of race and colour. It is surely absurd that Indians, as they so often do, should think and speak of themselves as 'Asians' closer to the Chinese than to the English. They look no more Chinese than they look English, and their close association with the English has, more than any other external influence, helped to make them the sort of people they are today. Their political and social ideals, though they have an authentic Indian character which marks them off from those of other peoples, are also very largely western. There have been Indian and Chinese civilizations very different from the civilization of the West, and their influence is still deep and strong, but there has never been an Asian civilization including both China and India. India today comes closer to being part of western civilization than of any other not originally Indian. Asia, much more than Europe, much more than the Americas, is 'merely a geographical expression'. The community of interests and beliefs which the Authority I have in mind would represent is altogether deeper than anything common to the peoples of Asia. There are causes, discussed in this essay, which now close our minds to this obvious fact. The setting up of this Authority would serve to open them.

The existence of the Authority would reassure the still dependent peoples that all the talk about preparing them for self-government and democracy was sincere. Over and above the ruling Power there would be an impartial body known to be impartial, because it would include countries which have or have had colonies and countries which have been colonies, and also because it would include coloured

o

and white peoples. At the moment, the ruling Power, no matter how good its intentions, is always to some extent suspect to the peoples it rules. It established its dominion over them in the first place much more for its own than for their benefit, and its reluctance to make concessions to them may be due to self-interest or pride. Whether or not it is so, the subject peoples will be inclined to find it so. If the ruling Power tells them to be patient in their own interest they are loath to believe that it is really their interest which weighs heaviest with it. If, however, they are told to be patient by a body much more obviously disinterested and impartial, they are more likely to be impressed. If they are told that the time has not yet come for them to be self-governing, they will be less ready to challenge that verdict on the ground that it puts a stigma of inferiority on them, for it is not the verdict of a 'master race' which in the past has too often behaved as if it had a birthright to rule over other races but of a body consisting in part of peoples recently in subjection and now recognized as equal to the others. By this means, too, the equality of recently subject peoples is recognized more strikingly even than when they got their independence, for they are invited to take part as equals in a scheme to strengthen and extend freedom and democracy. Their experience, as peoples who have not long been independent and are therefore faced with great difficulties peculiar to themselves, is recognized as likely to be of great help to the Authority. And certainly, that experience is as relevant as the experience of the older and presumably more mature and solid democracies.

The setting up of the Authority would be an admission of what is now obvious: that the future of the colonies is a matter of concern to more than the Powers that rule them and the peoples who inhabit them. It matters to all liberal and democratic countries that the colonies, when they get independence, should also be liberal and democratic, or be on the way to becoming so. To the authoritarian states it may matter that they should *not* become liberal and democratic; but that is no concern of ours. It is the colony-owning Powers which are primarily responsible for their colonies, and it happens to be the case that most still or until recently dependent peoples are or have been ruled by liberal states, and therefore (to the extent that they have explicit political ideals) come closer to desiring liberal democracy for themselves than any other viable system. But the liberal colony-owning Powers are now so placed that they can help these peoples get what they want more easily by sharing responsibility for their colonies with other liberal Powers than by refusing to share it. Legally, the responsibility is still only theirs, and they therefore have the legal right to share it with whom they please. If they choose to share it with some countries and not with others, they do no wrong to anyone. It is not their duty to share that responsibility with all countries if they share it with any; but it is their duty not to share it with countries which would prevent their helping the dependent peoples achieve their aspirations.

This Authority would enable the colony-owning Powers to get advice and assistance without subjecting them, as they are now subjected in the United Nations Organization, to ignorant, irresponsible, and even malicious criticism. The countries associated in that organization do not have the same political ideals, or a similar political experience. Many of the critics of 'imperialism' are much less interested in the fate of the colonies and dependent peoples than in making trouble for Britain or France or some other country denounced as 'imperialist'. Admittedly, some of this irresponsible criticism comes from countries which would be partners in the Authority I suggest. But in the United Nations they are differently placed than they would be in the Authority; for in the United Nations there is nothing to encourage them to think constructively about the colonies. The United Nations is the arena where the two protagonists of the 'cold war' try to gain diplomatic victories over one another. It is there that the United States is apt to be most put out by anything done by Britain or France which provides the critics of 'imperialism' with an excuse for raising a clamour; it is there that India, anxious not to be drawn into either camp, is tempted to deal her sharpest blows at countries belonging to the camp she needs to repudiate the more vigorously if she is to look as neutral as she wants to look. She was never a dependency of Russia but of a western Power, and her strongest links are still with the West; and it is therefore against the West that she feels the stronger need to assert her independence. It is in the United Nations too that the cold war is most apt to look like a contest for world hegemony between nations of European stock, between peoples misnamed 'white'. And it is also, to some extent, the dilatoriness and ineffectiveness of the United Nations which from time to time irritate the colony-owning Powers into taking the reckless courses which lose them the sympathy of countries which else might sympathise strongly with them.

The United Nations Organization is not useless, still less worse than useless. It would not exist if the nations belonging to it had not recognized the need for an enduring instrument for the peaceful settlement of disputes. It includes the two greatest Powers, and neither has shown any inclination to leave it. The aggressors in the last war all left the League of Nations before they had gone far on the courses which eventually led to war. The Russian Communists have belonged to the United Nations since it was created; they are now used to it and to its ways, and are probably rather more sensitive to world opinion than they would be if they did not belong to it. True, the nations all have one clear interest in common, which is to avoid war, and they do not need the United Nations to help them see it; but that body does help create the world opinion which discourages actions likely to lead to war and also makes countries more sensitive to that opinion. It is one thing to see the obvious, that a major war would now be so destructive that aggressors could achieve nothing useful by it, and another to be deflected by world opinion from courses which might lead to such a war. The United Nations is probably more useful in preventing conflicts arising than in settling them once they have arisen; the nations probably behave differently for belonging to it, more prudently and taking a longer view. They may not love each other the better for belonging to it, but they are probably more sensitive to one another's reactions.

But the United Nations, though it helps to preserve peace in the world, does not, I think, make smoother the coming of independence to dependent peoples or help to ensure that when they get independence they are fit for self-government. The nations assembled in that body have a common interest to avoid war, especially a war between the great Powers, but they have no common interest where dependent peoples are concerned. Some of them hope to strengthen their position internationally by using colonial troubles and the nationalism of 'backward' peoples to embarrass the old 'imperialist' Powers and their allies, while others, though in many ways they sympathise with these Powers, are against them in any difficulties they may have with their colonies. Everyone denounces war as an instrument of policy, and the denunciation is mostly sincere, for everyone has good reason to fear war. But this fear of war, though it has made the Powers move more warily, has not made them more friendly to one another, and they use against each other what weapons they can use at least risk to themselves. One of the most tempting weapons, because it can do great harm to the victim without much danger to the user of it, is the stirring up of subject peoples against their rulers.

This stirring up can be open or secret, whichever seems the safer or more effective; and it is easy to put a stop to it without losing face when to persist with it looks too dangerous. It is also possible, by diplomacy and propaganda, to create a situation which makes it difficult for a ruling Power to take vigorous action against rebels and those who help them. Precisely because everyone is so much more afraid of war, it is safer than it used to be to indulge in some kinds of provocation. A colony-owning Power exasperated by provocation into taking vigorous action can easily be made to appear to be endangering the peace of the world. In the United Nations, as I have tried to show, it is easy to divide the liberal Powers over 'colonialism', although they have at bottom the same interest that colonies should move smoothly towards independence in such a way that they too, in their turn, should become liberal states. This is certainly as much the interest of India as of Britain; and perhaps even more, for reasons which I shall discuss later. The United Nations Organization serves to obscure (or at the best does nothing to bring out) the fundamental community of interest of the liberal states where the future of the dependent peoples is concerned. But the Authority I have in mind would do precisely that; it would bring together the countries which care most about the dependent peoples and best understand their predicament, and would enable them to discuss their future without being distracted by the accusations and manoeuvres of countries always ready to denounce 'colonialism' because they have never had colonies of their own and do not much care what happens to other people's.

This Authority would not weaken the United Nations, for what it would do is not done by anyone. It would undertake what in practice the United Nations, because it contains countries differing so widely in their social and political ideals, cannot do; and by so doing, would diminish some of the tensions which now make the United Nations less effective.

The Authority would not be a military alliance, and would not be directed against the Communist Powers. No doubt, if it did its work properly, it would add to the number of securely established liberal democracies, and in that way *might prevent* the spread of Communism. I say *might prevent* deliberately, for the only alternative to liberal democracy is not Communism; it is perhaps as likely that the back-ward countries, if they do not become democracies, will become nationalist dictatorships as that they will go Communist. And even if the parties that got control over them were Communist, they might not long remain 'orthodox', that is, in political communion with Moscow. If that were to happen, the 'heretical' Communist countries might find the liberal states more tolerable than the 'orthodox' Com-munist countries.

In any case, the purpose of the Authority would not be to fight Communism but to extend and strengthen a certain kind of democracy. It would distract the greater western Powers, and especially the great-est of them all which stands most in need of this distraction, from the 'cold war'. It would cause them to devote rather more of their energies to achieving something they believe in, and rather less to trying to prevent something they fear. Instead of encouraging weak nations to form unstable alliances against possible Communist military attack, they would encourage them to ward off a danger which is perhaps more pressing and is certainly more within their power to arrest—the danger of falling victims to fanatical minorities eager to drive and whip them in the name of progress. The more the western Powers were dis-tracted from the 'cold war', the less the Communist Powers would have reason to fear their efforts on behalf of dependent and backward peoples. These efforts would not be directed to making these peoples militarily formidable but to bringing democracy and freedom securely to them. What the Communist Powers fear is war, and not what we call democracy. Our attempts to make our kind of democracy secure might not impress them, might appear to them doomed to failure, but would not seem to threaten them. The colonies are already ours, and we are responsible for them; the Communist Powers may deplore the fact but they also recognize it. Therefore, whatever we do *for* our colonies, however misconceived the Communists may think it, will not seem to them a serious threat to their cause, provided the help we give is not given for the purpose of raising up military allies for ourselves against Moscow. No doubt, the Communists will continue their subversive activities. But why should that worry us? The more effective our help, the less effective their subversion.

The Authority would give the recently independent countries a chance to work constructively for the cause they believe in, the emancipation of subject peoples. Instead of working for it largely against the western democracies, and by fits and starts as occasion offers, they would work for it with those democracies, continuously and responsibly. Liberal and democratic institutions are still, with them, less firmly established than in the West. They may be more attached to these institutions—those of them with settled views in the matter—than to any others; they may want democracy for themselves and for the still subject peoples. They may want it only less than they want national independence. Associated with the western Powers in the Authority I have in mind, they would be working for both these things, for the independence of subject peoples and for the spread of freedom and democracy. And they would be working for them in a way that would strengthen their own faith in democracy and enlarge their political experience. They would be associated as equals with the wealthiest, most powerful, and best-established democracies; and yet their own experience, as newly independent peoples with whom democracy is still far from secure, would be as relevant as any to the problems that would face the Authority.

This scheme might also dissipate one of the chief causes of misunderstanding between the western Powers. America has been a far from irresponsible critic of colonialism. She has shown more understanding than her allies, especially the French, have given her credit for. The fault has not been all on her side; far from it. But still, where one country has direct responsibility and another has not for something which matters to them both, there is almost bound to be misunderstanding and action at cross purposes. The Americans cannot help but be worried by the world's reactions to what Britain or France do in their colonies or to peoples 'protected' by them; and Britain and France, though they cannot brush this concern aside as impertinent (for they sometimes need American help even in their dealings with subject and protected peoples), are easily offended by what it moves the Americans to say or do. If America acquired a legal right and a duty to express this concern, and to express it within a circle of friendly Powers undisturbed by the manoeuvres of the unfriendly, she might say and do a great deal more than she does now and give much less offence.

There are obvious objections to the scheme.

India and the other newly independent countries might not wish to have anything to do with it. They are still suspicious of the 'imperialist' Powers. Moreover (and this probably matters a good deal more), they are naturally disinclined to do what might expose them to the same kind of criticism as they have been indulging in. It is pleasant to reproach others and to remain beyond reproach, and it is doubly pleasant to be able to score off people who in the past have treated you as inferiors. These countries might well say to the 'imperialist' Powers: this is your problem, you have created it and must solve it. Why should you expect us to help you solve it? We have enough to do solving our own problems, most of them bequeathed to us by you.

This would be a natural and perhaps a strong reaction, but it might not be the only one. In the first place, these retorts, addressed to the present rulers of 'imperialist' countries, are rather out of place. The British and French dependencies were acquired by Englishmen and Frenchmen long since dead, and if these dependencies are now well on the way to independence or autonomy, and perhaps also to democracy and freedom, it is largely because Englishmen and Frenchmen no longer think as their ancestors did about European rule over non-European peoples. They have inherited their dependencies and cannot decently let go of them now (when they have become liabilities rather than assets) without at least attempting to make some provision for their future.

What happens to the still dependent peoples (and indeed to backward peoples generally) will probably affect more deeply the newly independent countries than the western Powers. If, for instance, all the countries in Asia and Africa except India were to become authoritarian this would weaken democracy in India much more than in Britain. To the extent therefore that Indians care, not just for democracy in general, but for democracy in their own country, it matters even more to them than to the British that the dependent and poor peoples should get independence and make material progress in ways that lead to democracy.

Again, in Britain's African colonies there are now more settlers from Asia than from Europe. These settlers ought to be as much a concern to the men who govern the countries they came from as the European settlers are to the British government. Is India less interested than Britain in the fate of Kenya or Tanganyika? If our African colonies, when they get independence, are fanatically nationalist and authoritarian, will they treat settlers from India or Pakistan more considerately than European settlers? The European settlers may have powerful protectors; it may be dangerous to strike hard at them.

Or they may find it easier to move away and to get compensation for their losses. Who then will bear the brunt of resentment long pent up and suddenly let loose?

The feelings of the newly independent peoples towards the western Powers are mixed. They probably still feel more resentment towards them than towards anyone else. For every word spoken in India against the Russians there are probably a thousand spoken against the British. But there are probably also warmer and more generous emotions felt for the British than for the Russians. The present rulers of India have already, in ten years, had considerable experience of ruling reluctant or perverse or unresponsive subjects. They have, much more than they used to have, the thoughts and feelings of men accustomed to government. This has made them more moderate, more supple, more understanding than they were when they were merely opponents of British rule. They are still opposed to 'imperialism', but they are also aware that an empire in process of dissolution or transformation gives birth to painful and intricate problems. They are more than successors of the British; they are also, in many ways, builders on foundations laid by the British, and bearers of their traditions. Whether they are foreigners or natives, the rulers of poverty-stricken and illiterate peoples have many problems in common to bring them together in sympathy and understanding.

Another objection to the scheme is that the Powers having colonies would not accept it because they dislike outside interference. They think of the colonies as their own, and also believe that they have greater experience in dealing with them than anyone else has. This is true; but it is also true that their pride of empire is much smaller than it was. There are more kicks than ha'pence to having colonies today, and under these circumstances to share responsibility might be a relief. Besides, colonial problems sometimes get out of hand, and the ruling Power finds itself obliged to withdraw from a colony after squandering money on it and lives in a vain attempt to hold on to it. There may be more dignity lost in trying to deal with a colony single-handed than in getting help from others in dealing with it, especially if the help is asked for and given before the situation is desperate. Of course, to get the sort of help I have in mind is already, in a way, to lose that colony in part; it is to cease to have sole responsibility for its government. The scheme would be useless if the Power administering a colony took as little notice of the Authority as the Powers holding mandated territories took of the League of Nations. But this sole responsibility is in any case no longer what it was; the hands of the Power owning a colony are already much more tied than they used to be. The 'imperialist' Powers dare not, in practice, disregard world opinion, or the repercussions at home or in other colonies of what they do. They are already subjected to all kinds of irresponsible pressure. The Authority would at least make it easier for them to resist these pressures, and might also make their relations with their subjects smoother. At the moment the extremer and more violent nationalists can count on a good deal of sympathy from outside, for though the world may dislike their methods, it often condemns the ruling Power on the ground that it has driven them to use such methods. Anything that strengthens the belief of subject peoples that their rulers are seriously resolved to give them independence and are honestly trying to help them, weakens the extremists and encourages the moderates. What is the use of having sole responsibility for governing a people who are fast becoming ungovernable because they have lost confidence in your good intentions or in your power to carry them out? To share your responsibility is sometimes a good way of increasing your influence. It all depends on the circumstances. But what are, today, the circumstances of the colony-owning Powers? Might they not even, by pocketing their pride, save their dignity? Influence and prestige are not to be had today by the same methods as yesterday.

Yet another objection to the scheme is that the Americans would have nothing to do with it. Why should they pull other people's chestnuts out of the fire? Already, they are, so they think, more hated than loved for the help they have given other peoples.

This is, I think, the weakest of the objections. America is overwhelmingly the greatest of the democratic Powers, and whatever happens, she will not in practice turn a blind eye to her allies' difficulties. When the French lost control of the situation in Indo-China, the Americans felt they had to intervene. What more ungrateful role is there than to be irritated and embarrassed by the actions of your friends while they are getting themselves into a mess, and then in the end to have to clear up the mess after them? What is more likely to annoy your friends than this? Is it not far better to accept a share of the responsibility at an earlier stage, and so expose yourself to part of the blame should things go wrong? If you fail together with your friends, they will feel better towards you than if you watch them failing, and then run to their help when it is already too late, loudly blaming them for their folly. If America, despite her great generosity, has so often offended her allies, it is not by being too firm with them; it is by being sometimes urgent and at other times hesitant; it is by giving the impression that although she is at a loss what to do she is still censorious. The Americans, if they accepted a share of responsibility for the future of the colonies, would not be likely to agree entirely with the colony-owning Powers or with the newly independent countries. They would have their own opinions, which would necessarily carry great weight. But people whose deepest moral beliefs and whose interests are much the same can work effectively together even though they have definite and different opinions; for effective collaboration is as often prevented by people's not knowing what they want as by their wanting different things. Especially is this true if they are liberals and democrats, educated to respect opinions different from their own.

Index

References to Britain, France, Russia, and the United States are so numerous that I have not thought it useful to include them in the index